Letters Can Change Your Life.

With letters you can be just what you want to be—a supersalesman, a clever businessman, a charming friend, a gracious hostess.

Indeed, for many people, good letters have been the key to success in business and social life, in getting a better job, in conducting a romance.

THE COMPLETE LETTER WRITER shows you how to write the most interesting and effective letters and, above all, offers hundreds of samples showing just how this is done.

Books by N.H. and S.K. Mager

The Complete Letter Writer
A Guide to Tropical Fish
The Household Encyclopedia
The Office Encyclopedia

Also by N.H. Mager

How to Work with Tools and Wood

Also by S.K. Mager

A Complete Guide to Home Sewing

Published by POCKET BOOKS

The Complete

LETTER WRITER

• • • • • • • • • • • • • • • •

Compiled and edited by

N. H. and S. K. MAGER

POCKET BOOKS

New York   London   Toronto   Sydney   Tokyo   Singapore

An *Original* Publication of POCKET BOOKS

POCKET BOOKS, a division of Simon & Schuster
1230 Avenue of the Americas, New York, NY 10020

ISBN: 0-671-74419-4

First Pocket Books printing (revised edition) December 1968

26 25 24 23 22 21 20

POCKET and colophon are registered trademarks of
Simon & Schuster.

Printed in the U.S.A.

Acknowledgments

Although many of the letters in this volume were specially prepared or taken from the files of years of personal correspondence, the editors have not hesitated to seek the assistance of other professional letter writers. This book, therefore, contains scores of letters borrowed from the best correspondents in the letter-writing profession.

For advice and the use of some of their tried-and-tested business letters, the editors are indebted to officials of the following companies:

Ahrens Publishing Co.; Air Reduction Sales Co.; W. A. Alexander & Co.; The Allen Laundry, Inc.; American Automobile Association (Massachusetts Division); *The American Home* Magazine; American Tag Co.; Artwill Advertising Corp.; Autographic Business Forms, Inc.; Barber-Colman Co.; The Barrett Bindery Co.; Battle Creek Equipment Co.; Bostonian Shoe Co.; Leo P. Bott, Jr.; Broadway Maintenance Corp.; Burdine's; Burroughs Corp.; Carr, Dolan & Hahn, Inc.; Central Bergen Savings and Loan Association; *Changing Times*, The Kiplinger Magazine; Chesapeake & Ohio Railway Co.; Connecticut Mutual Life Insurance Co.; Craftint Manufacturing Co.; Crowell-Collier Publishing Co.; Crystal Tube Corp; *Cue* Magazine; Bachrach;

Dey Brothers & Co.; Dickie-Raymond, Inc.; Dictaphone Corp.; The Digest of Investment Advices; Don Barr Associates; Dun & Bradstreet, Inc.; the Egry Register Co.; Eli Bridge Co.; Fairy Silk Mills, Inc.; Filmack Trailer Co.; B. Forman Co.; Frank W. Horner, Ltd.; General Dental Supply Co.; General Motors Acceptance Corp.; General Motors Institute; General Services Administration; Green Giant Co.;

Gulf Oil Corp.; Hettinger Brothers; Hewig Co.; Henry Hoke; J. F. Horrigan Co.; Hotel New Yorker; Hotel Taft; Hudnut Sales Co.; The John Henry Co.; *Journal of Commerce;* E. M. Kahn & Co.; Kerr-McGee Oil Industries, Inc.; Kings Highway Savings Bank; Kleinhans; H. Kohnstamm & Co.; Kresge-Newark; E. Leitz, Inc.; Liberty Federal Savings and Loan Association; Lifschultz Fast Freight; Lindquist Tire Shop; Lit Brothers; Long Island College Hospital; *Look* Magazine; Henry C. Lytton & Co.;

McGraw-Hill Publishing Co.; *Mademoiselle* Magazine; Merchandise National Bank of Chicago; The Mersman Brothers Corp.; Miller Printing Machinery Co.; Monogram of California; the Morantz Mercantile Agency; The Mosler Safe Co.; Motor Sales Co.; Motor Twins, Inc.; Mullen & Bluett; National Audubon Society; Nephron Co.; New York Belting & Packing Co.; Ozark Fisheries; Palmer House; M. L. Parker Co.; Paulson-Gerlack & Associates; Pencil Specialty Co., Inc.; Peterson, Howell & Heather; S. Posner Sons, Inc.; *Printers' Ink* Magazine;

Reader's Digest; Orville E. Reed; Remington Rand, Inc.; Reply-O-Products Co.; *The Reporter* Magazine; Research Institute of America, Inc.; Revere Copper & Brass, Inc.; Al Robertson; Troy M. and Dorothy Rodlun; Roland G. E. Ullman Organization; Ross-Martin Co.; Sales Letters, Inc.; Science Research Associates; O. M. Scott and Sons Co.; Seamen's Church Institute; The Seaside Hotel; Seidletz Paint and Varnish Co.; *The Sporting Goods Dealer* Magazine; Standard Duplicating Machines Corp.; Standard Register Co.; Street & Smith Publications, Inc;

Taylor & Co.; TelAutograph Corp.; *Tide* Magazine; A. August Tiger; *Time* Magazine; Typesetters, Inc.; United Business Service; Universal C.I.T. Credit Corp.; Vestal, Inc.; *The Wall Street Journal;* Wassell Organization, Inc.; Weber Dental Manufacturing Co.; Weck Process Co.; Weiner's; White Haven Memorial Park; Wolf Envelope Co.; Yeck and Yeck; the Zeller Co.; Zippo Manufacturing Co.

CONTENTS

PART I
SOCIAL LETTERS

PART II
BUSINESS LETTERS

THE

COMPLETE

LETTER WRITER

PART I

SOCIAL LETTERS

CHAPTER 1

Letters and You

Everyone likes to receive letters, but practically no one likes to write them. For most people letter writing is one case in which it is far better to receive than give. Each of us has a hundred reasons why he can't write a letter. Rare indeed is the person who can sit down and dash off a wonderful letter without giving it a second thought.

But just stop a minute and think how vital letters are to us. Through letters we meet friends, make friends, and keep alive the warm glow of love. Letters bring friends and family together across the miles. If it weren't for letters, how difficult it would be to order merchandise, pay bills, borrow money, join a club, work on a civic committee, accept invitations or apply for a job—to name just a few of the things that are part of the routine of living.

And this essential portion of your life—writing a letter—is really based only on these two rules:

BE TIMELY

and

BE YOURSELF

¶

Be timely: This is such an easy rule to follow and yet, when broken, it can lose friendships, cause great inconvenience, and inflict hurt feelings. A letter whose aim is to fulfill a social obligation fails completely when it arrives late. A tardy letter of acceptance or regret can spoil a hostess's party and insures your not being invited again. A letter of friendship, like a visit with a friend, loses warmth and purpose when it is delayed. "Don't put off till tomorrow what you can do today" applies just as much to letter writing as it does to other human endeavors.

Be yourself: Too many letter-writing guides insist on originality at the expense of the writer's personality. The true secret of writing a good letter is to write as if you were talking. Before you actually put pen to paper, sit down and visualize the person to whom you are planning to write. Remember the last time you saw him and recall what you know of him—his interests, his hobbies, his work, his family. Think of what this person would want to hear, what you would tell him if you were in the same room chatting with him. Then write the letter in the kind of language and phrasing that is your everyday speech.

It is true, of course, that some correspondence, such as formal invitations and announcements, must follow certain rules of etiquette. Also, there are letters that even the most gifted person finds difficult to write—condolences, thank-you notes, complaints, and letters asking for favors. But with THE COMPLETE LETTER WRITER on your desk as a guide you will find letters are not only easy to write—but also fun.

For quick and effective reference, THE COMPLETE LETTER WRITER is divided into two parts and twenty-seven chapters. The first part deals with social correspondence, the letters the average person must write as a part of daily living—invitations, acceptances, friendship letters, job-application letters. The second part is devoted to business correspondence—sales letters, mailings, etc. Each category of letter is described in a separate chapter. And each chapter provides all the essential information and help you need in writing an effective letter of that type.

At the beginning of each chapter there is a short section devoted to the basic facts about the type of correspondence the chapter deals with. This is followed by a number of model letters, which you may wish to adapt or use as inspiration for your own thoughts. At the end of each chapter are lists of helpful phrases and sentences to guide you in finding the precise wording for the sentiments you want to express.

With these aids you will find letter writing easy and enjoyable—and you will lose all of your beloved, time-worn excuses for not writing promptly!

CHAPTER 2

The Form and Etiquette of Social Correspondence

Social correspondence falls into three categories: letters of obligation, letters of friendship, and letters of family business.

Letters of social obligation constitute a large part of everyone's correspondence, for they include invitations, announcements, acknowledgments, acceptances, thank-you notes, and condolences. Letters of friendship are the most fun to write because you send these chatty, newsy letters when you want to "talk in writing" with friends and relatives. Family business letters are the means of keeping the wheels of everyday family routine in good working order. In this category are the letters you write to order merchandise, seek professional advice, or explain a child's absence from school.

The tone of your letter, the type of stationery used, and the choice between pen and ink and typewriter is in good part dictated by the category of the letter.

A typewritten letter is a must for business matters. If you are one of the majority who has a handwriting that is neither clear nor beautiful, you'll be wise to type your friendship letters. However, formal letters that are not engraved, replies to formal letters and letters of sympathy and condolence should be handwritten in blue or black ink.

Just as you do not mix business with social matters in writing a letter, so you confine social stationery to social purposes and business stationery to letters of business routine.

The accepted types of social stationery are single sheets (8 x 10 inches), folded sheets, and note paper. The best colors for stationery are the conservative shades—white, gray, or cream-colored—appropriate for use by the whole family. A monogram or printed name and address are correct, although not essential.

Formal correspondence requires a white or eggshell paper

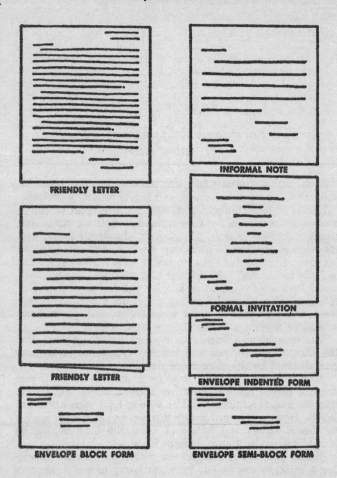

FRIENDLY LETTER

INFORMAL NOTE

FRIENDLY LETTER

FORMAL INVITATION

ENVELOPE BLOCK FORM

ENVELOPE INDENTED FORM

ENVELOPE SEMI-BLOCK FORM

in the standard sheet size. Cards or card-sized note paper engraved with your name are appropriate for short notes and invitations for at-homes, teas, dinners, and dances.

Personal cards (3 x 2½ inches for women, 3 x 1¾ inches for men) engraved with name and address are often used for simple messages of invitation, congratulation, or sympathy. They are usually delivered personally or enclosed with a gift. A slightly larger folded version—the informal card—is now widely used for brief informal notes.

The pages of a letter should be written on and numbered for the convenience of the reader. Letters that carry over to the second page of a folded sheet should be written on pages *one* and *three*. A longer letter should be written and numbered as in a book, in consecutive sequence. Only one side of formal stationery is written upon.

Fold letters neatly so that edges are even, with the first page inside. A carelessly folded letter, like paper and envelopes that don't match, indicates indifference and lack of personal pride on the writer's part. Insert the letter so that the salutation faces the flap of the envelope.

All letters are made up of five parts: the heading, salutation, body of the letter, closing, and signature. An additional part is the address on the envelope.

The heading consists of your address and the date. Except for informal notes written on small-size stationery, in which this information appears in the lower left-hand corner, and social stationery engraved or printed with your address, which carries only the date, the correct form is a three-line heading placed in the upper right-hand corner of the first page:

> Address
> City and State
> Date

In a social letter, the only abbreviation acceptable in the heading is the state name.

The salutation is a greeting to the person to whom you are writing the letter. It is the written equivalent of the conversational "How do you do" or "Hello." Except for love letters and intimate family letters, the form of the salutation is governed by tradition.

The very formal salutation for a social letter is *"My dear Mrs. Cortland."* For a less formal letter, *Dear Mrs. Cortland* is appropriate. Unlike business letters, in which the salutations *Gentlemen, Dear Sir, Mesdames,* and *Dear Madam,* are correct, a name must always be used in the salutation of a social letter.

A married woman is addressed as *Mrs.,* followed by her husband's first name (Mrs. John Saunders). A divorcee is addressed as *Mrs.*, unless she indicates otherwise. A widow is addressed as *Mrs.*, followed by her husband's first name (Mrs. John Saunders) or her own (Mrs. Sylvia Saunders), according to her preference.

A clergyman is addressed as *Rev.* or *The Reverend* (Rev. James White or The Reverend James White). If the first name or initials are not used, *Dr.* or *Mr.* may be substituted (The Reverend Mr. White). When *Reverend* is used in the inside address, use *Dr.* or *Mr.* in the salutation (My dear Mr. White.)

Avoid the use of *Hon.* and *Esq.*, but if they are used in the address then *Mr.* does not appear before the name. The complete etiquette governing the use and misuse of titles is fairly complicated, and when special problems arise on this score it is wise to consult one of the standard books of etiquette.

The body of the letter is, of course, the most important part, and its contents are a matter of your own choosing. But certain mechanical details will make your letter more pleasing to the eye and clearer to the mind. A letter should be written on a page as a picture is mounted in a frame—with attention to margins and pleasing placement. Indent the first line of the first paragraph and, for clarity as well as appearance, indent each following paragraph.

The closing is the complimentary ending with which you finish your letter. It is placed two or three spaces below the body of the letter and begins toward the center of the page. The first word is capitalized, and a comma is placed at the end.

The wording of the formal closing is rather rigidly set by custom. *Sincerely, Sincerely yours, Very sincerely yours* and *Very sincerely* are the correct phrases for formal social letters.

For informal letters, the appropriate closing varies according to the degree of friendship with the person addressed. In general, men are more formal than women. The forms of closing most usually used are, in order of decreasing formality:

Yours cordially,
Faithfully yours,
As ever,
Fondly,

Yours affectionately,
Lovingly yours,
Devotedly,

Your signature, written legibly in ink, is placed below the closing and somewhat to the right. It should end in line with the letter's right-hand margin. With the exceptions noted below, signatures never include titles, such as *Dr., Mr., Mrs.*

For a married woman the accepted forms of signature in a social letter are:

Very formal or legal—

   Joan Saunders Cortland

Less formal or business—

   Joan Cortland

or

   Joan S. Cortland

To avoid possible confusion or to indicate married status, a woman may use a double signature:

   Joan Cortland
   (Mrs. Milton Cortland)

An unmarried woman may place *Miss* in parentheses before her name. A new bride often uses the formal signature, showing both maiden and married name, to identify her to friends not familiar with her new name.

In addressing an envelope, the important elements are clearness, correctness, and completeness. Name and address are written in full on the envelope unless the address is long or complicated. In shortening an address, substitute figures for spelled-out numbers. The words *Street, Avenue, Road, Place, Court,* etc., are not abbreviated; neither is the name of a city.

Each line of the address should be indented, and an envelope should follow this form:

   Mrs. Milton Saunders
   224 Northwest Street
   Janesville, Ohio

The return address is placed in the upper left-hand corner on the front of the envelope. Although the return address is often seen written on the envelope flap, this is not considered the best form.

Before you put your letter in the envelope, read it over to see if it is everything you wanted it to be. Ask yourself if your letter is:

Clear

Will the reader understand what you mean to say? Watch your choice of words, sentence structure, punctuation, and paragraphing. Avoid unusual language and long, complicated sentences.

Unaffected

Remember that a good letter reflects your personality. Does the letter ring true? Have you taken the path of least resistance and started the letter with a rubber-stamp opening such as *How are you?*, *We are fine, This is in answer to your letter of June 14th?*

Complete

Have you provided all the essential information that you planned to convey? To make sure, do what the good newspaper reporter does and check the five W's and one H—what, who, where, when, why, and how.

Correct

Check your letter for the correct facts, address, grammar, and spelling.

Courteous

If you wish to make friends, keep friends, and influence people, avoid tactlessness, egotism, and inappropriate language.

Neat

Avoid erasures, cross-outs, overprints, unbalanced margins, and ink blots.

Friendly

Unless it is a message of complaint or indignation, your letter should leave the reader with a pleasant feeling. Don't complain, nag, bluster, or threaten. Avoid ridicule, sarcasm, and malicious gossip.

CHAPTER 3

Invitations and Announcements

Invitations and announcements play an important part in everyone's life. In the old days the etiquette surrounding such social events as parties, dinners, at-homes, dances, and luncheons was very much according to the rule book, and only two types of social affairs were recognized—the formal and the informal. Today, when life is so much more casual, the categories are less strict. But there are still reminders of the extreme formality of bygone days in such affairs as the formal dinner, dance, and wedding. Wedding invitations and announcements are in a category by themselves and will be dealt with on page 14.

Invitations to a large formal affair may be engraved or handwritten on one's most formal personal stationery. They are written in the third person and sent out approximately two weeks ahead of time. If the stationery used for a handwritten invitation does not have the address at the top, the address is written on the invitation.

A formal invitation is addressed to husband and wife if both are expected. A single daughter may be included in the parents' invitation, but two or more daughters must be invited individually or as a unit (the Misses Saunders). With the exception of the husband, the men of the family receive separate invitations.

Engraved invitation to a formal dinner

Mr. and Mrs. John Cortland
request the pleasure of your company
at dinner
on Friday, June the second
at eight o'clock
100 Grove Street
Janesville

Engraved fill-in invitation to a formal dance

Dr. and Mrs. Robert Silvers
request the pleasure of
Mr. and Mrs. Johnston's[1]
company at a dance
on Friday, the fifteenth of October
at half after ten o'clock
Island Beach Club

R.S.V.P.
One Elm Place

Handwritten invitation to a formal dinner

*Mr. and Mrs. Lawrence Curley
request the pleasure of
Mr. and Mrs. Fitzwilliam's
company at dinner
on Tuesday, April the twelfth
at eight o'clock*

R.S.V.P.   *21 Shaw Place
Oakmont*

Most social occasions today are informal and require only
simple notes, in some cases only an invitation by telephone.
However, there are certain rules all invitations should follow,
for both the hostess and guest. Indicate what kind of party is
planned—shower, birthday, open house, etc. Make it clear
where the party is to take place and at what time guests are
expected to arrive. Ask for an acknowledgment, and be sure
invitations are mailed at least a week in advance.

In making up invitations for an informal party, you can let
your imagination be your guide in creating clever and original

---

[1] Italic type indicates handwriting.

invitations. For instance, invitations to a bridal shower are often written in appropriate verse on little cut-out umbrellas.

A party for newlyweds or a couple celebrating an anniversary may make use of a wedding-band invitation. Cut out a strip of paper eight inches long and four inches wide from a piece of mat stock, and fold it in half to form a booklet. On the cover paste the center of a four-inch round paper doily. Then cover a small piece of wire with gold crepe paper, shape it into a circle two and one-fourth inches in diameter, and paste it on the cover of the booklet. Your invitation now has the attractive effect of a gold wedding band on bridal lace. In the center of the ring write the invitation, specifying the type of party and the guests of honor. Inside the booklet write the date, time, place, and an *R.S.V.P.* note.

Informal invitation to dinner

Dear Miss Mannering,

Will you and Miss Nevins have dinner with us at our home on Wednesday, April the seventh, at seven o'clock?

It has been a long time since we have had the pleasure of seeing you, and we do hope you will find it possible to be with us.

Yours sincerely,

Dear Mathilda,

Will you and Helen Nivins have dinner with us on Wednesday, the seventh of April, at seven o'clock?

We want to hear all about your trip to New York, and have you meet Sidney and John Milton, who are visiting here.

Cordially,

Informal invitation to lunch or tea

Dear Jean,

Will you come to lunch on Tuesday, June the sixth, at one o'clock?

Lillian Roberts is bringing a surprise dessert from her bottomless recipe file, which should be reason enough to bring you out!

I am looking forward to hearing all about your vacation. So do say you will come.

Yours affectionately,

Dear Mrs. Adams,

I have asked a few friends to come for tea on Wednesday, April the eighth, at four o'clock. Will you join us?

My new neighbor, Martha Simmons, will be here, and I think you will enjoy meeting her. She is widely traveled, witty—and very good company.

I know that the Women's Club occupies much of your time, but I hope you are not too busy to join us. I am looking forward to seeing you.

Cordially yours,

Informal invitation to bridge

Dear Jean,

Can you and Bill join us for bridge on Thursday evening, May the ninth? The Maitlands and the Darlings are coming, and as you know, they are top-flight players.

We plan to start playing at about eight-thirty, and we are looking forward to seeing you. Do try to make it.

Affectionately,

Week-end house guests

Invitations to house guests must be by letter, since there are many things your guests need to know. House guests must know when they are expected to arrive and when they are expected to leave. They should be given clear instructions for reaching your home by car or train (include a train schedule with your letter and write if they will be met at the station). Let the guests know what activities are scheduled, so they can bring proper clothes and equipment. Be sure to give your guests sufficient notice, so they can make any necessary arrangements.

Here is a typical invitation:

Dear Cynthia,

John and I would love you and Milton to join us for the week-end of January the twentieth. We've had real winter weather up here, and we think we can promise you some good skating.

Sylvia and Tom Darling will be with us, and I know you won't want to miss their pointers on figure-skating. Just bring country clothes and your skates. We have a full supply of heavy sweaters, scarves, and mittens.

Our train service is exceptionally good, as you can see by the enclosed schedule. The afternoon train leaving town at four-thirty, on Friday, gets you here in time for dinner. There is a choice of late trains returning on Sunday night.

We are looking forward to seeing you again, so please write and say you can come. Do let us know what train you will take, and John will meet you at the station.

Affectionately,

Occasionally it is necessary to recall an invitation. The form used for the recall should follow that used in the invitation. If time does not permit engraving, a "recall" should be written by hand.

Recalling an invitation—formal (handwritten)

Mr. and Mrs. James Saunders regret that they are obliged to recall their invitations for Tuesday, the third of April, owing to the illness of their son.

Mr. and Mrs. James Saunders regret that, owing to the death of Mrs. Saunders' mother, they are obliged to recall their invitation for Wednesday, the third of June.

Informal

Dear Peg,

As you may have heard, John's grandmother has been taken to the hospital. Naturally, all of us are very worried about her.

Under the circumstances, I have called off the dinner party we had planned for Wednesday, the third of March. I know you will understand.

I will be in touch with you again soon.

As ever,

Wedding invitations and announcements

Invitations and announcements for a formal wedding must be engraved on paper on the very best quality. The usual size is a folded sheet measuring 7½ inches by 5½ inches. To insure correctness, have the engraving done by a reliable and reputable stationer. Three weeks are usually required for the engraving, and all invitations should be mailed out at the same time—at least three weeks in advance of the event.

A formal invitation requires two envelopes. The outside envelope follows the form for all formal correspondence. The inside envelope contains the actual invitation (usually covered with a thin tissue to protect the engraving from smudging) and bears the title and family name of the person invited.

A separate invitation is sent to each adult member of the family except the husband and wife. When the family includes young children to be invited, their names are omitted from the outside envelope and their given names only are written under their parents' names on the inside envelope.

> Mr. and Mrs. Young
> Sally and Jonathan

Sisters may receive a single invitation addressed in the form *The Misses Ruth and Louise Young*. The same rule holds true for grown sons, who are addressed in the form *The Messrs. Lawrence and James Young*.

Unless the parents are divorced or one of them is dead, the wedding invitation is issued in the name of both parents. If neither parent is alive, the nearest relative or closest friend issues the invitations.

The accepted form for a formal church wedding issued by the bride's parents is:

> Mr. and Mrs. James Saunders
> request the honour of your presence
> at the marriage of their daughter
> Margaret
> to
> Mr. Thomas Cortland
> on Wednesday, the seventeenth of June
> One thousand nine hundred and sixty-eight
> at twelve o'clock
> Saint Anne's Church
> Janesville

When not all those attending the wedding are to be invited to the reception, a reception card of the same paper and half the size of the invitation is included with the tissue. The reception card follows this form:

Mr. and Mrs. James Saunders
request the pleasure of your company
at the wedding breakfast
following the ceremony
at
One hundred Grove Street

R.S.V.P.

When all those attending the ceremony are to be invited to the reception, the invitation may combine church ceremony and reception in this form:

Mr. and Mrs. James Saunders
request the honour of your presence
at the marriage of their daughter
Margaret
to
Mr. Thomas Cortland
on Wednesday, the seventeenth of June
One thousand nine hundred and sixty-eight
at twelve o'clock
Saint Anne's Church
Janesville
and afterward at
One hundred Grove Street

R.S.V.P.

A small informal wedding assumes an air of inappropriate pretentiousness if engraved invitations are sent. Although engraved announcements are often sent to relatives and friends at a distance after an informal wedding, the actual invitations are written on conservative note paper in blue or black ink. Mailed two weeks in advance, the informal invitation gives the time and place of the ceremony and reception.

The accepted form for an informal wedding invitation is:

100 Grove Street
Janesville, Ohio
June 3, 1968

Dear Jean,

Margaret is being married at home to Thomas Cortland, Wednesday, June the seventeenth, at four-thirty. We hope you will be with us and will be able to stay for the reception afterward.

As ever,

Wedding announcements

The formal engraved wedding announcement is sent only to those not invited to the wedding ceremony. It reads as follows:

Mr. and Mrs. Timothy Smith
have the honour of announcing
[*or* have the honour to announce]
the marriage of their daughter
Barbara
to
Mr. John Paul Jones
on Saturday, the fifth of December
One thousand nine hundred and sixty-eight
St. Bartholomew's Church
Janesville

An at-home card is often included with the wedding announcement. Of the same style as the reception card but smaller in size, it gives the new address of the couple.

At Home
after the first of January
2208 Poplar Lane
Janesville, Ohio

Although the parents of a young divorcée or widow issue the announcement of her wedding, a more mature divorcée or widow may issue her own announcement in conjuction with her husband:

Mrs. James Blue
and
Mr. Sidney Wheeler
announce their marriage
etc.

When it is necessary to call off a wedding the guests must be informed promptly by notes or printed or engraved cards. The wedding recall reads:

Mr. and Mrs. Sidney Thelan
announce that the marriage of their daughter
Marilyn
to
Mr. Anthony Stuart Kent
will not take place

Birth announcements

There are many novel ways other than by letter to announce the birth of a child. A charming way is to attach a small engraved card bearing the baby's name and date of birth to the parents' calling card with a pink, blue, or white ribbon.

Mary Ann Walters
May 10th, 1968

Mr. and Mrs. Jay Walters

Very often novel birth announcements can be tied in with the vocation or avocation of the parents. A journalist might create a miniature newspaper or news report. A travel agent could stress the "new arrival" or "launching." A lawyer might present a brief.

A novel announcement in booklet form could follow this pattern:

ANNOUNCING

THE

WORLD PREMIERE

ON

MAY 10th, 1968

OF

MARY ANN WALTERS

Produced by
Marjorie and Jay, Inc.
Released by
Dr. John Pearl
Edited by
Rev. Martin Sohn
Sound effects by
MARY ANN
Preview
St. Anne's Hospital
Regular Showings
3365 Cedarlawn Avenue
starting May 24th
after 3 P.M.

(picture)

MARY ANN WALTERS

Invitation to a christening

Dear Martin,

Our son is to be christened at St. Anastasia Church next Sunday. He is to carry his father's name, Joseph.

For so many years we have considered you as almost one of the family. It would make Rosemarie and me most happy if you would consent to be Joseph, Jr.'s godfather. Timothy Donlon has already consented to join in the ceremony.

After the service, a small group will be gathering at our house for luncheon and I will trust you will be able to join us.

Cordially,

Announcement of a death

When someone in the family dies, etiquette performs a real service by providing an orderly list of things to be done and by assuring that they are done with proper dignity. Those members of the family who are not present and a few intimate friends should be notified immediately. This is usually done by telephone or telegram. However, it is often necessary to write a letter. Such letters require tact and dignity.

Dear Mr. Johnson,

I am writing to let you know that my father, Sidney B. Balister, died on Thursday, June the fourth, after a short illness.

He had mentioned you as a friend so often that I knew you would want to be informed.

Sincerely,

Dear Uncle John,

Something has happened that was a great shock to us and I am afraid will be to you. Mother, who, as you know, had been ill for some years, passed away last night in her sleep.

The funeral is to be held at St. Anastasia Church on Forest Avenue, Janesville, Tuesday at three o'clock. Burial will be at Fairlawn Cemetery.

We know you join in our prayers and in our sorrow.

Affectionately,

CHAPTER 4

Acceptances and Regrets

Letters of acceptance or regret are sent out promptly. An invitation is accepted or declined with the same degree of formality with which it is issued.

Following are the traditional forms for a letter of acceptance and a letter of regret. These are suitable for any formal occasion except a wedding.

Formal acceptance

> Mr. and Mrs. Rufus Johnston
> accept with pleasure
> the kind invitation of
> Dr. and Mrs. Silvers
> to a dance
> on Friday, the fifteenth of October
> at half after ten
> Island Beach Club

Formal regret

> Mr. and Mrs. Rufus Johnston
> regret exceedingly
> that because of a previous engagement
> they are unable to accept
> Dr. and Mrs. Silvers'
> kind invitation for the fifteenth of October

In accepting or declining an informal invitation, it is of the utmost importance to give a prompt and definite answer, to imply a "thank you," and to convey the thought that you were pleased at being invited. A note of regret should give the reason for declining and imply one's sincere regrets.

Informal acceptance to dinner

Dear Mrs. Cortland,

Miss Nevins and I will be delighted to dine with you on Wednesday, the seventh of April, at seven o'clock. Thank you so much for asking us.

We are both looking forward to seeing you and Mr. Cortland again.

Very sincerely,

Informal dinner regret

Dear Mrs. Cortland,

Miss Nevins and I are so sorry that we cannot dine with you on Wednesday, the seventh of April. Unfortunately, we already have an engagement that evening.

We do appreciate your asking us and hope we will have the opportunity to say yes at some future time.

Sincerely yours,

Informal acceptance to lunch or tea

Dear Ruth,

I can't think of anything I'd rather do more than come to lunch with you on Tuesday, June the sixth. You can be sure that I will be there promptly at one o'clock.

One of Lillian's special desserts would tempt a saint, but most of all I am looking forward to seeing you again!

Affectionately,

Informal lunch or tea regret

Dear Meg,

How nice of you to ask me to tea on Wednesday, the sixteenth of May. I only wish I could be with you, but unfortunately Wednesday is now my day to work at the Women's Club Canteen.

Thanks so much for asking me, Meg. You know how sorry I am to miss being with you.

Affectionately yours,

Informal acceptance to bridge

Dear Helen,

You can most certainly count on us for your bridge party on Thursday, May the ninth. It's been months since we've had a really exciting game of bridge.

Bill and I are both glad of the opportunity to see the Maitlands and Darlings again, and we will brush up on our rules so we can offer some real competition.

Thanks for asking us. We'll see you promptly at eight-thirty.

Fondly,

Informal bridge regret

Dear Helen,

I wish I could accept your invitation to play bridge on Thursday, May the ninth, but since we are not sure we will have that evening free I think it would be wisest not to count on our coming.

As you know, this is Bill's busy season. He has been bringing work home every evening, and he can't guarantee that he will be all caught up by the ninth.

I know a last-minute change of plans would ruin your bridge party, so I must say No, but with the hope that you'll ask us again soon.

Affectionately,

Informal week-end acceptance

Dear Marge,

The minute Milton read your invitation he made arrangements to have our skates sharpened. So tell Sylvia and Tom to look to their laurels. We are delighted that you asked us and won't let anything prevent us from coming.

As you suggested, we will take the four-thirty train from town Friday. And we'll take the ten-twenty express back to the city Sunday night.

Thanks so very much for asking us. You know how much we are looking forward to seeing all of you again.

Fondly,

Informal week-end regret

Dear Marge,

We feel so badly at the thought of turning down your wonderful invitation. But I'm afraid it's a case of business before pleasure. An important client of Milton's company is coming to New York the week-end of January the twentieth, and Milton will be called upon to devote full time to this Very Important Person.

Thanks so much for asking us, Marge. I know we'll be missing a wonderful time. Do remember us to the Darlings and tell them how sorry we are not to see them.

Affectionately yours,

An invitation to a church wedding does not require an acknowledgment unless an invitation to the reception is included. When an acceptance or regret is called for, it is written on the best conservative stationery and follows the wording and the spacing of the original formal invitation:

Mr. and Mrs. Walter King
accept with pleasure
Mr. and Mrs. James Saunders'
kind invitation to
the wedding breakfast of their daughter
Margaret
and
Mr. Thomas Cortland
at twelve o'clock
One hundred Grove Street

A formal regret to a wedding reception reads:

Mr. and Mrs. Walter King
regret that they are unable to accept
Mr. and Mrs. James Saunders'
kind invitation for
Wednesday, the seventeenth of June

The acceptance to an informal note of invitation for a small informal wedding and reception might read:

Dear Ruth,

Tom and I wouldn't miss Margaret's wedding for anything in the world. You may be sure that we'll be there on Wednesday, June the seventeenth, at four-thirty.

Thanks so very much for including us among the friends you want to have with you at this wonderful event,

Fondly,

An informal regret could say:

Dear Ruth,

Tom and I regret so very much that we will not be able to attend Margaret's wedding on Wednesday, June the seventeenth.

It was so thoughtful of you to ask us, but our Caribbean cruise starts on June the seventh and we will not be back in time for the wedding.

We send our very best wishes to Margaret and Thomas, and we shall be with them in spirit on the happy day.

Fondly,

Asking for another invitation

Dear Joan,

Out of a clear sky, we learned today that Nat's cousin Joe will be in from the West Coast next week. Of course, he will be staying at our house most of the time.

You have never had an opportunity to meet Joe, but he is a very interesting part of the family—an adventurer as well as a businessman.

May we bring Joe along to your dinner party on the tenth? I am sure you will find many things in common.

Of course, Joan, if it will be inconvenient or for any reason you'd rather not have an extra guest, don't hesitate to say so. We can make other plans for him at the Club and arrange to meet him there later.

Cordially,

Helpful Sentences

To say no

I shall have to say No to your kind invitation of . . .
Very regretfully . . .
Unfortunately it will be impossible for . . .
I regret I cannot accept . . .
Because of Jonathan's illness, we find that we cannot . . .
I am sincerely sorry that John and I cannot join your dinner party . . .
Nothing would please me more than to join you for lunch on Tuesday, but unfortunately . . .
If it were possible, I would be delighted to . . .
Please accept my sincere regrets at not being able to join . . .

To say yes

We are delighted to accept . . .
It is with great pleasure . . .
We look forward with pleasure to joining you . . .
We are sincerely happy to join you . . .
Nothing would give us greater pleasure than accepting your kind invitation . . .

CHAPTER 5

Letters of Congratulation

The key to success in writing a letter of congratulation is promptness. Write the letter as soon as you hear the good news and are still filled with initial pleasure at hearing of the birth of a child, an engagement, an honor.

We all like to share someone's good fortune, and for that reason the letter of congratulation is especially pleasant to write. And it is the kind of letter that goes a long way to making friendships warm and lasting.

Here are 20 typical reasons for writing a letter of congratulation.

A person receives recognition for any achievement, passes a birthday, plans an interesting vacation, gets promoted, takes a public stand on an issue, gets a new customer, recovers from an illness, has a happy family event, plays a good game of golf, joins a new organization.

A company passes an important anniversary, creates a new product or service, establishes a new policy, gets a new account, lowers or raises prices, runs an interesting advertisement, changes a business policy, designs a new package, takes a stand on a political issue, or joins a trade association.

A few basic rules to remember, aside from the all-important necessity of being prompt, are sincerity, cheerfulness, mentioning the occasion, and in most cases, brevity.

Congratulations on an engagement

Only the man receives "congratulations" on his engagement. The woman receives "best wishes."

Dear Dick,

Your brother told me the great news about your engagement to Anne. All I can say is that some men have all the luck!

Anne is a wonderful girl in every way, and I congratulate you on your good fortune and wish you both the best of everything in life.

As ever,

Dear Dick,

Uncle Ed and I were delighted to hear of your engagement to Anne—although to tell the truth we have been expecting it.

We've known you both since you were toddlers, and you have all the qualities that go toward making a marriage successful. The best of all good wishes to you both.

Affectionately,

Dear Anne,

The best of luck to you and Dick!

I heard the good news this morning and called George right away to tell him. We think it's really wonderful, since we can't think of two people more suited to each other than you and Dick.

I know you'll both be happy, always.

Fondly,

Dear Anne,

Mother wrote us the good news of your engagement, and you just can't imagine how pleased we are. Everything we've heard about Richard points to his having the qualities that make an excellent husband.

Uncle Henry joins me in sending best wishes and in offering an invitation to bring Richard to see us soon. Please send him our congratulations and sincere good wishes.

Affectionately,

Congratulations on a marriage

Congratulations are sent to the bride and groom when a wedding announcement is received. Although the letter is usually written and addressed to both, it may be written individually to the bride or groom.

Dear Isabel and George,

Tom and I were thrilled to hear about your wedding!

We both send you our love and best wishes for all the good things in life.

Do let us know when you will be back in Janesville, so we can deliver our congratulations personally.

Affectionately yours,

Dear Isabel,

It seems only yesterday that you told me you were engaged, and now you are married! I haven't met George, but from everything I've heard I know that both of you will be very happy.

Congratulations to George and my very best wishes to the two of you for a marriage filled with all the good things in life.

Sincerely,

Dear Mrs. Clarence,

Mr. Stafford and I take this opportunity to wish you and Mr. Clarence happiness on your recent marriage.

With every good wish,

Sincerely yours,

Dear George,

Martha and I were delighted to receive the announcement of your marriage in today's mail.

Please accept our most sincere congratulations and very best wishes for all the good fortune in the world.

Cordially,

Congratulations on the birth of a child

A letter of congratulation on the arrival of a baby is sent to the mother. It should be cordial, gay, and a little on the flattering side if the proud mother is a close friend or relative.

Dear Peggy,

Uncle Ben called today to tell us the wonderful news. We are all as delighted as you and Henry to have a baby girl in the family at last.

I hear little Susan is a real heartbreaker even at the young age of five days. It is certainly a case of like mother, like daughter!

Henry must be bursting with pride. Tell him that Dick and I send you our very finest brand of best wishes and congratulations.

Fondly,

Dear Peggy,

Congratulations on the new baby. I couldn't be more excited if it were my own!

Henry tells me you are calling her Susan. It's a charming name for a little girl who, according to all reports, is a real charmer already!

I can't wait to see you and the baby, so please let me know when you will be able to have visitors. In the meantime, all my love to you both.

Affectionately,

Birthday congratulations

Although birthday cards are in almost universal use, a handwritten letter of congratulation shows more sincerity and sense of real friendship. To your closest friends and your dearest relatives a birthday note, no matter how brief, always will mean more than a ready-made card, no matter what its cost or sentiment.

Dear George,

If I were called upon to rewrite the definition of "birthday," I would change it to read—"the day we are glad you were born."
HAPPY BIRTHDAY TO YOU!

As ever,

Dear Cecile,

Congratulations on this happy day. The best of all good things for this birthday and all the many more to come.

Affectionately yours,

Dear Isabel,

If only you lived a little closer I could come and bring my happy birthday wishes to you in person. But I will do the next best thing and send you my love, congratulations, and warmest wishes for this day and every day.

Fondly,

Dear Aunt Sophie,

To most people March is a reminder that spring is on its way. But to me it means the month that holds the birthday of my favorite aunt.

All of us in Janesville miss you particularly at this time of the year, although we try to console ourselves by remembering when you lived here and shared all the fun of family parties and picnics.

But near or far, you know, Aunt Sophie, that on your birthday as on every day we are all thinking of you with love and affection.

A very, very happy birthday and many, many more of them to come.

Love,

Congratulations on graduation

Dear Ned,

It seems only yesterday that Aunt Nora and I were helping you learn your ABC's—and now you have graduated from Janesville High and been accepted at Ohio State!

We are both very proud of you, Ned. We have followed your high-school career with joy and pleasure and know that your four years at college will be even more rewarding. A word of congratulation just doesn't seem enough, so I am sending you a gift that I'm sure you will find useful—an unabridged dictionary. Aunt Nora says you'll not only find it handy in your studies, but a great argument-saver at Scrabble!

Mother and Dad are coming here for a week-end next month. Please try to take a few days off from your exciting life and come along too. We are looking forward to seeing you.

Affectionately,

Dear Clarice,

Please add my warmest congratulations to the large chorus of friends acclaiming your graduation.

I heard all about the honors you won, with delight but not surprise. Everyone knew you would distinguish yourself at college as in high school.

I understand that you are going to Zenith to join the staff of *The Daily Press*. My very best wishes go with you. I'm sure you will conquer the world of journalism with the same ease and charm as you did the campus world.

The best of luck to you!

As ever,

Congratulations on winning an honor or prize

Dear Mrs. Stafford,

All of us at the office take great pleasure in sending congratulations to you for winning the Women's Club Citation. I know of no one who deserves it more than you.

Our very best wishes to you.

Sincerely,

Dear Ed,

I was delighted to hear that you won second prize in the Thomas Jefferson Essay Contest. It must feel good to know that you ranked among the best in a state-wide contest.

All of your friends are proud of you.

Cordially,

Dear Thomas,

My warmest congratulations to you on receiving the regional scholarship to the State College of Engineering.

It is an award that you richly deserve. I know you will be a credit to the traditions of that fine school and to your chosen profession.

You have my very best wishes for your continued success.

Sincerely,

Congratulations on a business promotion

Dear Mr. Tompkins,

It was with mixed feelings of pleasure and disappointment that I read of your promotion to sales manager of the Louisville office—pleasure at seeing a long-standing business friend get the promotion he deserved, and disappointment in knowing that from now on you won't be passing through Zenith every month.

I don't have to tell you that all of us in this area wish you the best of luck in your new position.

We know we will be reading more good news about you in the trade papers.

Very cordially,

Dear Charlie,

Mort told me the good news about your being appointed Merchandising Manager of the Omicron Company.

It's the kind of news I like to hear, Charlie, because it proves once again that a good man always gets ahead.

Let me offer my warmest congratulations. I know you are going to be tops in the merchandising field.

Sincerely,

Congratulations on military promotion

Dear Bill,

So the Navy finally realized what a great sailor you are. I could have told them the minute I saw you in uniform!

Now that you're Ensign Thomas, don't look down your nose at your old civilian friends. We are mighty proud of you and are sure you will end up with a lot of gold braid on your sleeves.

Keep up the good work and take care of yourself.

As ever,

Dear Ralph,

Everyone in the office joins me in sending congratulations on your new rank. Gladys, particularly, thinks being a sergeant is just about the most wonderful thing in the world.

Please be sure to put the office on your itinerary when you're home on furlough. We'd like to see you in uniform and hear all about Army life.

Cordially,

Dear Alex,

You should have seen Dad's chest swell when he heard the news of your promotion. I thought he would just about burst!

All of us are really proud of you. Please write and keep us posted on how it feels to be a First Lieutenant.

Fondly,

Unsolicited compliments

One of the best ways to make friends is to send a complimentary letter when it is not necessary—an unsolicited compliment.

This is especially true of a business and for a business. So few people send such letters that they can have important effects on the career of an employee, on business policy, and on your relationship with a firm.

Helpful Sentences

Congratulations

What exciting (wonderful) (thrilling) (happy) news!

It's good (great) (sensational) news (the most joyful news I have heard for a long time).

Mother just told us the (momentous) (cheerful) news.

I was delighted (thrilled) (pleasantly surprised) to hear (to receive) the news (to receive the announcement) (to read in the newspaper) . . .

So you've done it (gone and got married) (been promoted)!

So you and Tom are engaged!

I congratulate you . . .

Congratulations on . . .

Warm (sincere) congratulations . . .

Congratulations, good luck, and best wishes—all in one breath.

I was (I am) (we were) so exited (delighted) (thrilled) to hear (by the news) . . .

Congratulations and all good (best) wishes!

You have no idea what a thrill (kick) (great pleasure) I got when I heard . . .

Accept my heartiest congratulations . . .

Permit me to congratulate you . . .

It is always a pleasure to say . . .

My warmest (heartiest) (sincerest) congratulations . . .

I am gladder than glad . . .

We want you to know how happy we were . . .

May I join in the chorus of congratulations . . .

May an old friend congratulate you . . .

It gave me a great deal of pleasure to learn . . .

I was delighted to learn . . .

Good wishes

I wish (let us wish) you all the happiness in the world (every happiness life can bring) (every happiness) (all possible joy and happiness) (increasing happiness as the years go by) (continued joy and contentment) (the best of luck) (a hundred years of happiness).

We hope you will have nothing but joy and happiness (in your life together) (in your chosen career).

I wish you many more anniversaries—each happier than the last.

I hope that each year finds you happier than the one before.

Many happy returns!

We hope you will (both) be very happy (always).

Sidney and I join in sending (both send) our love (best wishes).

Best wishes from all of us on . . .

Our very best wishes . . .

Best of the best wishes . . .

We certainly wish you all the happiness in the world . . .

The best of everything (to both of you).

The heartiest good wishes . . .

Loads and loads of good luck (good wishes) (happiness).

All the luck in the world to you.

She's a fine girl.

We have heard so much about her (we are eager to meet her).

I think you're a lucky guy.

I think it's swell.

She's a wonderful (fine) (splendid) (marvelous) (charming) (very lovely) (pretty) girl in every way.

She will make you a wonderful (excellent) (charming) wife. She has everything a young man would hope for (both feet on the ground) (good sense).

If you picked her, she must be a winner.

You're the luckiest guy in the world!

He's a fine fellow!

We have known Tom for years and have always known he's (thought of him as) tops (considerate) (dependable) (steady) (unusually fine) (a good provider) (lucky fellow) (fine fellow).

He's a swell (lucky) man (fellow) (chap) (guy)!

He has everything a girl could want in a husband (both feet on the ground) (a good background)!

He comes of a good family.

I don't know anyone who would make you happier (I would rather have you marry).

I don't know Tom, but from everything I've heard about him he's quite a fellow. I want to meet him soon (everyone has a good word to say for him) (he has an excellent reputation) (he's reputed to be one of the best).

Both of you

We never knew two people better suited to each other.

You were made for each other. I knew it as soon as I met her (him).

It's a wonderful baby!

Dad must be busting with joy (pride) (happiness).

He must be wonderful if he's yours (from all the reports I've had) (if I'm to believe Mother) (if he's at all like his parents).

I hear she's just like her mother (simply beautiful) (very lovely) (charming) (the prettiest baby in the world) even at ten days old.

I hear he's just like his father (the biggest baby in the hospital) (cute as can be) (the handsomest guy in the world).

I hope she grows up to be everything you want her to be (just like her mother) (as charming and beautiful, etc., as her mother).

For one so inexperienced in the ways of the world, she shows remarkable judgment in the selection of her parents.

He's the handsomest little gentleman I've ever seen!

Happy Birthday!

It's your birthday, and once again . . .

It's a very special occasion again . . .

To some people it's only July 6th, but to me this day will always be remembered as the birthday of my favorite cousin.

I couldn't let February 12th go by without sending my "Happy Birthday" wishes to you. May this birthday be an especially happy one.

Congratulations (greetings) and sincere good wishes on your birthday.

The best of (all my) love to the best mother (dad) (sister) a guy ever had. Your son sends you the biggest kiss and the tightest hug a letter can carry.

I know you don't count birthdays any more, but I'm sending my love, just as before.

Here's a word of cheer on your birthday (warm birthday greetings) from an old friend (your ever loving Aunt) (old faithful).

Congratulations and all good wishes.

Hearty congratulations and all good wishes on this milestone (wonderful day) in your life.

I want you to know that we are thinking of you on your birthday and wishing you the best of everything life has to offer.

With gifts

I hope this (little) gift will add a bit to your enjoyment (happiness) on your birthday (during the years ahead).

I hope you received the little remembrance I sent. When you use it, you may remember the trout we used to catch when there weren't so many distractions to keep us at our desks.

Anniversary geetings

I look forward to greeting you on your golden wedding anniversary. May you have many golden (happy) (good) years.

May each year bring you new (greater) happiness (joys).

Congratulations and best wishes (every good wish) to you both for a long life, health, happiness, and prosperity (many more anniversaries).

May you always have everything you wish for (happiness and contentment) (fair weather and smooth sailing) (a rich life together).

I couldn't let this happy occasion go by without allowing myself the pleasure of sending you my sincere good wishes for many happy years ahead.

Many happy returns of the day!

May the years ahead fulfill all your hopes (dreams).

All of us, wish to both of you

The wishes you wish will all come true.

A great accomplishment

My hat's off to you!

I'm proud of you.

My enthusiasm about you prompts me to write . . .

The careful planning and hard work is reflected in a job well done.

The recognition you have received is well deserved.

Permit me to send my enthusiastic congratulations.

Three cheers for you and for the Omicron Company—an outfit that knows a good man when it sees one.

It was a tough assignment, and you handled it with credit.

It was a splendid performance (great triumph) (brilliant speech). I liked especially. . . .

It is a superb (fine) (record) . . .

I admire your judgment (planning) (perseverance) (ingenuity) (achievement) (capacity to get things done) (impressive record).

It's wonderful to know that you have achieved the goal you set for yourself (completed the dream of a lifetime) (won the recognition you deserve).

A great honor

How does it feel to be famous!

I am delighted (thrilled) (very pleased) (excited).

I can think of no one who deserves it more (no way in which we could express our opinion of you more sincerely) (no honor that can do justice to the fine work you have done).

We are fortunate in having you among our members (friends).

It is a well-deserved recognition of your excellent work (accomplishments) (leadership) (achievements in the field).

I am basking in the reflected glory that I gather from knowing you (your achievement brings to the organization) (your honor brings to all of us).

I am sure you must be very happy and proud (thrilled) (excited) (pleased) at the great honor (selection of your work) (recognition).

From a distance

My thoughts are with you in Janesville, even though I cannot be present.

I wish I could be with you to share the occasion (in the celebration) (the joy).

CHAPTER 6

Letters of Condolence

Letters of condolence are particularly difficult for most people to write. But there is probably no time when a letter is so deeply appreciated.

Write such a letter promptly while the shock of the news is still with you. Be brief, tactful, and sincere. Avoid gushy sentiment, morbid details, and discussions of the philosophy of death. Don't say "She was too young to die" or "Life will be desolate without him." A letter of condolence has only one purpose—to give comfort tactfully and sincerely.

Dear Shirley,

There is little one can say at a time like this. But I'd like you to know that I'm thinking of you and that you have my heartfelt sympathy.

Sincerely,

Dear Sid,

I heard of the loss of your father today, and I know how you must feel. I just can't tell you how sorry I am.

I know that nothing I can write can dull your sorrow since only time can do that—and it will, Sid.

Please call me if there is anything I can do to help.

Sincerely,

Dear Jane,

Your father had a rich full life and lived every minute of it without regrets. Let the thoughts of a life well-spent be your consolation now. Knowing your father as I did, I am sure that is the way he would have wanted it.

You will miss him, as we all will. But time will bring comfort in the fond memories of your many good years together.

George and the boys join me in sending our deepest sympathy.

Affectionately,

Dear Mrs. Cortland,

Mrs. Tompkins and I are deeply sorry to hear of your great loss. Please accept our sincere condolences and call on us if there is anything we can do.

> Sincerely,

Dear Mrs. Rose,

If I knew the magic words that could comfort you at a time like this, I would write them today. But I know how little anything I can say can be of real help at a time like this. Jim was so much a part of your life and he was a small part of mine.

I feel for you in your sorrow and extend my sincere sympathy.

> Very sincerely,

Dear Cynthia and Paul,

Although there is little consolation in a note, Milton and I want you to know that our thoughts are with you at this sad time.

We would do anything to ease your sorrow if we only could. Our love and heartfelt sympathy to you both.

> Affectionately yours,

Dear Anne,

The news of Dickie's death came as a shock to all of us. We loved him very much and our deepest sympathy goes out to you.

Mother feels that it might be best for you to join us this summer at Cape Cod. I think you will find the peace and quiet of the country restful and soothing.

Meanwhile, if there is anything we can do please don't hesitate to call.

> Affectionately,

Dear Ruth,

The news of Jim's passing is a great sorrow to all of us in Janesville. How can we say how much he meant to us and how much we will miss him and his jolly stories and good spirits.

There is, of course, little comfort in knowing that so many of his friends join in your loss, but you must know that you have our heartfelt sympathy.

> Sincerely,

Dear Clarice,

We know there can be no real consolation on the sad loss of your sister. Daisy was so bright and charming that no one who knew her will ever forget her.

But for the sake of your mother you must be brave, Clarice. For now more than ever she will turn to you for comfort and courage.

To both of you, Ralph and I send our love and deepest sympathy.
Affectionately,

Dear Charles,

I have just heard the sad news.

May I add my sincere condolences to those of your many friends? I know there is not much one can say at a time like this, but you can take comfort in the knowledge that your mother had a full life and shared in the pleasures of your own successful career.
Very cordially,

Dear Mr. Tennyson,

May I extend to you my sincere sympathy at your loss.

Although I never had the privilege of knowing Harriet, I know how deeply you must be affected.

Please accept my heartfelt condolences in this hour of sorrow.
Very sincerely,

Helpful Sentences

I was extremely (terribly) (so) sorry to hear of the death of . . .

We have just heard (learned) with profound sorrow (regret) the sad news.

Mother told us of the sad news today.

It was a profound (sad) (great) shock to hear the tragic (sad) news.

I don't have to tell you how much we regret . . .

It is with the greatest disappointment . . .

I want you to know how much I sympathize with you and your family (how deeply we feel for you in your sorrow).

I wish there was something I could say or do to soften your grief (to help you).

I can't (must) tell you how sorry I am (how saddened we were) . . .

We were deeply saddened . . .

May I add my sincere sympathy (small word of consolation) to that of the many who knew and admired her (to that of her countless friends).

You have (know you have) our deepest (sincerest) (heartfelt) sympathy (you are in our thoughts).

Please accept my deepest sympathy (sincere condolence) on the death of . . .

Your sorrow is shared by everyone who knew and loved . . .

We want to offer (most) sincere (heartfelt) (deepest) sympathy.

There are no words that can express my great (overwhelming) (sincere) (deep) sorrow at . . .

I know words are not much comfort at a time like this (there are no words that can be a comfort to you now).

We wish it were in our power to soften your (great) (deep) sorrow.

I wish there were some way in which we could lighten your grief (burden of sorrow) (soften the blow that has come to you).

I hope the sympathy of your many good friends can in some way lighten your burden of sorrow.

Although there is little solace (consolation) in a note from a friend, I want you to know we all share . . .

Just now it seems impossible for you ever to be happy again. But time heals the wounds.

About the deceased

You have the consolation of knowing your brother went quickly without suffering (has come to an end of his long suffering) (had time to arrange his affairs and say good-by to you all) (had a rich, full life) (lived without regrets) (left a heritage of achievements that will be long remembered) (lived every minute of his life, richly and fully).

Everyone who knew Jean loved her.

He died as he lived, simply and quietly (surrounded by affection) (happy in the memories of life fully lived) (loved and respected) (admired by countless friends).

It isn't everyone who has had such a father, who held the esteem of every one (could count so many among his friends) (understood his children so well and was so close a companion to them).

Although I never met your father, I had heard you and your brother speak of him so often that I felt that I knew him.

We who knew him had a genuine love and respect for him.

He will be long remembered for his steadfast service to his host of friends and to the community.

I remember talking to your father while we were working together at the Center. He was always so willing to pitch in and lend a hand when a job had to be done.

I hope you can find a little comfort in the knowledge that your grief is shared by so many of Tim's friends (by the many friends who are thinking of you).

Kinship of a similar bereavement

When Mary died three years ago, I, too, felt the world was at an end, but time, in its own way, heals our wounds.

Offer of help

Please let me know what I can do to help.

Please call on me if there is anything I can do to help (for any help I can give).

Please don't (I hope you won't) hesitate to call on me if there is anything I can do (now and always).

There is, I know, little that even a good friend can do to help at a time like this, but . . .

You know you can always count on me (our friendship) (our affection).

Closing

I know you will be strong and brave for the sake of the children.

I know Sidney would not want you to grieve, for his sake and for the children's.

Please accept my love and sympathy.

We all join in sending you our heartfelt love.

I want you to know I am thinking of you.

CHAPTER 7

Letters of Sympathy and Good Cheer

People who are ill especially appreciate a letter of sympathy and good cheer. Although such a letter, like a letter of condolence, must be tactful and sincere, it needn't be as formal or dignified. Let the circumstances be your guide as to the tone of your letter. A friend recovering from an appendectomy would probably enjoy a light, witty note. But a person who is seriously ill would have every right to feel resentful of a letter written in a comical mood.

Not that a letter of sympathy should be gloomy. It should radiate warmth and friendliness and a sincere understanding of the person's bad times.

In writing to a person who is ill, convey the idea that everything will be all right, that he is well on the road to recovery. Minimize the illness, avoid dwelling on morbid details, and don't tell how a friend died of the same illness! Your letter may be as brief or as chatty as you wish.

Dear Mr. Thelan,

I was so sorry to hear you were in the hospital. Do hurry and get well! Everyone at the office misses you and hopes you will be back at your desk very soon.

Sincerely yours,

Dear Mrs. Neville,

Mrs. Saunders and I are mighty sorry to hear of your illness. Your many friends here in Janesville are thinking of you and won't be happy until we hear you're completely recovered.

I understand you will be hospitalized for a few weeks, so I'm sending you the new best-seller to help you while away the time. I hope you will enjoy it.

Cordially yours,

Dear Margie,

Sylvia called today to tell me you have decided to have your operation immediately. If Dr. Koenig tells you it is advisable, then it is sensible to have it over with once and for all. With all the modern facilities at City Hospital, you should be up and about in a few weeks minus all the old aches and pains.

Hurry up and get well soon. We're skipping our bridge nights till you get back, and you know how much of a strain that is on Sylvia!

Affectionately,

Dear Joe,

I always knew you loved your sleep, but this is the first time I've heard of anyone going to the hospital just to stay in bed. It must be those pretty nurses!

Jerry and I are pitching in to keep your work covered, so you may rest easy on that score. Both of us will be up to visit you on Saturday with all the news of the week and the best wishes of the entire staff for a speedy recovery.

As ever,

Dear Anne,

The Women's Club just isn't the same without you. So hurry up and beat that virus infection!

Have you heard the latest news about Harry and Liz Carter? They bought a house out on Lakeshore Road that's supposed to be a showplace. It's ultramodern, with a sunken living room, a patio, and the most up-to-date kitchen in Janesville.

Norma Bing just announced her engagement to Charlie Southern. We're planning a surprise shower and look forward to your being there.

All the girls send their best wishes, and we all hope to see you very soon.

Fondly,

Dear Keith,

Doc Peterson dropped into the club tonight and vouched for the fact that you weren't just playing hooky. We almost persuaded him to take your favorite chair for a game of poker, but doctors don't get much time for recreation these days. Bill Nolan sat in for you and, as luck would have it, won most of the money.

Sam Sheridan asked me to send his special greetings. He'll be out on the road again before you get back on your feet, and he wanted you to know that he's waiting for a return match. He never did get over that run of luck you had in February.

Your brother has promised everyone you will be well enough to attend the picnic on June the twelfth. Don't disappoint us—we're all rooting for a fast recovery.

As ever,

Helpful Sentences

Your many friends are hoping for your quick return to health (early recovery) (rapid recovery) (return from the hospital).

All of us are awaiting your return.

We expect to see you back soon (as good as new in a few weeks).

We hope your convalescence will be rapid and pleasant.

We hope you will soon regain your health (be up and about) (be feeling a lot better).

We hope you will have a speedy convalescence (quick recovery).

Hurry up and get better.

We're sure it won't be long before you're back on your feet again.

Hurry up and lick that old germ!

CHAPTER 8

Thank-You Letters and Acknowledgments

We all know when we are supposed to write a thank-you letter, but too often we delay the writing so long that it becomes a chore rather than a pleasure.

A thank-you note should be, above all, sincere. This quality translates itself easily into words when the pleasure of receiving a gift, favor, congratulations, or hospitality is still fresh in your mind.

Although there is no hard-and-fast rule that you must acknowledge birthday greetings or letters of congratulations, it is a gracious and charming gesture and one that attests to your good upbringing. In writing this kind of letter, always mention the gift or the occasion that prompts it.

Thank you for gifts

Dear Aunt Gert and Uncle Jules,

Thanks so much for the truly magnificent sugar and creamer. They will be the *pièce de résistance* of every dinner we give.

George is as delighted with them as I am. We have decided that you and the boys will be our first dinner guests so you can see for yourselves how handsome your gift looks on our table.

Again thanks for the lovely present and the thoughtfulness that inspired it.

Fondly,

Dear Janet,

What a terrific Christmas present those Argyle socks were! You certainly know my tastes and my insatiable appetite for hand-knit socks.

Thanks so much, Janet. It was very thoughtful of you to remember me, and I really do appreciate it.

Your affectionate cousin,

Dear Donna,

How did you know that we wanted a Toulouse-Lautrec poster!
Max and I have been shopping for weeks, but we just couldn't
seem to find exactly what we wanted. Then your lovely gift arrived
on Saturday.

Of course we hung it up immediately. Do come over Friday
afternoon and see for yourself how beautifully it complements
the living-room color scheme.

Thanks so much for taking the time and the trouble to get
us just the right thing. We love it.

Affectionately,

Dear Ted,

Now that I'm able to write again, I want to thank you for the
lovely flowers. They helped cheer me up on several gloomy days,
not only because they added color to the room but because they
reminded me of a good friend's thoughtfulness.

The day nurse put them in a pretty vase with the comment that
flowers have more scents than people. As for me, I like both flowers
and people like you!

Fondly,

Dear Ginnie,

The blanket is the prettiest one I've seen, and Carol is a lucky
baby to be its owner. We used it at her christening, so you know
how truly lovely we think it is.

You must come and see the latest addition to our family. We
think she's getting to be quite a little girl—but of course we're
prejudiced! Sunday afternoon would be a good time for us, and
we'd love to see you and thank you personally.

Affectionately,

Dear Jane,

If you had been able to read Tommy's mind you couldn't have
selected a gift that would have pleased him more than a catcher's
mitt.

Tommy's handwriting is still a bit on the wobbly side, so he
asked me to say "thank you" for him and then added, "She's a
peach!"

We are all looking forward to seeing you again soon.

With love,

Dear Sam,

How am I ever going to be able to dissuade you from sending such elegant Christmas presents? The contents I can cope with, but the decanter is so lovely that it far surpasses my middle-class liquor cabinet. The only answer I can think of is to drink it quickly so as not to put the rest of the stock to shame.

Thanks and Happy New Year.

Cordially,

Dear John and Mary,

Thank you so much for that simply superb decanter of brandy. It is far too good for my unsophisticated taste but I shall try to live up to it.

Happy New Year!

Sincerely,

Thank you for a favor

Dear Lillian,

Many thanks for allowing me to use your sewing machine over the week-end. It saved me hours of work and made my new spring dress look really professional. But perhaps most important of all, it persuaded Fred to think seriously of getting me my own machine.

Again thanks, Lillian, for being such a very good neighbor.

Fondly,

Dear Mrs. Norman,

My wife has just told me of your courtesy in returning my brief case this morning.

I want you to know that I am deeply grateful for the trouble you took on my account.

Sincerely yours,

Dear Sid,

Thanks to you, I'm now assistant to the sales manager of The Gorgon Products Company.

Everything you told me about Mr. Gorgon is true. He wanted to know all about me, what subjects I liked best at school, what I had done since I left school, and what I thought about half a dozen varied topics. Then he read your letter over again, and I knew I had satisfied him that I could do the job.

I don't have to tell you that I'm sincerely grateful for all your help in finding a place for me. The mailman will bring you a package tomorrow that's a small token of a carload of appreciation.

Cordially,

Dear Fred,

I wish there were a better word than 'thanks" to express my appreciation for your letter of May the first and the generous contribution to the work of the Boys' Foundation.

Thanks for giving me the thrill of bringing your letter to the attention of the Trustees at our next meeting.

All my best wishes.

As ever,

Home from a hospital

Dear Sandra and Jim,

Now that I can sit up, I do want to say thanks for the beautiful flowers you sent while I was in the hospital. Your comical cards and cheerful notes were a helpful morale-builder in those dismal days.

Both of you have been so kind in so many ways that I want you to know how much I appreciate having you as good friends.

Love,

Thank you from a hospital

Dear Mrs. Neighbor,

Kenny has told me of your many kindnesses while I have been in the hospital. I want you to know that I do appreciate it.

Sometimes I worry just a bit that you are too good a "substitute mother" for I'm not quite sure I can keep up with the wonderful cooking Kenny tells me about. Perhaps I can borrow some recipes?

The doctors tell me I am getting better every day so I hope to be home and to see you soon.

Cordially,

Dear Fred and Nancy,

Joan asked me to say thank you for the lovely roses and good wishes. They add a note of cheer to her room. She was particularly happy when she saw they came from you.

The doctor says Joan will be able to leave the hospital in a week or so and we hope she will be able to have visitors soon after.

Sincerely,

Bread-and-butter letters

A thank-you note for hospitality received for a week-end or longer must be written to your hostess within two or three days after you return home.

Dear Mrs. Timothy,

Thank you so much for the marvelous week-end at Skytop. I can't remember when I have had a more pleasant or relaxing time.

It was most thoughtful of you and Mr. Timothy to invite me, and I warmly appreciate your hospitality.

Sincerely,

Dear Adele,

If you don't know it already, I want to tell you how very much Joe and I enjoyed the week-end with you. Everything was perfect —the weather, the beautiful countryside, and above all the company.

Joe has been talking about moving to the country for months, but it took three wonderful days in Westport to persuade him to start house-hunting. He loved every minute of the fresh air and quiet.

It was grand seeing you all again, and our visit was an event we'll long remember with appreciation and pleasure.

Affectionately yours,

Dear Selma,

Although Billy is going to write you himself, I still want to thank you for the grand time he had at Shady Ridge.

He came back bubbling over with stories about boating and swimming and the enormous pickerel Sid helped him to land.

You two always had a way with youngsters, and I cannot tell you too often how very much I appreciate the wonderful time you gave Billy. You've been more than kind, and I won't forget it.

Fondly,

Acknowledging congratulations

Dear Joan,

Our anniversary would not seem complete without the thoughtful card you always send. Thank you again for remembering us and for the sentiments, which I know come from the heart.

Sam and I look forward to seeing you again soon.

Affectionately,

Dear Tim,

One of the best things about winning a scholarship to Cornell was getting so many nice letters from my friends.

Thank you ever so much for your congratulations and good wishes. I hope I can live up to them.

My best wishes to all your family.

Cordially,

Dear Uncle Sid,

Thank you for your wonderful letter. Frankly, I was the most surprised fellow in the world when I learned I had won the essay contest.

School is keeping me so busy nowadays that I scarcely ever get time to write the letters I plan. With baseball practice almost every afternoon, games on Saturdays, and the usual quota of homework, the days run into weeks before I know they've passed.

Mother, Dad, and Sis are all well and join me in sending best wishes to you and Aunt Sylvia

Sincerely,

Dear Miss Smithers,

I was both surprised and grateful at winning the Women's Club Citation. Thank you so much for your kind congratulations and good wishes.

Sincerely,

Dear John,

Thank you very much for the lovely note and good wishes. You must know that we are delighted at Joe's promotion and we are happy that our friends join in the feeling.

We will be home all next week so if you can drop by Joe will be able to say good-bye personally.

Cordially,

Dear Helen,

Your charming note of congratulations capped a wonderful day. It was good of you to send it. I am flattered that you noticed and I sincerely appreciate your good wishes.

Cordially,

Dear Marian,

It was thoughtful of you to remember my birthday. And thanks most of all for losing track of the number!

Fondly,

Dear Tony,

You may go to the head of the class for remembering my birthday!

Seriously, I really appreciate your good wishes and great letter. I can't recall when I've had such a good laugh.

It was grand hearing from you again. Dot joins me in sending our warmest regards to you and Marie.

As ever,

Acknowledging condolences

Although they are widely used, engraved cards are not considered in the best of taste for acknowledging letters of condolence. A personal letter of thanks, brief and sincere, should be written to every person who sent a message of condolence. It needn't be written as promptly as other thank-you letters—within six weeks is considered correct.

Dear Cynthia,

I want you to know how very much your thoughtfulness at the time of Mother's death has meant to me. Your sympathy and kindness will always be remembered.

Affectionately,

Dear Mr. Gould,

Thank you for your kind expression of sympathy. Mother and I appreciated your thoughtfulness.

Sincerely,

Dear Sophie,

Thank you for the kind letter you sent when you heard of John's death. It is only a person like you, who knew him so well, who could have sent so comforting a letter.

My gratitude goes to all of John's good friends who join in missing him and who knew him as the wonderful man he was.

Sincerely,

Dear Ray,

Thank you from the bottom of my heart for your good letter of sympathy and your many kindnesses during these trying months.

The condolences of friends like you have helped to ease the long nights of tension and loneliness and I do appreciate it.

Cordially,

Helpful Sentences

Thank you

Thank you very much (very, very much) (ever so much) (most sincerely) (indeed) (from the bottom of my heart).

Many thanks for your kind and warm letter.

Thanks a million (ever so much).

An oceanful (trainful) (carload) of thanks.

Please accept my (I wish to express) my sincere (grateful) (profound) appreciation for . . .

I sincerely (deeply) (warmly) appreciate . . .

I am very sincerely (most) (truly) grateful to you for . . .

There is nothing more important (satisfying) (gratifying) to me than to receive one of your letters.

Your letters are so much fun (comfort) (entertainment) (company).

Your most courteous (considerate) (delightful) letter . . .

Your lovely long (fascinating) (charming) letter . . .

I cannot tell you how much your letter delighted (relieved) (amused) (enchanted) me.

I love the way you say (put) things in your letters. You make even the smallest incident seem so interesting (important) (charming) (mysterious).

It was good (fine) (charming) (thoughtful) (nice) of you . . .

It was good (characteristically thoughtful) (more than kind) of you . . .

At the outset, I want to thank you for your kindness to me and for your compliments.

Believe me, I am truly grateful for . . .

We were deeply touched by . . .

It is a hopeless (definite) (positive) understatement to say that I am deeply (sincerely) (truly) grateful.

It is generous of you to take so much interest in my work (to give me so much of your time) (to show me so much consideration).

We are indebted to you . . .

Thank you without end . . .

Thank you from the bottom of my heart.

I regret very much that I did not have an opportunity to thank you personally for . . .

Thanks for a gift

As soon as I opened your package, I felt that I must sit right down and tell you . . .

To indicate, in a small measure, my gratitude for your co-operation (kindness) (friendship) (courtesy) . . .

I just wish you could have seen . . .

You were kind to send a gift . . .

Your lovely gift came this morning (was waiting for us when) . . .

Expected gifts are a pleasure to receive, but unexpected remembrances are an even greater joy.

You couldn't have given me anything that I wanted (would enjoy) more.

You must be a mindreader.

Alice is in seventh heaven.

The wedding gift you sent to us is one of the most beautiful we received. It now occupies the most prominent place on our mantel.

Sidney and I were overjoyed with the exquisite vase . . .

I find an ordinary "thank you" entirely inadequate to tell you how much . . .

It was most thoughtful and generous of you to send the beautiful clock.

Your desk lamp is a perfect gift.

Acknowledging an announcement

It was good of you to send us an announcement of your marriage. We were delighted to receive . . .

Bread-and-butter letters

I don't know when I have had such a delightful (pleasant) (memorable) (enjoyable) week-end as the one . . .

This is to thank you again for your wonderful hospitality and to tell you how much I enjoyed seeing you again.

Thank you for one of the most memorable days of my trip.

Thank you for one of the most enjoyable visits we have had in many months.

Thank you for doing so much to make my trip to New York interesting (pleasant) (resultful).

Thank you for contributing so much to the pleasure of our stay in . . .

Thank you so much for your generous hospitality.

I hope something will bring you to Janesville soon so that I can reciprocate your kindness.

You must give me the chance to return your kindness when you visit here.

For a favor

I appreciate very much your . . .

I realize that the task took a great deal of precious time.

Thank you for doing me a real favor.

Your generous spirit of cooperation . . .

Your offer of assistance . . .

Your generosity in . . .

You may be sure that I appreciate . . .

Acknowledging congratulations

That was a mighty fine letter you wrote me.

Your note of congratulations is deeply appreciated (gave me a great deal of pleasure).

I appreciate your kind words.

Your kind letter . . .

We acknowledge with gratitude your message of good wishes.

Many thanks for remembering (our anniversary) (my birthday) and for your very flattering remarks.

How cruel of you to remember my birthday, but how kind to do it in so charming a way.

It was good (fine) (thoughtful) (nice) (kind) (wonderful) (swell) of you to write me as you did (go out of your way to write).

Thanks for the good word. I certainly received some good wishes from my really good friends, and it is my great pleasure to list yours among them.

Acknowledging sympathy letters

It is almost worth going away (being ill) to receive . . .

Thank you very much for your lovely (warm) (newsy) (charming) (encouraging) (flattering) letter.

It was thoughtful of you to . . .

I hope to be on my feet again within a few days, and I look forward to seeing you.

CHAPTER 9

Letters of Apology

Since none of us is perfect, there are occasions when it is necessary to apologize for a mistake, error, or oversight. A letter of apology must be written promptly. If there is an explanation, devote a few sentences to it. If there is none admit it, since a lame excuse will do little toward smoothing ruffled feelings. Express your regrets and assurances that such an incident will not happen again. Offer to arrange for repairs or to pay for damages. The letter should convey a sense of sincerity and cooperation on your part.

Dear Mrs. Morrell,

The superintendent informed us that you were annoyed by our television last night. We certainly do not want to cause you any disturbance, particularly in view of Mr. Morrell's condition. If you had called the matter to our attention immediately, we would have lowered the volume and closed the windows.

The boys are extremely interested in night baseball games, and though I do not wish to ask them to forego that pleasure, I will see to it that they take every precaution to keep the sound from disturbing you.

If at any time you should find our activities bothersome, please do not hesitate to let us know. We shall try to cooperate in every way we can.

Sincerely yours,

Dear Mrs. Sommers,

The first thing I did this morning was to telephone the best rug weaver in the city. He has assured me that he can repair the burn I so carelessly made in your beautiful rug yesterday.

Mr. Mantino will call you tomorrow and arrange to see the rug and match the color. The bill will be sent to me, of course.

It was most understanding of you to make so little of the accident. My carelessness was unforgivable, and the least I can do is see that the damage is repaired.

Sincerely,

Dear Evelyn,

I was heartsick when Alison told me about the accident to Shelley's china doll. I know how long it had been in the family and how much sentimental value it had for you.

If I could replace the doll and all the memories it had for you, I would certainly do so. Unfortunately, that is impossible, so I have asked Parson's to send up the prettiest modern doll in the store. I know Shelley will love her, and I hope that in time the new doll will replace the old one in her affections.

Please explain to Shelley how sorry we all are.

Very cordially,

Dear Mr. Jackson,

Peter has explained to us the unfortunate coincidence of your windshield's being directly in the path of his baseball. He wanted to go immediately and apologize himself, but didn't quite know how to go about it.

I have checked with Bob Kuhn's Service Station, and they tell me it will cost $6.00 to replace the glass. Peter has agreed to pay for this out of his allowance, and I am advancing this sum for him with the enclosed check.

We are sincerely sorry that the accident occurred, and I know that all the boys will be more careful in the future.

Very sincerely yours,

Dear Mrs. Saunders,

Jane Eichelberg has just told me about our cat's adventure among your day lilies. I don't know how to tell you how sorry I am, for the lilies were so lovely and I know how proud of them you were.

Nibbles is usually such a good cat that I can't imagine what got into her yesterday. Perhaps it's the first sign of spring. At any rate, we've taken measures to keep her where she can't possibly run off again.

Unfortunately, there is no making amends for the flowers you worked on so carefully. If there is anything that can be repaired, I'd like to have our gardener see what he can do. He comes on Thursdays, so if you'll let me know what time is convenient, I will arrange to have him see you.

In the meantime, please accept a few of my begonias as a compensation. They are potted and just ready for transplanting. Richard, who is bringing them over, will be happy to plant them for you wherever you wish.

Sincerely yours,

Dear Mrs. Cortland,

I was fortunately at home yesterday when our dog scratched Sonny. I cleaned the scratch immediately and bandaged it, so there should be no cause for worry.

The boys were wrestling in the back yard when Lucky decided to get in on the fun. I guess he didn't realize his nails were so sharp, for he is always very gentle with children.

Lucky has been properly punished, and I'm sure he won't scratch again. The boys have agreed to keep him as club mascot with the promise that any wrestling in the future will be out of Lucky's sight.

Very sincerely,

Dear Selma,

My face has been red all morning! How can I apologize for missing our luncheon date yesterday?

You know my mind has been on Margie's wedding. I was so absorbed in the details of the reception that I completely forgot about our date.

Please forgive me. Let's make it next Tuesday. I promise to tie a string around my finger so I won't forget.

Affectionately,

Dear Harry,

It wasn't till I got to the office this morning that I realized this was Thursday and I had missed our lunch date yesterday. The peaked hat you will see me wearing next time we meet will have "Dunce" written across the band.

I honestly don't know how it happened, since I had been looking forward to seeing you all week. Can you make it for lunch next Monday at the same place? I'll be there at one o'clock unless I hear from you.

As ever,

Helpful Sentences

How to say you're sorry

I was (so) (mighty) (very) (extremely) (ever so) sorry . . .
I can't tell you how sorry (embarrassed) (ashamed) I was . . .
I hope you will accept my sincere apologies . . .
I certainly owe you an apology for . . .
I (sincerely) regret (very much) . . .
How can I apologize for . . .
I was heartsick (angry with myself) (much disturbed) sin-
cerely sorry) (terribly upset) (ashamed) (embarrassed) to hear
(discover) (learn) . . .
I wish to apologize (offer my sincere apologies) (say I am
sincerely sorry) . . .

Apologies for delayed letters

Delays in writing a letter are not only a lapse of good taste
but bad manners. The least you can do to make amends is
indicate that you know you are late and make an apology. If
there is an explanation for your tardiness, give it.

Suggested starters

Now that I am finally able to sit up and write again . . .
Business in New York delayed my return to the office until
today.
By now everyone in the world except me has written to con-
gratulate you, but I have been . . .
By now I'm probably the only one you know who hasn't
written . . .
It seems only yesterday . . .
I have delayed answering your letter because . . .
This is a letter I had intended to write months ago, but . . .

CHAPTER 10

Friendly Letters

The letter you get the greatest pleasure in writing is the one that springs from no particular duty or social obligation. The friendly letter is the one you want to write—the newsy letter to a far-off friend or relative, to the folks back home, a cousin in service, a child at camp.

If such an enjoyable letter has a purpose, it is to make people feel better. Intimate, informal, gay, and conversational, a friendly letter is the reflection of your own personality. If the reader feels your presence, then it is a good letter.

Isn't it surprising, then, that some people find a friendly letter hard to write? All you have to remember is to write the person what you would tell him if you were in the same room talking to him—the small incidents of everyday life, pleasant happenings, a really funny joke, news of mutual friends—any and all news that would interest a person of his particular age and personality. But if you still feel there is absolutely nothing to write, remember that your friends and relatives are interested in you, and follow the advice of one of the most famous letter writers of all times, Pliny the Younger, who wrote: "There is nothing to write about, you say. Well, then, write and let me know just this, that there is nothing to write about; or tell me in the good old style if you are well."

Although a friendly letter should be light-hearted and avoid pet peeves and personal problems, there are times when you have to tell bad news. Don't use the shock approach. Prepare the reader with some introductory hints, then tell the full story, so your letter won't give the impression that there is worse to come. Don't cause the reader needless worry by dramatizing the event, but rather assure him that the operation was successful or that the fire caused little actual damage.

Letters to friends and relatives

Dear Len,

We've been having a taste here of the kind of weather I always associate with Syracuse. That got me to thinking about college and, naturally, of you and Cecile. You can imagine how pleased I was to find your letter in the mailbox.

It was great hearing all the news about you two and the gang in Syracuse. Compared to you Syracusans, we New Yorkers lead pretty tame lives! Jean and I have been seeing quite a bit of Jack and Rita Diamond—and you know what a mine of information they are. Jack hasn't changed a bit since he was leader of the midnight bull sessions at the Omicron Nu house.

Jack tells me that Milt Willets, the old legal beagle, has opened an office in Washington. When I read in your letter that you're thinking about going into Government service, it occurred to me you might do well to drop Milt a line. He always was a particularly well-informed fellow. His address is 4423 Connecticut Avenue, N.W., Washington, D.C. 20010.

Fred Williamson finally decided that he was tired of being the only bachelor in the class of '49 and popped the question to Adele Hughes. Remember her? She was the freshman cheer-leader in our senior year—and a mighty pretty girl.

Jean and I both feel it's been too long since we've seen you and Cecile. I know you're busy and that your trips down here have to be few and far between, but how about coming down for a really big event—the Fordham game on November the sixth? We've got room for two extra now that we've moved into a larger apartment, and we're planning a party the night of the game that won't be complete without Mr. and Mrs. Len Crothers.

Do try and tear yourself away from those law books.

As ever,

Dear Bob,

Your last letter went the rounds of the whole family. They were all tickled pink to know that you are really enjoying yourself in the Army. Aunt Sadie was particularly pleased, since she'd felt you'd never be able to stand G.I. cooking after living with her for four years.

Uncle Tom and Aunt Martha dropped in the other day on their way to the country. As soon as they saw your photograph, they exclaimed that you had put on weight and that the uniform was very becoming. Uncle Tom had Mother a bit worried with his stories about what he did when he was in the Army. If you should get a long letter from Mother telling you what *not* to do, you'll know she learned it all from Uncle Tom.

The most exciting news in these parts concerns Nibbles and her eight kittens. Three of them are orange and five are black. Two of the males have been spoken for by Peter's pals on the block. We don't quite know what to do with the others, but I'm sure we'll find homes for them. They are so cute that it's hard to part with them, but Mother says her budget won't allow eight more mouths to feed—even little ones. Maybe you can bring some C-rations home on your furlough!

Your loving cousin,

Dear Louise,

Uncle Sol came into town last week to do his annual shopping. He asked me so many questions about you that it reminded me I hadn't written in a month of Sundays. Actually, there has been very little to write about. All of us are growing older, the children are getting cuter, and the days seem to be getting shorter.

The other day when Mrs. Robinson dropped in to bring us a piece of her delicious green-apple pie she commented that it seemed just yesterday that you and I were stealing apples from her orchard. The orchard isn't there any more, unfortunately. A split-level house is being built over the roots of our favorite tree.

Sandy goes into junior high next month. She is going to be quite a gal from the looks of things. Her hair is getting blonder and her eyes bluer, and she has that pert turned-up nose that runs in the family. I think she gets to look more like your mother every day.

I ran into Jill Mantell last week. She always has the latest word on the crowd we went to school with. All she could report this time was that Sam and Tuck Devine have reconciled. I'm glad for both of them because they're really swell people. Jill is still a bachelor girl. She has shown excellent taste in her choice of boy friends, but none of them has been able to get her to say yes to that all-important question. I saw her out with Jim Mason a few times last year, and the gossip had them going steady. But so far no serious news.

Everyone in the family is in good health, including Pete, who has his tonsils out last month. He was looking forward to the operation for weeks because his friend Charlie Bing had told him he could have all the ice cream he wanted after the operation. Pete had his share, but he was a bit disappointed that the operation wasn't a more pleasant experience. He'll never quite trust Dr. Spindell again after that whiff of anesthetic.

I hope all is well in your end of the state. Please write and give us all the news.

Fondly,

Dear Betty,

The big news here is our new car. Sally, Bobbie, and I finally convinced Paul that the old tin can would fall to pieces if it was driven up Slate Hill once more. But just wait till you read what my serious, conservative husband bought—a bright blue-and-yellow hard-top convertible with white-wall tires and leather upholstery! The kids are in seventh heaven and, frankly, I'm pretty thrilled myself.

Paul gets his vacation in August, so don't be surprised to see this vision on wheels come honking at your front door.

And as if that wasn't excitement enough, Bart Evans came home from his military service overseas with a wife! Lisa's a lovely girl right out of one of those gay Viennese operettas. They have rented the little yellow house on the corner of Orchard and Maple. We were over for a buffet dinner Friday night, and can Lisa cook! We all kissed our diets good-by that night. I am enclosing her recipe for a wonderful cake called a linzer torte. I've tried it, and it just melts in your mouth.

Aside from the usual drugstore gossip to the effect that Jenny Newsom is going steady with Dave Broder and that Mrs. Thelan has painted her house shocking pink, there is nothing new here in Janesville.

Let us hear all about Zenith. I'm sure Stan loves his new job, since nothing but a chance to work on *The Daily Press* could have induced you all to move away. We really do miss you, so please write a long long letter.

Affectionately,

Letters to the folks back home

Dear Mother and Dad,

Well, we're really in the Big City! And it really is big and impressive. We got off the train at Grand Central Station just five minutes behind schedule and took a cab to our hotel a few blocks away. It was lucky that Sid had insisted on our making reservations long in advance, for there were a half dozen people at the desk trying to get rooms.

As soon as we unpacked we decided to take a walk along Broadway and see the Gay White Way. You won't believe it until you see it yourself! There must be a million electric light bulbs and a thousand miles of neon lights within sight when you stand at 42nd Street and Broadway. The traffic is worse than Main Street on election night. There is a sign on the New York Times Building that carries the news on what looks like a belt of electric lights. One building has a waterfall in electric lights that looks as grand as Niagara. All in all there is a tremendous amount of ingenuity shown in the advertising displays.

Before returning to the hotel for dinner we walked to Rockefeller Center, an imposing group of buildings of fifty or more stories. They are beautifully designed, with a series of geometric setbacks. Right in the center of all these giant structures is an ice-skating rink flanked by two restaurants. A tremendous Christmas tree, probably 70 feet high, overlooks the rink. The lights had just been turned on, and it was something to see!

Today we went to the Hayden Planetarium, and it was like visiting another world. Dad, you would love it. It's just like one of those science-fiction stories you're always reading. Afterward we strolled along Fifth Avenue and window-shopped. They say not even Paris can beat New York when it comes to fashions, and I wouldn't doubt it. The stores had their windows fixed up for Christmas, and they were like a storybook come to life. One of the most elaborate displays was entitled "Christmases of Yesteryear," and the windows were like a charming peek into the pages of history. I particularly liked the Gay Nineties window, with its children in pinafores and high-button shoes playing with quaint old-fashioned china dolls and hobbyhorses.

Tonight we are going to see the new musical with Rex Harrison, and I don't have to tell you how much I'm looking forward to that.

Give the folks back home our love and tell them they should all plan on visiting the big city.

Lovingly,

Dear Millie,

Each day of my vacation I have more reasons to thank you for recommending Ogunquit as the perfect vacation spot.

The Sea Spray Inn is every bit as good as you said it would be, and the food is wonderful. I don't know when I've had better boiled lobster and steamed clams. The people at the inn are lovely, and I've already made some good friends, particularly among the bridge players. I met a very nice couple, Mr. and Mrs. Gerald

Whyte, who remembered you from last summer and send their regards.

But perhaps the best thing about Ogunquit is the scenery. There's nothing quite as beautiful as Maine's rugged, rockbound coast, is there? I've already done a few water colors of the view near the lighthouse, and when I return home I want you to choose one for yourself.

Send my love to Marty and Bess and do write if you get a chance.

Affectionately,

Letters to a child at camp or school

Dear Peter,

Your bus had hardly pulled away from the curb when Mother remembered a half dozen things she meant to tell you. I know she must have reminded you about watching out for poison ivy, but she insists that she forgot. So now you've been warned again. She also asked me to send along your catcher's mitt. She meant to give it to you to carry, but it stayed behind in the excitement.

Sis was terribly disappointed to see you go off. She didn't realize how much she would miss you until you were actually gone. Perhaps next year she will be able to go to camp, too. In the meantime, she has embarked on a new fad—riddles. Did you teach them to her? Her latest is: "What begins with P and ends with E and has a thousand letters in it?" Mother and I were stumped, and she had to tell us the answer. I have written it on the back of the page, so you can guess, too.

We spent a quiet week-end at home over the Fourth, since I never like to go away when the traffic is so heavy. On Sunday night the town had a fireworks display in City Park. It wouldn't match your campfire for fun, but Sis had a good time and was thrilled every time one of the skyrockets went off. There were all kinds of shapes and combinations of colors—red, white, and blue, yellow and purple, orange and green. The climax was a beautiful tableau of two American flags topped with a large star and surrounded by revolving pinwheels of various colors.

Uncle Al and Aunt Mary dropped in Monday afternoon and left a few comic books for you. We'll bring them, along with a box of cookies, when we come up to see you next week-end.

With love,

Dearest Josie,

Dad and I must have read your last letter a dozen times. You can't imagine what a thrill it gives your proud parents to share with you all the joys of your freshman year at college.

I'm glad you found the books we sent you useful for your English exam. We are so pleased that you got an A. Keep up the good work, dear. We have every confidence in your ability to get the most out of your college years.

Your description of the Freshman Hop was priceless. I could hear the band playing rumbas, see those sophisticated upperclassmen with their crew cuts and gray-flannel suits taste the grape punch, and unfortunately, feel that six-foot-six forestry student stepping on my feet! I'm glad you had such a good time with Stu Drake. His father, you know, was a school friend of Uncle Paul's, and if Stu is anything like his father he must be quite a fellow!

Dad and I are both pleased that you have gone out for the tennis team and the school paper. Extracurricular activities add so much to the pleasures of college life and in your case, since you are interested in journalism as a career, working on the paper will provide valuable experience. Don't forget to send us a copy of the college paper.

Betsy Sarton dropped by after school on Tuesday with a bushel of news to send along to you. She says that Janesville High has the best chance ever to win the Janesville-Charlton football game. Also, it seems Sally Marks and Tom Rogers are going steady, Pat Parker has given Fred Warner's class ring back to him in no uncertain terms, and the Waring twins have been accepted at Ohio State. So even more of your Janesville friends will be joining you next year.

Dad sends his love, and we both look forward to your next letter.

With love,

Dear Tim,

Your letter came while I was out shopping, but I guessed you would be asking for good things to eat. So, in appreciation for your writing so promptly, I have made up a package with most of the gourmet delights that you listed.

Of course, we are very happy that you have made some nice and interesting new friends. But I knew you would because Antelope Hill attracts so many people who have the same interests as you do. From what I have heard, the facilities for all kinds of craft work are excellent, and you will find no end of fascinating things to do. Uncle Tom tells me the native rocks in the area are quite unusual and are especially excellent for sculpture.

Mary James stopped by yesterday to ask how you were spending the summer, and when I told her you would be away, she volunteered to look after Tangerine. I told her Yes, for a while. She loves him so.

Jim Brown dropped in to let you know his brother made the football team at Dartmouth and was taking a trucking job for the summer to build up his muscles. Jim is working for the first month and will visit the West Coast with his parents in August. . . .

If you have trouble writing a newsy letter, imagine what you would say if the reader were with you. Think of what he would like to hear.

1. What has happened that concerns him?
2. What has happened that concerns his friends and family?
3. What has happened that concerns you?
4. Whom have you met that he would know or want to know?
5. What are you planning that concerns him, his friends, or you?
6. What are you thinking, planning, hoping for, that concerns him?
7. Interesting anecdotes or jokes you have heard.

Write about your work, hobby, sports, spare-time activities, pets, collections, friends; games you've played or seen, movies, funny things you've done or thought about, even the weather.

Helpful Starters

The first sentence of any letter should be interesting, and this is particularly true of the friendly letter, which is the least inhibited by formalities. Avoid starting with an apology for not writing sooner, unless it is really valid. Here are some good beginnings:

So much has happened since I last wrote you.
It was great news about your promotion.
I wanted you to be the first to know.
Hold your hat! I have news for you.

Bermuda is charming!

It has been some time . . .

Just today I heard . . .

One of these days . . .

As soon as I heard . . .

When I last saw you . . .

Just a few months ago . . .

Mother called me today to tell me . . .

Thanks so much for the letter about . . .

I am going to answer your letter immediately and with pleasure.

Nothing could have made me happier than getting news of you.

I was so glad to see your handwriting.

I have just returned from . . .

I am sending this short letter today, so I can look forward to another note from you before I leave.

Your last letter was priceless.

In closing

Close your letters on a cheerful, positive note. Don't let your note just peter out with a lame excuse as "Mother's calling" or "Nothing more to write so that's all for now." Here are some good endings:

Have a good time and write often.

Please write and tell me all the news of . . .

You always have my best wishes for . . .

All your old friends send their love.

CHAPTER 11

Love Letters

How does a sedate, ordinary person go about writing a love letter? There is only one rule—write what your heart dictates! Spontaneous, sincere, unselfish, a love letter should be individual. In other words, a love letter should be you. Flowery phrases, affected statements, cloying sentiments that are not the real you, are better left unwritten.

In writing a love letter, keep the receiver in mind and avoid the selfish viewpoint. Remember the little things you have done together, the dates, the picnics, the walks, the dances. Say you miss your loved one, but don't complain of loneliness.

Although it is not a very romantic thought, love letters are sometimes a bombshell that can injure the writer. Nothing should be written that can be misconstrued. Many of the greatest love letters rely on subtlety for their charm rather than on blunt, overpowering statements that can all too easily be misunderstood.

Dearest Joe,

Next to you I think the mailman is my favorite person, for he brings me your wonderful letters. And your letters fill my days with sunshine and happiness.

Have I told you that I love you, recently? You're in my thoughts every minute of the day, in my dreams every hour of the night. Yesterday at the office when I was taking dictation I almost wrote the words "I love you, Joe" right in the middle of a business letter. Luckily, Mr. Forbes didn't notice my embarrassment!

Most of my lunch hour was spent at the record store looking for our favorite song. The old record has just about worn out from being played over and over again. Remember (as if you could forget!) the night we first heard it and waltzed to its lovely melody?

Right now, having just re-read your letter, I feel as if you were here with me, and I'm the happiest girl in the world at the mere thought of you.

Take good care of yourself and do rush that job!

Lovingly,

Fred darling,

I can still hear your voice. It was wonderful speaking to you last night and even more wonderful (if possible) to know you'll be coming here on Friday.

I'm still walking on a great big cloud, so when I meet you at the station don't be surprised if you can't see me for the rays of happiness surrounding me.

Everyone in the family wants to meet you, but there just won't be enough time to visit all of them on this trip. Besides, I want you for myself most of the time. There are so many things to talk about and so many exciting plans to make. Let's spend Sunday afternoon walking by the lake. I love the lakeside more than any place in the world, for it was there that you first told me you loved me.

Oh, dear, there I go getting my eyes all filled with stardust when I wanted to be very practical and tell you the week-end plans Uncle Dave has suggested. He would like to give one all-inclusive family dinner at his house, which is the biggest. I didn't say Yes or No, since I want to do what will make you happiest. So in your next wonderful letter, squeeze in among those three little words I love so well what you think of Uncle Dave's idea.

Dearest, I'll be counting the minutes till I see you Friday.

Devotedly,

My dearest,

A million kisses to you for that beautiful letter. I shall never tire of knowing how much you love me. Indeed, that is all I live for, all that means anything to me now.

You ask me if I love you. I could quote the lovely poem that begins "How do I love thee? Let me count the ways." But, Tom, there would never be space enough for me to list all the ways I love you!

Your letter was waiting for me when I got back from trousseau shopping. I bought some beautiful things, including a gold bracelet for those gorgeous charms you gave me. I also bought something for you. After all if a girl has a trousseau, then why not a man? I'll give you a little hint—it will look really dashing with your new tweed suit!

Since you went away on what seems like an endless business

trip, we've received even more lovely wedding gifts. The Harlans sent a beautiful cocktail set from Tiffany's in New York City. Now we'll be able to give the most sophisticated parties in Zenith!

Good night, my darling. I hope morning will find another long, wonderful letter from you. Till then,

> All my love,

Dear Susie,

There is nothing more difficult for a matter-of-fact engineer like me to write than a letter that will tell you how much you mean to me. You are the dearest thing in the world, you're wonderful, terrific, and tops.

I know a lot of logarithms and axioms, but not the language of love. I wanted this letter to be beautiful and poetic, but all I can say, and it comes from the bottom of my heart, is I love you.

Susie, I've loved you ever since the evening of the dance, and I would never have had the courage to write you if our talks and our wonderful times these past few months hadn't held the promise that you care for me as deeply as I for you.

I am sending you my class ring. It was a tradition at college that a man only took it off to give to the one girl who was everything in his life. If you are wearing it when I come home next week, then my happiness will be complete. If you are not I will understand and admire your honesty, for whatever you do I will love you always.

> Devotedly,

Darling Ruth,

I think of you always and have a thousand things to say to you. But they can all be summed up in a few heartfelt words—I love you to distraction, my precious fiancée.

If it weren't for your beautiful letters, each hour would seem like a day. But just when I think I cannot live another minute without you, a letter comes. Immediately it seems that you're in the room with me. I hear the sound of your beloved voice saying you love me, and I feel I am the luckiest man in the world.

This coming week is going to be pretty tough, since we've come to the trickiest part of the whole construction job. I'm sure I'll be able to do my part and make you proud of me, dearest. And best of all, as soon as the week has passed I'll be seeing you again.

A thousand thoughts of love.

> Your own,

Marge, sweetheart,

Please write and say you forgive me. It was all my fault that we quarreled, and I'm heartbroken that my love has caused you unhappiness.

It's not that I don't love you, darling, but that I love you so much that my heart rather than my head is my master.

Say you still love me as I adore you, for without your love I am a man without life.

Devotedly,

To your wife

My own dear girl,

Only six more towns to visit, darling, and I will be on my way home. However, it will seem a dozen years before I get through them. I just can't wait to be back with you and Betty.

I visited with the Petersons yesterday. You remember Johnny Peterson—we had him for dinner when he was in Janesville last year. He signed a new three-year contract, which makes the trip a bang-up success. I have already filled up my quota for the month, and I still have a dozen good customers to see.

It will be great to be home again! Even the best hotel seems desolate without your adorable presence.

You'll be delighted with a little gift I picked up at Marshall Field's yesterday. I know how you love surprises, so I won't even give you a hint as to what it is.

Love and kisses from

Your devoted husband,

To your husband

Tom dear,

You are the most wonderful husband in the world! Your letter was waiting for me when I got back from marketing, and it was like sudden sunshine on a cloudy day. If you were here this minute, I'd hug you to pieces.

Time seems to just creep by when you're gone. And although I'm proud as punch of the success you are having, I'm still counting the minutes till you come home.

Everything here is fine. The new television set arrived, and it works perfectly. Bob helped me put it near the sofa, where you wanted it. You were absolutely right—the screen is visible from every part of the room. My, what a smart husband I have! Bob looks wonderful, thanks to your sister's cooking. Marriage has really made a new man of him.

You're not the only one with a surprise. Wait till you get home and take a peek into your study! I won't say any more, but I'm sure you will like what you see there.

Good night, my dearest. Dream of me as I will of you, and wake up in the morning with the happy thought that we are one day closer to seeing each other again.

Lovingly,

Helpful Thoughts

Salutations

My dearest darling; My precious; My wonder girl; My morning star; Beloved; My angel; My adorable; My adored; Sweetheart; Darling; Honey darling; My heaven on earth; My heart's delight; Hello, honey; My lovely wife.

What to say

I have been making plans all week (for our new home) (for our honeymoon).

You're a dear to write so often.

I've been practicing calling (you) (myself) Mrs. Cortland.

Your letters are wonderful.

Your letters make me so happy.

I have missed you from the minute we said good-by.

I can't wait until the mailman rings in the morning.

I am counting the hours till I can be with you.

Each hour I am away from you seems an eternity.

I can't wait to crush you in my arms and cover you with a million kisses.

How is my lovely wife today?

What is my darling doing today?

Don't forget about . . .

I dreamed of you last night.

Take good care of yourself.

I can't wait to see you again.

I am sending you . . .

Have I told you recently I think you're wonderful (you're the most beautiful girl in the world) (you're lovely) (you're swell)?

And of course:

I love you (forever) (and always will).

I adore you (with my whole heart).

I shall love you forever.

Our love will last as long as our lives.

There is no limit to my love.

I think of you always.

Your love is the cornerstone of my existence.

My first thought is of you in the morning.

You are everything to me.

Oceans (carloads) of love to you.

I stayed awake all last night thinking of you.

I love you because you are so beautiful (fascinating) (lovely) (sweet) (modest) (affectionate) (warm) (good-hearted) (generous) (courageous) (charming) (captivating) (intelligent) (have such good judgment) (energetic) (nice-mannered) (good-natured).

Home is heaven with you but a desolate desert when you are gone.

I can't be happy anywhere without you.

Kiss the children for me.

Nothing can erase the memories of those few days we spent together.

No man has ever loved a woman more than I love you.

I shall love you always.

I cannot stop loving you.

Sleep well, my heart and soul. My prayers are with you.

These are classic sentences:

I am hungry for your letters as for food. I am thirsty for them, and my thirst is overwhelming.

A thousand, thousand tender thanks for not having forgotten me.

I did not write because you had not written and because I wished only what should be agreeable to you.

Think of me sometimes, while alps and ocean divide us—but they never will, unless you wish it. *(Byron)*

Ever thine. Ever mine. Ever for each other. *(Ludwig van Beethoven)*

My thoughts are with you.

Remain my true, my only treasure, my all, as I am yours. *(Beethoven)*

Be my good angel to the extent of throwing me a scrap of your beloved writing. *(George Bernard Shaw)*

Closings

Good-by for now,
Always yours,
With love,
Lovingly yours,
Devotedly yours,
Adoringly yours,
Your most affectionate,
Your own,
Ever yours,
Yours ever,
Forever yours,
Tenderly,

CHAPTER 12

Children's Letters

Children, just like adults, have letters that they must write. Although parents often write the letters for them, it is an excellent idea for a child to handle his own correspondence as soon as he is able. It is particularly important that a child write his own thank-you notes for gifts and hospitality.

In guiding a child, let him express himself freely. Tactful hints and suggestions are helpful, but never dictate a letter. For, as in adult correspondence, sincerity and warmth are of the utmost importance.

Thanks for gifts

Dear Aunt Rae,

Thank you very much for the new doll. I call her Linda Sue. She is just the doll I wanted.

I hope you and Margaret will come to visit us soon.

With love,

Dear Uncle Tom,

How did you know I wanted electric trains for Christmas? I've been hoping for them all year.

I wish you could have come to my birthday party last Sunday. Daddy showed movies of the whole family and some Western pictures. It was lots of fun.

Please come to visit us soon.

Love,

Dear Grandma,

Thank you very, very much for the wonderful bicycle. It is the gift I wanted more than anything else in the world.

Daddy is teaching me to ride it. I fell off twice this morning, but I didn't hurt myself. I expect to be whizzing off to the park on it pretty soon. All my friends have bicycles, and now I can ride with them.

I hope you will come to my party on Sunday. By then I think I will be able to ride real well.

Lots of love,

Dear Aunt Portia,

I can't tell you how excited I was when I opened your package this morning and saw the lovely dress you sent. It's gorgeous! And it fits like a dream. I will be able to wear it for a party tomorrow night.

It was terribly sweet of you to send such a wonderful gift. I do hope you will be able to visit us soon and see how well it looks on me.

Affectionately,

Thank you for hospitality

Dear Mrs. Cortland,

This is to say thank you for the wonderful time I had at your house. I enjoyed the Friday-night party tremendously, and the exciting baseball game on Saturday was something I'll never forget. The week-end was one of the best I ever spent.

Sincerely yours,

Dear Margie,

I want to tell you that the week-end at your house was just swell. I had a wonderful time. It was just grand to be able to dress in the house and jump right into a swimming pool without having to ride for hours.

Please tell your mother I think she's a wonderful cook, and I would like the recipe for her barbecued hamburgers. I've told my mother all about how delicious they were, and she's agreed to make them as soon as I have the recipe.

I'm counting on having you visit us for the Fourth of July week-end. Dad bought a half dozen records for my birthday that you'll love to hear, and the crowd is planning a picnic at Bear Mountain.

Your loving friend,

Invitations

Greeting-card publishers make up so many intriguing in-vitations that no one need go beyond the nearest stationery store. However, if your child wants to give free rein to his imagination he can create his own invitations with just a few simple supplies.

The motif should be adapted to the type of party. Here is a suggested birthday invitation: Cut out from a piece of colored construction paper the outline of a birthday cake, a candle, or the number of the birthday. The front may be blank or have a pasted picture clipped from a magazine. The inside page may contain a straight invitation such as this:

> Will you come to my birthday party
> on Saturday, October the third
> at 2 o'clock
> Margie Saunders
> 100 Grove Street

or a rhymed invitation like one of the following:

> Come up to my house
> Next Saturday
> To help me celebrate
> My tenth birthday.
>
> We will be having
> Much food and fun
> And many prizes
> For games you've won.
> 3 to 5 P.M.   Tommy Cortland
>   21 New Street

> On Thursday next, when I'll be ten
> I'm giving a party for girls and men
> So if you'll join us for food and fun
> There'll be a good time for everyone.
> Thursday after school, March the tenth
> Peter Allison   10 Lawn Street

Teen-agers particularly appreciate novel invitations. A black disk made to look like a phonograph record is a popular idea. Plain white cards with pressed flowers pasted on are also intriguing. An invitation in verse adds to the fun.

Here's a call for everyone
Who likes to dance
And eat, have fun,
And join the game of chance,
Perhaps romance
With music to delight
At my house Friday night

| Margie Saunders | November the first |
| 24 East Tenth Street | eight o'clock |

Or a double candle folded over may carry the message:

This Candle	To the
Bright	Sanders Party
Will Light	On
The	Saturday
Way	―――――
June 4	Marie Saunders
Five O'Clock	24 East 10th Street

If you want to cut out a hat shape, color it, and add a feather, you can write your invitation on an inside fold:

Put On Your
New Spring Bonnet
With A
Big Flower
On It
And Join
The
Easter Parade Party
At 3 O'clock March 27th
Alicia Sullivan
24 Maiden Lane

An attractive St. Valentine's Day invitation is a heart cut from red paper, with silver paper as lace. The invitation is written in red, white, or gold ink, depending on the color of the paper.

For Easter invitations, use egg-shaped cutouts. Or make a conventionalized bunny by pasting a small circle above a large circle and adding two ears and a spot for the tail.

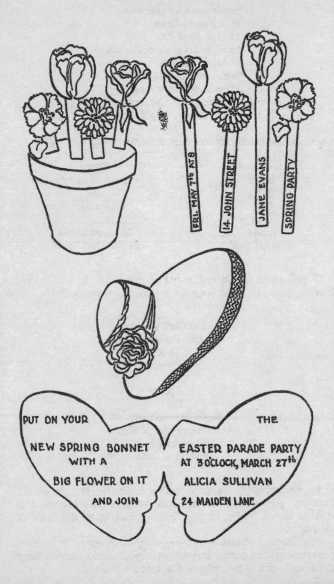

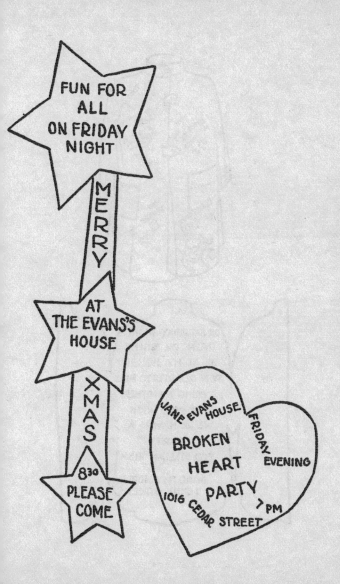

A firecracker, a sky rocket, or an American flag are touches that will make your July 4th invitations different. If you can get very small firecrackers, remove the powder from them and paste the empty tubes on the invitations. Or make a giant firecracker by cutting and rolling up red construction paper into the proper cylindrical shape. Paste on a piece of cord to resemble a fuse. Write the invitation in red ink on a white card or in red and white ink on a blue card.

> This is an invitation
> To join the celebration
> Of our nation's birthday!
> So come and have a lot of fun
> At half past one
> At our house next Thursday
> July 4th.
>> Milton Saunders
>> 24 East 10th Street

Colorful Hallowe'en invitations are available in the stores, but it is much more fun to make your own from colored paper cut-outs shaped like a jack o'lantern or a witch's hat. As an added novelty you may make the witch's hat removable, with the invitations attached underneath the hat. The written message may be placed right on the cut-outs or on a piece of enclosed white paper. Light-hearted verse or a spooky message is equally appropriate. The text may read: "Come to the house of Saunders at four hours before midnight on October 31st, wearing your best disguise. Give two short raps and one long. Ask for Vampira. Broomsticks will be carried.—The Witches."

The same cut-out idea may be adapted for Thanksgiving by making invitations in the shape of a turkey, cornucopia, pine cone, acorns, or an autumn leaf. Or you may buy turkey stickers and paste them to your note paper for a holiday atmosphere.

Make novelties for Christmas by cutting out a stocking, Santa Claus (sack and all), holly wreath, bell, or Christmas tree. The invitation to the party may be in the sack or the stocking. Or you may write it out in the shape of a tree. A peppermint stick attached to the invitation, a sprig of pine, acorn, or bit of holly adds a further festive note. But be certain the message is prominent so the invitation won't be placed on the mantel with Christmas greeting cards.

If it is desirable to send a more formal invitation, a short note from Mother will usually suffice:

Dear Mrs. Saunders,

Tommy is celebrating his sixth birthday with a little party on Saturday afternoon, June the sixth. He particularly wants to have Margie come.

We plan to start the games about half past one and show movies until about five.

Very cordially,

A child's own invitation might read:

Dear Joan,

Please come to my eighth birthday party on September the ninth from three to five o'clock.

We are going to have cake and ice cream and play games. I hope you can come.

Your friend,

Acceptance

Dear Mrs. Cortland,

It was very kind of you to ask Margie to Tommy's party on Saturday, June the sixth. She will be most happy to be there.

Cordially,

Dear Mary,

Thank you for inviting me to your party. I wouldn't miss it for anything!

Your pal,

Regrets

Dear Mrs. Cortland,

Margie was delighted at the invitation, and she would like very much to go to Tommy's party. Unfortunately, she has not entirely recovered from her virus infection and the doctor thinks she should not leave the house for another week.

Thank you very much for asking her.

Very cordially,

Dear Susie,

I wish I could come to your party on Wednesday, but we are going to visit my grandma that day.

I hate to miss your party. I know it will be lots of fun.

Happy birthday and thanks for inviting me.

With love,

Letters home

If your child goes away for the summer, he will probably write more letters home during the two vacation months than he will write during the rest of the year. In most children's camps, three or four letters a week are compulsory. A letter home is often the admission ticket to the dining hall. If you want really informative letters, ask your child to answer a specific set of questions about matters of interest to him.

What to say in writing home:

1. What did you do since you wrote last?
2. What have you learned? read? seen?
3. Whom did you meet?
4. What happened regarding the things you wrote about last time?
5. What curious or funny stories have you heard?
6. How is your health?
7. What has happened to some of your friends? relatives? counselors? pets?
8. What do you hope or expect to do?
9. What would you like to have done for you?
10. Whom do you care to hear about?

Many parents have reconciled themselves to a postcard with a single sentence about the day's activities and "Send me . . ." These samples may help you get better results:

Dear Mother,

Camp is very nice. It was very cool when we arrived, and all of us had to wear heavy pajamas the first night.

The counselor in my bunk is the nature counselor. We took a long nature walk today, and she caught an eight-inch garter snake! It is in the nature house now.

Please send a canteen. I need it for longer hikes. We may take a canoe trip to Pine Island next month.

Janet Brown is in my bunk. We plan to go horseback riding tomorrow.

Love,

Dear Mother and Dad,

I am feeling fine today, and the touch of sniffles I had when you were here last week is all gone. The counselor sent me to the infirmary on Monday morning for a check-up and the doctor gave me a yellow pill. That ended my sniffles.

The boys in Bunk Five beat us at baseball yesterday. They have a crackerjack pitcher who wins most of the games for them. But we expect to beat Bunk Seven tomorrow.

I am making some ash trays in arts and crafts. If I can work on them this week, I'll be able to show them to you when you come up next time. My swimming is getting along fine. Pop Hausser says I can try for the canoe test a week from Wednesday. If I pass, I'll be able to go out on the lake with Dad when he comes.

When you can, will you please pick up some flashlight batteries for me? The canteen here is all out.

Give my love to Toady and to Aunt Martha. I miss seeing them.

Love,

CHAPTER 13

References and Letters of Introduction

Letters about people—introductions and references—present problems of delicacy, tact, and sometimes legal considerations. The letter of introduction serves to bring together people you are sure will find pleasure or profit in each other's company. Such a letter is never lightly requested nor casually written. Unless you know both parties well and are sure that they have mutually compatible interests and personalities, it is best not to write a letter.

A letter of introduction should be brief and relevant. Since it requests that kindness and hospitality be offered to a stranger, it must include a sincere expression of thanks for the courtesies requested. This kind of letter may be mailed or given to the person to be introduced for personal presentation. In the latter case, the envelope is left unsealed. Of course, particular tact must be used in writing such a letter.

Letters of reference have to be written, since withholding such letters implies an obviously negative opinion. An employee, unless seriously inefficient and extremely dubious of character, should be given a chance to find employment with someone else whose requirements may differ from yours.

Write the good things and omit the bad. Condemn with faint praise in an oblique rather than a direct manner. For example:

"Her work was satisfactory enough."

"Her typewriting is almost satisfactory."

"Since Miss Wheeler has taken a refresher course in shorthand, her work should now show an improvement."

"I believe he has now stopped drinking and should prove more trustworthy."

Letters of introduction

Dear Sandra,

My cousin Matilda Dunn will be in Chicago next month to take a summer course at the Art Institute. As you know, I've often wanted you two to meet, and this seems like an excellent opportunity.

Besides sharing your interest in painting and music, Matilda is as devoted a baseball fan as you are!

I know how busy you are with your new job, so please don't regard this as an obligation. But if you have any free time, do give Matilda a ring at the Statler. I know once you've met her you will really enjoy her company. Anything you can do will be sincerely appreciated on my part and on Matilda's also.

Affectionately,

Dear Bob,

You've often heard me speak of Mark Wilder, my former roommate at college. I've always wanted you and Mark to meet, but the two of you have never been in the same place at the same time. Well, that's about to be rectified. Mark, like you, is the proud possessor of a Fulbright fellowship and will be studying in Paris for eight months, beginning this September.

I've asked him to give you a call, since he has no definite address as yet. Of course, I would never have taken this liberty if I hadn't been sure you would enjoy the meeting.

Although Mark is a very serious student, he is one of the wittiest men I know—a good conversationalist in both French and English. I'll really appreciate any kindness you can show, and I know Mark will, too.

As ever,

Dear Sidney,

The bearer of this note, Robert Saunders, plans to be in New York for about a month. A good friend of mine, he is a crackerjack copy writer for one of the agencies here. I think you two advertising executives will have a lot in common, and I'm sure you will enjoy meeting him.

Thanks, Sidney, for any kindness you may extend to Robert. We will both appreciate it.

Cordially,

Dear Mrs. Santangelo,

This note will introduce my good friend and co-worker Miss Dorothea Wills, of whom you've heard me speak.

Miss Wills is in Zenith to study your child-guidance program, and as a former social worker, you will undoubtedly share many interests with her. Besides, you are both expert bridge players.

I will appreciate any courtesy you show Miss Wills, and I am sure she will, too.

Please send my best regards to Mr. Santangelo. I look forward to seeing both of you before very long.

Sincerely,

Business introductions

Dear Milt,

The bearer of this letter, Robert Saunders, is a bright young man from Janesville who is determined to seek his fortune in the big city.

Bob worked on the local daily here for all the years he went to high school and during his summer vacations while at Yale. The editor, who is an old friend of mine, considers him the best rewrite man he has ever had and a demon for accuracy in the smallest details. He was largely responsible for uncovering discrepancies in a news story that led to the solution of one of the few crimes we have had around here in years.

I know that occasionally you look for talent to add to your staff. If this is one of those periods, I wish you would talk to Bob and see for yourself whether he can fit into your organization. If you can't use his talents yourself, will you give him the benefit of your experience and steer him into the proper channels?

Martha and I plan to be in New York for a few days in June. Perhaps we can have dinner together one evening.

Cordially,

Dear Mr. Bruse:

I am writing this letter for Miss Joan Bridges of Janesville, Ohio. She arrived in New York only a few days ago with the highest recommendations from an old friend, Miss Nannette B. Furness, Dean of the Milwaukee College for Women.

Miss Bridges was an outstanding student at school, president of several societies, and editor of the college newspaper. She showed exceptional talent in writing advertising copy and has come to the city to make a career for herself. I have read some of the ads she wrote for local advertisers, and they impress me as showing a sound command of language and good imagination.

Miss Bridges has no grandiose ideas of what she can do. She realizes that she needs some experience with a big advertising agency, and she is willing to fit into any position she can fill. She types well and has a little knowledge of shorthand.

I think you will be interested in talking to her and perhaps in finding her a place in your copy department.

Sincerely,

Asking for references

Dear Mrs. Saunders,

Jane White, whom I am considering for employment as a house-keeper, has given your name as a reference.

Would you be good enough to let me know your opinion of her character, efficiency, and ability to get along with small children?

I shall appreciate any information you can give me and will keep it in strict confidence.

Thank you.

Sincerely yours,

Dear Mr. Lawrence,

Although it has been several months since I left Martin's, I have not as yet found the type of work I wish to follow as a permanent career.

In making applications at several places, it has been necessary to present a complete business résumé, including references. Would you be kind enough to let me use your name as a reference when the occasion arises in the future?

Sincerely,

Dear Mr. Hall:

Miss Eleanor Silver has given your name as a business reference. I am considering hiring her as my secretary, and I need a young woman who, besides proficiency in secretarial skills, has the ability to get along with others and work well without supervision.

Any information you care to give will, of course, be held in the strictest confidence.

Thank you.

Very truly yours,

Response to a reference request

Dear Mrs. Childs,

Jane White was in my employ for three years, during which time we found her work and character most satisfactory, although we did have occasional differences of opinion about her time off. Whenever I was away from home for the day or week-end, she took care of my five- and eight-year-old sons. The children were very fond of her. If we were not planning to move to another city, there would be no reason to dispense with Jane's services.

Sincerely yours,

Dear Miss Wheelock,

I shall be pleased to let you use my name as a reference. We found your work more than satisfactory and regretted the circumstances that led you to leave Martin's.

I know that any company you work for will get the same kind of loyalty, intelligence, and efficiency that you displayed during your three years with us. Be assured that I will not hesitate to recommend you to any prospective employer.

The best of luck to you.

Cordially yours,

Dear Mr. Amsterdam:

I am happy to have the opportunity of answering your letter about Eleanor Silver. She is a rare find as a secretary; a young lady who is accurate, intelligent, and personable.

Miss Silver came to us about five years ago as a graduate of one of Zenith's best secretarial schools. She moved from one department to another as the work required, accepting added responsibilities with cheerfulness, efficiency, and dependability. When she left us a year ago to get married, she was secretary to the president of the company. We were sincerely sorry to see her leave.

Yours truly,

Dear Mr. Barclay:

James Method worked as a saleman in our grocery department from April 1964 to November 1965. He was a hard worker, ambitious, intelligent, honest, and full of initiative. At the end of a year his record was a little better than that of the average salesman in the organization.

However, the same qualities that contributed to Mr. Method's effectiveness as a salesman led to a great deal of friction with his co-workers. There were constant disputes about overlapping territories, delegation of responsibility, and interpretations of regulations. When his contract expired, we felt it would be wise to replace him.

I believe that Mr. Method will have considerably less difficulty in a smaller organization such as yours, where he can be left on his own. He has the qualities to make him a good producer for the company that can give him the freedom he needs.

Very truly yours,

References in blank

Eva Smith was with us for the past three years as a housekeeper. She is trustworthy, pleasant, good with children, and a fine laundress. We are truly sorry that our moving to another state necessitated her leaving our employ. I shall be happy to answer any inquiries about Eva.

Anne Walker Willis
(Mrs. Edmund G. Willis)

Roberta Morris was employed by the Janesville Emporium from June 1957 to January 1965. In that time she held positions of increasing responsibility, progressing from salesgirl to section manager, and finally to assistant buyer of the book department. At all times Miss Morris showed a great aptitude for merchandising. Her campaigns were always executed with great originality and effectiveness. It was with great regret that we accepted her resignation to seek broader opportunities with a larger organization.

Ralph L. Atkins
Merchandising Manager

Helpful Sentences

Introductions

Tom is the sort of fellow you'll like (want to know) (find interesting) (find no trouble at all) (find is a lot of fun).

Jane is a wonderful girl, full of enthusiasm (is a blithe spirit) (is the type of girl you enjoy having around) (is helpful, gay and full of fun) (is a serious girl, self-sufficient, and thoughtful) (embodies all the old-fashioned virtues).

References

Mr. James Doe is an asset to any organization (the type of assistant an officer manager will find indispensable) (a meticulous record keeper) (a man who can handle details without losing sight of the over-all situation).

Miss Nancy Roe has all the qualities of a perfect secretary. She is efficient and discreet (a careful worker who seldom makes a mistake yet is the first to admit any error on her part) (has been helpful in a hundred different ways beyond the requirements of her job) (has a fine ability to deal with people, particularly where tact is required) (has never left a job undone, regardless of how difficult or time-consuming).

CHAPTER 14

Community, Club, and Civic Correspondence

If you take an active part in the affairs of your community, you will have occasion to write letters in connection with public matters and the business of the organizations with which you are associated. In general, club correspondence follows the same rules as business correspondence. It should be friendly, tactful, brief, and to the point.

Models of the letters you would be most likely to have to write are given below:

Proposing a member

Dear Mrs. Saunders,

I wish to propose Mrs. Thomas Cortland for membership in the Janesville Civic Club.

Mrs. Cortland has been active in community affairs since she moved to Janesville five years ago. She has been a leading spirit in the Whittier School P.T.A. and an associate director of the Community Chest Drive for the past two years. Those of us who know Mrs. Cortland respect her ability and her energy on behalf of so many worthy causes.

I am certain Mrs. Cortland will be a credit to our organization.

Sincerely yours,

Inviting a member

Dear Mr. Cortland:

Your name has been suggested to me by John P. Saunders as a person who is actively interested in the affairs of Janesville and particularly in the important work the Taxpayers League is doing to maintain good government in the community.

You will recall that it was the work done by the League that led to the adoption of the city-manager plan of government for Janesville six years ago. This was only one of the many measures sponsored by the organization. Some of our other accomplishments, our purposes, and our present program are described in the enclosed booklet.

If you agree with the principles for which we are working, I should like to have the privilege of proposing your name for membership at the next meeting on Friday, September 27th, at eight o'clock. In any case, you are cordially invited to be my guest at the meeting. I would like to meet you personally and discuss any questions you might have about the League.

Very cordially,

Notifying a candidate of his election

Dear Mr. Bates:

I am happy to notify you that you have been elected a member of the Executive Committee of the Tonkawanna Club.

Installation ceremonies will be held at the Clubhouse on Tuesday evening, May 24th, at 8:30. Judge Ferdinand Smith will be the installing officer and will address the group on current community problems.

I hope to have a chance to talk with you at length on Tuesday about some of the activities of the club for the coming year and about the program we plan to develop for the young people.

Very cordially,

Acknowledging an invitation for membership

Dear Mr. Saunders:

Please express to the members of the Board of Directors my sincere appreciation and thanks for selecting me to head the Executive Committee of the Janesville Society.

I am honored to accept, and I shall make every effort to continue the good work traditional with the committee.

Very sincerely yours,

Accepting a nomination

Gentlemen:

I am proud and happy to accept your nomination to the Board of Directors.

Of course I will be delighted to accept your invitation to join the IQ Society. I consider it a privilege and an honor.

Your invitation to join the PDQ Circle is a pleasant surprise. I am delighted to accept.

It is with great humility that I accept your nomination as Man of the Year for the MPB Society.

Very sincerely,

Declining a nomination

Dear Mr. Chatworth:

I was gratified and honored to receive notification of my nomination as a candidate for the Civic Association Board of Trustees.

Unfortunately, I must decline this honor. I have not yet recovered completely from a recent illness, and my doctor has suggested that I limit my activities.

I trust that in a year or so my health will permit me to be active in community affairs again.

Sincerely yours,

Letter of resignation

Dear Mr. Martin:

It is with sincere regret that I must tender my resignation as a member of the Greenville Community Center.

Since moving to the country, my family and I find that our interests and community activities are now centered around Janesville. Thus we feel it would be mutually beneficial to join the Janesville Center.

Please be assured of my appreciation for the many courtesies shown to me and my family.

Sincerely,

Accepting a resignation

Dear Mr. Johnson:

Your letter of resignation was read to the Board of Trustees at the last meeting.

All of us heard with regret your decision. Your resignation was accepted with the understanding that membership will be open to you at any time you might wish to rejoin our organization.

We hope that you and your family will enjoy your membership at the Janesville Center.

Cordially yours,

Letters of appreciation

Dear Mr. Herbert:

We know that you do not ask thanks for your generous expenditure of time and effort in behalf of the Association. But we want to express to you, at least in this small way, our thanks and appreciation for the time and trouble you took to make the annual bulletin so successful.

We are certain that your fine example will serve to inspire others to give of their time to our common cause.

Please extend our thanks to your wife for her unselfish cooperation.

With all my best wishes,

Very cordially,

Dear Mr. Jacobs:

At the Executive Board Meeting of the Greater New York Council on Wednesday, March 17th, I was instructed to express to you the deep gratitude of the Council for your company's sponsorship of the Washington's Birthday Luncheon. The luncheon was a great success, and all the Board members are most appreciative of your kind cooperation.

Cordially yours,

Dear Mr. Wallace:

On behalf of the Janesville Board of Education, permit me to thank you for your invaluable assistance as a member of our Public Relations Advisory Committee. Particularly let me express our appreciation for your generous donation of time and effort in the preparation of the referendum brochure.

Most sincerely yours,

Dear Mr. Mager:

Please accept our heartfelt gratitude for your gift of $25.00 which has been forwarded through the kindness of our mutual friend, Mr. James Bright.

Through your gift you are helping maintain the unbroken continuity of more than 73 years of uninterrupted free care of the tuberculous needy of our land in this pioneer hospital.

Your generous aid will help us to extend sorely needed medical and surgical service to even more patients. It will help to expend our important research program.

Each day in our laboratories our scientists are moving closer to our ultimate goal—the control and eradication of tuberculosis, asthma, and other chest diseases.

Our patients, young and old alike, join in sincere appreciation. To you they say, "Thank you."

Faithfully yours,

Acknowledging a letter of appreciation

Dear Mrs. Saunders:

Thank you for your kind letter of February 12th.

It was a privilege to help the Civic Group. Janesville is, after all, my town, too, and it is a pleasure to pitch in and help keep it the wonderful place it is.

Very sincerely,

Fund-raising letters

For many civic-minded people, fund raising is both a necessary and onerous part of community work. Since civic projects cannot succeed without financial support, fund raising is the cornerstone of any worth-while project. Fund-raising letters are most effective when they appeal to the emotions. Here are the beginning paragraphs of several letters that have been notably successful:

Dear Mr. Saunders:

There are few causes that are so close to my heart that they could induce me to write you a letter like this; but on this occasion I feel I *must* appeal to you.

My home town of Janesville is one of those expanding communities that has outgrown its recreational facilities. We are, therefore, building an addition to our Community Center that will be almost entirely for the use of children. To keep them off the streets, we are planning classrooms, game rooms, hobby rooms, a gymnasium, and other facilities for supervised activities.

In order to provide the necessary funds, we are publishing a journal in connection with a dinner-dance to be held on March 4th. This letter is to ask you to buy advertising space in this journal.

It is not easy for me to write to you in this way, but I am sure you understand the importance of the cause.

Please say Yes!

With sincere thanks,

P.S. Of course the advertisement is a deductible item on next year's income tax.

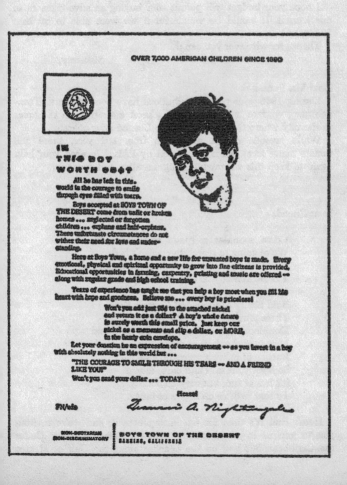

Gentlemen:

This year we are trying to finish the job of raising money for building the additions of our Janesville Community Center.

The people in Janesville have done a magnificent job of fund raising, and we now have $78,500. That's a lot of money, even in these days.

We are striving for a $20,000 journal this year. If we make it, we'll go over the top, and the new building will be finished before the summer is out.

I hope your budget will permit your buying an advertisement in our journal. It would be wonderful if we were able to hit that $20,000.

Thanks for whatever you can do.

Sincerely,

Dear Mr. James:

During 1960 your past contributions have been at work. Teenage gang warfare has disappeared almost entirely from the areas in the city where the Police Athletic League now operates.

While juvenile crimes are down from last year, there still remain many areas not now covered by PAL. We need your help again to keep this worthwhile program alive and growing.

Sincerely,

Dear Friend:

> Come shoulder a spade and heave the lead,
> We're going to search the ocean's bed
> For silver and pearls and diamond rings,
> The sunken hoards of pirate kings.
>
> Bold Henry Morgan and Captain Kidd
> These jeweled treasures pirated—
> Doubloons and ducats, guineas and gold
> Minted in the days of old,
> Burden of many a mermaid's song—
> So hoist your sails and come along!
> It's lots of fun, but may be chancy
> To soar with us on flights of fancy.

Here's fun! It's time for our spring benefit, and we're inviting you to join us in an imaginary game—a Treasure Hunt. Under the Caribbean Sea and on the beaches along the Gulf of Mexico lie vast riches, lost in the days when bold buccaneers preyed on Spanish galleons.

So just put on your diving suit and helmet and sail in your imaginary ship to the Southern Seas. In return we'll give you the privilege—for a price—of staking out your claim on our PIRATE MAP and taking your chances at the treasure of your choice.

The money you send us will be used for a good cause: to continue in your behalf the work of the Seamen's Church Institute of New York which, for 107 years, has provided a wholesome and spiritually healthy atmosphere for merchant seamen of all nationalities and creeds.

We hope the treasure you "discover" will bring you real happiness.

> Sincerely,

It *hurts* to be rejected . . .

. . . but there is hope for these children and thousands of other tragic victims of rejection—

hope as bright and shining as this new-minted penny—

hope that *you* can bring with your help.

The little boy and girl are not rejected through any fault of theirs. They have no contagious disease. They are not disabled.

When you are not soliciting funds

Dear John and Sylvia,

In previous campaigns you certainly have been very helpful.

Bette and I, in talking it over this time, felt that it was really not right to bother the same people again. So we have generally been involved with others during this campaign.

I do feel, however, that we may have slighted our friends of past years by inadequate attention. Let this then be a thank-you note for your early and continued support.

> Sincerely,

Refusing to take

Dear John,

Your interest in writing to us about the catalog which will be issued in connection with National Festival is appreciated, although we regret that we are unable to be represented as advertisers in the book.

The very limited amount of advertising of this nature which is allowed in our budget is taken up entirely by allocations for trade journals in connection with local events. Although many suggestions similar to yours have come to us in the past, we have never been able to take advantage of them.

While our reply cannot be favorable, we hope you will be generous enough to understand our position and to realize that this answer by no means indicates any lack of interest or goodwill in the publication you are issuing.

Sincerely,

Sample letter and paragraphs

This is a grim message.

It cannot be otherwise on the subject of cancer. As unpleasant as this might be for me, I'm drawn into it by the thought that someday, somewhere, somebody might live because I am overcoming the usual inclination to let another do the job.

City Hospital was ready to serve you the moment you needed its help. Now the hospital needs your help . . . urgently.

Have you ever seen a small child stricken with heart trouble? Looked into a tiny face from which all traces of childhood have vanished—all hope fled? Held this child's pain-racked body in your arms, trying in vain to find just one word of comfort? And felt that you would do anything to bring even a fleeting smile to that solemn little face?

A poor woman brought us five dollars in dimes, nickels, and pennies. "It took me a long time to save this," she said. "Perhaps it will tell you how grateful I am. Your hospital saved my life."

CAN I BE YOUR BOY, MISTER,
'TIL MY ARM'S FIXED?

I was just getting so I could walk again when I fell and broke my arm, and Mommie couldn't take care of me 'cause she has two babies younger than me.

Response to a request for funds

Dear Mr. Cortland:

I enclose with great pleasure our advertisement for the journal of the forthcoming dinner-dance of the Janesville Community Center.

It is certainly gratifying to see what an effort you and your com-

Dear Father,

I've got to write this letter to you. Teacher says so. It's supposed to be a bit of a composition! You see, every boy in the class has to write a letter to his father for Lincoln's Birthday. And he has to make believe he is Abraham Lincoln's son writing a letter to his Dad to cheer him up on his birthday while a terrible war is raging all around him.

Gee! I have to laugh before I start. You'd look awfully funny in chin whiskers, Dad — but seriously, you're the famous President for tonight and I'm your not so famous son. Make believe, can't you?   Here goes.

Dear Father Abraham, on this your birthday your brow is wrinkled with care at a time when it should be crowned with laughter. A war is on. And you and I and millions of Americans are in it. Ours is a just cause. We are fighting not for conquest but for freedom; for the foundation of your Democracy, the rule that all men are created equal. It's a man's job, a big man's job — to fight and to win. And you are that big man who will inspire and lead boys like me to give all we can in our small way to win that fight. Count on me.

Gosh, Dad, such a message would hold good today too, wouldn't it? And, as I write it, it isn't make believe any more. I mean it.

All homework aside now, let's commemorate Lincoln's Birthday together! Know how? Not the ordinary way, at a show or a movie! Do you mind if I suggest a grand and original way? The way a father and son ought to get together! You know, dining out in company, like at a banquet!

(turn page please

mittee are making to insure that this will be the most successful dinner-dance we have ever had. Now that our plans have definitely taken shape, it is up to each of us to do his part so that we can go over the top.

Sincerely yours,

Letter to the press

To the editor

Dear Sir:

People are so quick to write a letter of complaint and so slow to write a letter of praise that I feel it is only fitting to commend our Police Department.

I have been a resident of Janesville for five years and have had three occasions to ask assistance of the Police Department.

I can only use superlatives when I speak of their promptness, courtesy, and efficiency.

Last month, I had the misfortune to fall and break my ankle. A friend called the Police Department, and in a few minutes I was surrounded by policemen to help me.

Although I am leaving Janesville, I shall continue to talk about the Janesville Police Department, and I wish to take this opportunity to thank them.

Sincerely,

To The Editor of the Janesville Times:

The news story in your issue of March 4th quotes Mayor Tomlinson as urging the erection of a new junior high school in Central Park, just north of Route 22. The mayor has explained in detail the viewpoint of the city, and it boils down to just one point: saving the taxpayer's money.

Although every resident of Janesville will concede that this end is much to be desired, I wish to point out that it is not the whole story. As chairman of the Taxpayer's League Town Planning Committee, I was partly responsible for setting aside the present Central Park area as a place for public recreation some twelve years ago. The purpose set forth at that time was to provide a place where all the citizens might find relaxation and a retreat from the ever encroaching buildings, which now appear to cover every other sizable plot in town.

Using a portion of this park—even twelve of the total of sixty acres—for a junior high school would entirely defeat the purpose for which the park was originally created. The rural atmosphere would be entirely lost. The quiet and peace would be no more. The small animals that still abound there, away from the built-up areas, would flee or die. And Janesville could never again create such an area.

Condemning twelve acres of built-up property would undoubtedly be expensive. However, this cost can be amortized over a period of many years. Is it wiser to sacrifice the beauty and tranquillity of Janesville's only large park to save the cost of a comparatively small school site?

Very truly yours,

Letter to the mayor

My dear Mayor Walker:

This morning I found on my doorstep a note informing me and other home owners in this area that a proposed change in the zoning laws would permit the building of a 100-family apartment on the site adjoining my property.

Such a change in zoning would be grossly unfair to my neighbors and myself. Not only would it substantially depreciate the value of our property, it would create costly problems for the city.

All of us built our homes in the Bloomingdale section with the understanding that the area was zoned exclusively for one-family homes. The section is entirely occupied by such homes, valued between $15,000 and $25,000. If an apartment house were to face these homes, they could not be sold for even a fraction of their present market price.

I note that the change in zoning makes no provision for garages to house the cars that 100 families in a suburban community would necessarily have. This would create street-parking problems as well as traffic hazards to the children of the neighborhood.

From the point of view of the community, the addition of 100 families would require immediate construction of a new school in the area. It is a well-known fact that income from taxes on the apartment building would not nearly meet the cost of building and maintaining school facilities for the 130 to 150 additional school children who might be expected.

As a matter of fair play to the home owners of Bloomingdale and as good tax sense for the people of New Cape, I strongly urge that the proposed change in zoning be denied.

Very truly yours,

CHAPTER 15

Letters About Family Business

Advice, complaints, purchases, money matters, Junior's relations with school, are but a few of the many phases of family business that require letter writing. Such letters should be businesslike and cordial. Although they may reflect your personality, they should contain a minimum of irrelevancies and a sufficient amount of detail to make your purpose crystal-clear. Always keep in mind what such a letter aims to accomplish. After you have written the letter, read it from the point of view of the person to whom it is addressed. Then decide if it can and will accomplish what you want it to do.

Asking for advice

Dear Tom,

With your visits to the Midwest so few and far between, it has been a long time since we had a chance to sit down and have a chat together. I've missed the old bull sessions no end, particularly now, when, to coin a phrase, "I have a problem." Because I know you have a good sense of logic and can see things more objectively than I can, I am taking the liberty of asking for your advice.

You know how I am situated in Janesville. I earn a good salary working for my father-in-law, and I have all the security a man can want. Cynthia has many friends in town, and we are about as deeply rooted as a family can get.

On the other hand, because of its size, Janesville has definite limitations for an ambitious young man. With my engineering degree and the three years of experience I have had in the plant, I think I can get a job with one of the larger companies in the East. Although this may mean a cut in salary for the present, I believe that in the long run I'll earn more money and find a better position by leaving town.

Cynthia is leaving the choice entirely up to me. It is a difficult decision to make, and I shall appreciate any comments or advice you'd care to give. I do hope you'll write soon.

Cordially,

Dear Judge Manville,

I know how busy you are these days, and I am writing to you for advice because you are the only person I can turn to.

You will remember my brother Jimmy as a teen-ager who delivered newspapers to your door until about four years ago. After two years in the Army, Jimmy went to work for the Martin Manufacturing Company in Greendale. In his spare time he developed a process for spraying metal parts so that they would not rust under ordinary conditions.

Before he tells anyone about the process I believe he ought to take some measures to protect it. Would you be good enough to suggest how he can best do this and what precautions he should take in his relations with his company?

I will be most grateful for your help and so will Jimmy.

Sincerely,

Answering a request for advice

Dear Tim,

I have thought over very seriously the questions you raised about going to college. Weighing all the factors involved and appreciating your personal difficulties, I am nevertheless convinced that you should try to make it.

Given the choice of two young people to hire for the same salary, ninety-nine out of one hundred employers will pick a college graduate. In the long run, a college education is a solid financial investment that will pay a lifetime of dividends in increased earning power, as well as in personal satisfaction. If you fail to enter college this year, the probability is that you will never get around to going, and for the rest of your life you will feel that every college graduate has a big advantage over you.

The financial difficulties are very real, Tim, and I don't want to underestimate them. But such difficulties have been overcome by a great many young people, some of whom have gone on to win national prominence. It isn't at all unusual for a boy to work his way through college. The biggest sacrifice is being made by Mother, who has a right to expect you to help with the household expenses at your age. Mother is, I am sure, more than willing to make that sacrifice.

I am not going to tell you that working your way through college is easy. It means that you will have to work hard for four years, perhaps five or six. You will have to miss some of the fun that other boys get out of college. But I think that the fun you will miss in the next few years will be more than made up by the practical advantages you get from a college education. You have, after all, only one life to live, and what you do in these next few years will determine just what kind of person you will be and what kind of life you will be able to live. It's up to you to decide whether it is worth some years of hard work and sacrifice to make yourself a better-educated and more effective person.

I hope you will make the kind of decision that you won't ever regret.

Affectionately,

Asking to borrow money

Dear Sy,

This is the kind of letter I hate to write, and I know it is the kind that you hate to get. But I think you know that if it wasn't necessary, this letter would never have been written.

Frankly, I am in a tough spot and need four hundred dollars. I am writing to you as one of my oldest friends and one whom I could always depend on in an emergency.

You know about most of the bad luck I have been having. After Mary returned from the hospital last month, Jim took sick with an illness that mystified the doctors. He's better now, but the doctors haven't been paid. Being laid off for six weeks during the strike ate up most of our reserves, and it will be several months before I can pay off the more pressing bills. After that I can return the money to you in installments of one hundred dollars a month.

I don't have to tell you that I am asking for a loan only as a last resort. I know you won't let me down.

Sincerely,

Dear Tom,

It is never easy to write a letter of this sort, and it is particularly difficult for me because I have never had to write one before.

As you know, we had a fire in the store last month that ruined almost everything. The insurance we collected paid the outstanding bills for merchandise, and two creditors attached the balance. Meanwhile, the store has been closed and we have had no money coming in to meet our household bills.

Right now I'm desperate for funds to tide me over the next month until the store can open up again. I have already arranged to finance my new inventory and I have every reason to expect to be back earning a living by April 15th. It has taken every bit of business credit I had to make this possible. Now I need about five hundred dollars to take care of our personal expenses. I will be able to return it to you before June 15th from the regular store income.

Because of the urgency, I have to count on you. Please don't let me down.

Cordially,

Response to a request for a loan

Dear Tim,

As soon as I received your letter I went into a huddle with Ruth. We're sending along a check for one hundred dollars, which is not quite what you asked for, but a lot for us to manage right now. Frankly, it's our Christmas fund. Under the circumstances, we're glad to send it along to you.

I hope things will pick up in the next few months as they usually do in the fall. If you can see your way clear to returning the money before the holidays, please try to do so.

Our best wishes to all of you.

Cordially,

Dear Selma,

As difficult as it must have been for you to ask, it is equally difficult for me to have to refuse. I am sincerely sorry, but I just can't spare any cash at this time.

I know you must have tried the ordinary sources of loans like the banks and the finance companies, but perhaps Sid's boss could advance a few weeks' salary to him.

I wish I could be more helpful, but circumstances simply don't permit it.

Cordially,

Dear Bob,

I'm sorry, Bob, but I have to say No at this time. A number of personal problems have drained me of ready cash, and I'm just not in a condition to spare any money.

Would it be of help to you if I offered to endorse a note at your local bank? I will be glad to accommodate you if this will solve your problem.

Cordially,

Asking for the return of a loan

Dear Rose,

I'm frankly embarrassed to ask, but I know it must have slipped your mind. When I lent you the ten dollars last Friday, you said you'd return it after the week-end. Will you please send Robert over with it today?

As ever,

Dear Steve,

What would you do in my place? Several months have gone by since you asked me to lend you twenty dollars for a few days. If I could afford to forget about it, you know I would.

However, like most of us, I depend on money to buy the things I need. There are twenty good reasons why I must have the money this week. Please make certain I have it by Friday.

Sincerely,

Dear Martha,

I hate to have to write a letter like this to an old friend, but I just don't know what else to do. When you borrowed fifty dollars from me for your Christmas shopping, you assured me it was only for a few days. The "few days" have stretched into several months, and you haven't even tried to send me part of the sum.

Perhaps I should have been firmer months ago. Please understand that I must have the money you owe me this week.

Sincerely,

Request for delay in payment

Gentlemen:

I am enclosing my check for twenty-five dollars towards the sum of one hundred dollars, which is currently in arrears on my account.

Please accept my apologies for failing to keep my account up to date. Recent unexpected expenses have placed a financial burden on me that I did not foresee when I made the purchases last spring.

Let me assure you that I will make every effort to catch up on my payments at the earliest possible time. I appreciate your courtesy in bearing with me.

Very truly yours,

To enclose with payments

Gentlemen:

Enclosed is my check for $90.25 covering your statement of May 15th amounting to $97.50.

I have deducted a charge of $7.25 for a set of draperies, which were returned to you on April 27th.

Please acknowledge receipt of this payment and mark my account paid in full to this date.

Very truly yours,

Opening a charge account

Gentlemen:

I should like to open a charge account at your store for me and members of my family.

Will you please have two bottles of Grade A milk delivered daily, and a dozen of your best white eggs delivered once each week until further notice. You may begin deliveries immediately after Labor Day, September 3rd.

Thank you.

Very truly yours,

Ordering merchandise:

Please send C.O.D. to
John P. Saunders
2748 Booth Street
Rego Park, Pa.
two boxes of white note paper as advertised in today's Times.

Thank you.

Yours very truly,

Complaint regarding apartment service

Gentlemen:

I have complained to the superintendent on several occasions during the past three weeks that water is leaking through our bathroom ceiling. Nothing has been done, and the plaster has already started to fall.

Please see to it that the leak is stopped and the ceiling repaired immediately.

Very truly yours,

Complaint regarding damaged merchandise

Gentlemen:

I received today a package (Sales Slip No. 42751) in response to my order for the set of leather-bound luggage advertised by you in last Sunday's Times.

As soon as I opened the package, I noticed that the 26-inch case had been seriously damaged by a big gash.

Will you please see that this case is picked up and replaced? If a duplicate case is not available, please arrange to have the entire set picked up and the cost credited to my account.

Very truly yours,

Complaint regarding delayed merchandise

Gentlemen:

Please check on the delivery of my order for one dozen spun-aluminum glasses from your houseware department.

The order was placed by telephone on May 15th and was to have been delivered before Saturday, May 20th. It was to be charged to my account.

If delivery of the glasses cannot be made by May 25th, please cancel my order.

Very truly yours,

Complaint regarding personnel

Gentlemen:

I know that your company, like every business that deals with the public, tries to maintain a standard of courtesy and service among its employees. Therefore, I am writing to bring to your attention an incident that occurred last week on the Paterson bus leaving Dixie Terminal at 7:10 P.M.

The bus was apparently behind schedule, and the driver failed to stop at Bridge Plaza although two passengers wanted to get off there. One of the passengers, a middle-aged lady, protested that she would not be able to walk back from the next stop, a quarter of a mile away, because of a leg injury. The driver thereupon stopped the bus suddenly, causing the lady and several other passengers to lose their balance and fall. He then opened the door and insisted that the lady leave the bus.

I am writing this letter not only on my behalf, but at the suggestion of several other passengers, including Mr. Norman Person, of 271 River Road, Capeville, and Mr. Joseph Johnson, of 156 Cornelius Drive, Greenlawn.

I am sure that you will take steps to see that such an incident is not repeated.

Very truly yours,

To cancel a contract

Dear Sir:

This is to give you thirty days notice of our desire to vacate Apartment 7D at 12 Cedar Lane on September 30th. Such notice is in accordance with our lease, dated October 1, 1967.

Please acknowledge receipt of this letter.

Very truly yours,

Registered mail

Making reservations

Gentlemen:

Please reserve a double room with bath for my wife and myself for the period from April 14th through May 7th. We would prefer a room overlooking the lake and not higher than the second floor. If possible, we would like a room furnished with twin beds.

Please confirm this reservation by wire today, since I plan to leave the city by Tuesday. We expect to arrive at about 7 P.M. on April 14th.

Very truly yours,

Change of address

Gentlemen:

Please change my address on your subscription rolls from:

> Jonathan Greenhouse
> 27-14 Terrace Street
> Janesville, Ohio
>   to
> 431 Grand Avenue
> Englewood, N.Y.
> Thank you.

>   Very truly yours,

(Make certain to give your old address. Most files of large companies are maintained on a geographical basis.)

Excuse for absence from school

Dear Miss Buckley,

Please excuse Peter's absence from school on Thursday and Friday, May 7th and 8th.

Peter had the sniffles and an intermittent cough, and I felt it would not have been fair to the other children to allow him to attend school.

As you can see, he has now entirely recovered.

If there is any work that should be made up, will you be good enough to tell Peter or send me a note about it?

Thank you.

                        Very truly yours,

Excuse for future absence

Dear Mrs. Keener,

Peter will be absent from school next Thursday and Friday, March 27th and 28th. These days are important religious holidays in our faith.

If it is possible to give Peter assignments that will allow him to make up the work covered by the class during these days, he will attempt to catch up on his studies over the week-end.

                        Sincerely,

Excuse for tardiness

Dear Miss Buckley,

Please excuse Mildred's tardiness today.

She had not been feeling well yesterday afternoon, and could not fall asleep until well into the night. I felt it was wiser to let her sleep in the morning than to wake her. The additional rest appears to have done her good, for she is feeling better now.

Mildred didn't want to miss the day in school, so I have allowed her to go at this time.

Very truly yours,

Asking for a special consideration

Dear Miss Buckley,

In a routine check-up by Dr. Bond yesterday, he discovered that Cynthia's hearing was not quite up to par. He suggested that this might account for her occasional lapses of attention and her unsatisfactory grades in some subjects.

Would it be possible to have Cynthia's seat changed so that she would be well toward the front of the classroom? I shall sincerely appreciate any help you can offer.

Cordially,

Helpful Sentences

Asking a favor

You have been so good to me in the past . . .

I am in a rather difficult situation . . .

May I ask a favor of you—one that I would gladly do for you if our positions were reversed.

This is a letter I hate to write . . .

Only the difficult situation I now find myself in . . .

Saying no

I wish I could say yes, but . . .

Nothing could be more difficult . . .

I know how difficult it was for you to ask, but . . .

It is particularly difficult for me to have to say No.

Your request comes at a particularly difficult time . . .

CHAPTER 16

Getting, Holding, and Leaving Your Job

Probably the most important personal letter you will ever write is the one that will get you the job you want. Indeed, the effectiveness of your job-application letter may well determine your entire career.

There are two basic types of job-application letters: 1. a letter in response to an advertisement; 2. an unsolicited letter of application. Usually a résumé of your education and business background is enclosed with or is part of the application letter.

The first objective of any letter of application is to obtain an interview. Since this kind of letter is basically a sales letter and is usually in competition with many others, your letter must be different enough to attract immediate attention and arouse interest. But it must not be so unusual as to appear eccentric and gimmicky. Above all, it must convince the prospective employer that he can profit from the talents and services you can offer. An application letter and résumé should be tailored to the viewpoint of the reader, and the first step is to make a work sheet.

Making a work sheet

A work sheet is a rough draft listing all the assets you have that will be of value to a prospective employer. From this complete analysis of what you have to offer, you will be able to draw material not only for your letter and résumé but for your interview as well. Don't list merely the bare facts of your education and work experience, but put down your hobbies, travels, high-school and college activities, and those character traits that can be of value to an employer.

It is always a good idea to list on another sheet of paper the qualities you think the prospective employer wants and needs.

Thus you can pinpoint your own personal qualities and assets. For example, if you are applying for the position of comptroller, you might list:

1. Experience in accounting
2. Ability to analyze facts and figures
3. Ability to presents facts clearly and simply
4. Ability to supervise others
5. Ability to get along with people
6. Ability to address a meeting
7. Honesty
8. Accuracy
9. Neatness
10. Industry

In digging into incidents of your past, ask yourself these questions:

What did I do on my last job to help increase my employer's profit? What ideas did I suggest? What work brought me compliments? How did I solve specific problems? What work did I do besides the routine jobs? How did I do my job better than it was done before?

Here is an outline of some of the factors to include in your work sheet:

What have I got that an employer can use profitably?

Personal character

1. Productive factors—Intelligence, imagination, ideas, industry, accuracy, speed, enthusiasm.
2. Personal factors—Honesty, loyalty, judgment, initiative, alertness.
3. Special abilities and interests—To get along with people, to supervise, to sell.
4. What I know—My trade, related trades, business in general.

My tastes and aptitudes.

My education.

My ambitions.

My wages.

Don't limit your list to a bare outline. Describe what you have done. Give examples that illustrate these points. Dramatize your abilities by describing actual problems you have solved.

One approach is to tell what conditions you met on the job, how you dealt with various situations, and what results you obtained. If you think constructively, you will find you have an asset to offset each of your liabilities.

With this work sheet in front of you, proceed with the creation of your job application.

The application itself may include several parts:

1. The letter of application, which carries the burden of attracting attention, creating interest, and doing a substantial part of the job of selling you to your prospective employer.

2. A résumé that gives the essential facts about yourself, your education, experience, personal qualities, and what you have actually accomplished. All these factors are presented in a manner aimed at proving that you can make a profit for the company that hires you.

3. Sometimes you may send along samples of your work.

4. In certain circumstances you may wish to include references, endorsements, or a photograph.

Your letter must be easy to read. It should be typewritten on good-quality business stationery and, of course, must be free of erasures, overtyping, and errors in spelling, grammar, or punctuation. If you are in doubt about the latter factors, have your letter checked by someone who knows these subjects.

There are a few additional technical devices that can help to make your letter more attention-getting. Use a business typewriter with a distinctive type face, such as one that resembles printing. Use a No. 10 envelope, the long size. Send the letter by special delivery or in the form of a night letter. Remember that in writing a job-application letter the idea is to be businesslike but different.

Answering an advertisement

As in any letter, the first paragraph of a job-seeking letter must attract favorable attention. The most common method (and therefore not the most effective) is to mention the point of contact:

Your advertisement in the Sunday Times . . .

A more effective opening is one that offers a specific fact about yourself:

Four years of specialized training in selling advertising have equipped me to be an effective addition to your staff.

My five years in the bookkeeping department of the Pacific Sales Corporation have given me sound and varied experience that can be of value to your company.

Words are my business, for I am a working newspaper woman with six years experience.

Your advertisement intrigued me because it offered advancement in a field for which I am particularly qualified by experience and aptitude.

Can you use my seven years experience in rating the credit standing of mercantile firms in New England?

For eight years I have been saving substantial sums for big shippers in Janesville.

As traffic manager for the A.B. Corporation and before that as shipping manager for the B.C. Corporation, I rerouted thousands of shipments to cut delivery charges by more than 50 per cent.

Here are my seven assets to help you make bigger profits:
1. A thorough academic training in accounting, culminating in a degree from Jones Institute.
2. A conscientious training in . . .
3. A sound understanding of . . .
4. A sincere desire to . . .
5. A wealth of friends in . . .
6. A creative imagination trained to think in practical terms of . . .
7. A good sense of public relations developed by . . .

Here's a record that speaks better than anything I can say about my abilities.

During the two years I was advertising manager of the C.D. Company, sales jumped more than 150%, to over four million dollars.

I have four years of training in accounting plus good business judgment and the ability to get along with people.

I have behind me 28 years of experience in magazine and newspaper publishing and advertising, commercial research, and agency work. This has involved the planning and execution of creative and profitable plans for the sale of advertising space and the management of sales staffs as advertising sales manager and district sales manager.

Once you have secured the reader's interest you have the task of convincing the prospective employer that you are the one and only man for the job. To accomplish this, your letter must give the basic information about yourself: business experience, education, record, character, marital status, age, etc. If the reason for leaving your last job does not place you in an unfavorable light, you may mention it.

The basic information must be presented in a manner that will consistently point up your assets. Always remember that your letter must appeal to the self-interest of your prospective employer. Your objective should be to present your qualifications so as to convince your prospective employer that 1. you can justify your salary and 2. return a profit to him.

Unless you are specifically asked to mention salary, it is best to avoid this subject in your first letter.

Try not to make your letter too long, since brevity invites reading. The bulk of the factual material may be included in the résumé. Put only the highlights in your letter.

Response to an advertisement

Dear Sir:

In my office there is a sign that shouts in letters of increasing size: Results—RESULTS—RESULTS.

As far as I am concerned, there is only one qualification for a letter or a mailing piece—the return it brings. And in the course of many years of copy writing, I think I have learned what clicks. I have written hundreds of direct-mail circulars and letters, checked each against the return, and gradually developed the style and the rules that bring my average return well over two per cent.

My work has been largely concerned with mail-order services and publications, and has consisted principally of free-lance work for organizations, printers, and private business concerns. I studied advertising at New York University, and although I value this training I think I have learned more from trial and error and checking returns.

The best way for you to judge what I can do for you is to let me write a letter to fit your problem. If you think it is worth a test, try it against any previous mailing. Then compare the results. I know I can get them for you.

May I see you to tell you more about myself and what I can do?

Very sincerely yours,

Dear Sir:

Four years as secretary to the sales manager of the Omega Products Company in Minneapolis have, I believe, given me the experience to qualify for the job you advertised in Tuesday's Times.

Since 1956 I have been responsible for all office details in the administration of sales, including writing much of the correspondence. In the course of my work, I have become familiar with the various sales territories and with the problems of handling a group of twenty-seven salesmen on the road.

The year before I was employed at Omega, I was a typist for B.C. Cortland, an accounting firm. There I became familiar with accounting terms and procedures.

I was graduated from Janesville High School in June 1953. I am twenty-four years of age and single.

I am leaving my present position because I feel I can use my capabilities more fully in a posiiton with wider scope. My present employer knows of my ambition and is helping me to find a new place.

May I see you at your office to tell you more about myself and show you just how well I can do the work you require?

Very truly yours,

The following formula is a popular attention-getting device used in sales letters. It is easily adapted to job applications.

$4 \times 7 = \$100,000$ in sales

That is an equation that has proved itself in profits for my present employers. I believe it can open new avenues of profit for your organization.

> **4** represents four years of intensive technical training in engineering, leading to a B.S. degree.

> **7** represents seven years of sales experience with three manufacturers of industrial machinery.

This combination of my technical training and sales experience has made me intensely aware of the situations in which machinery can be adapted profitably to industrial requirements. My net sales last year for the A & B Corporation exceeded $100,000.

May I show you how I can top this record for your company?

> Very sincerely,

The unsolicited letter

Unsolicited letters of application are generally sent to all or a selected group of companies in the field of your major career interest. By checking through trade and professional directories, you will find not only the companies in your field but also the names and titles of the men you will want to direct your letter to.

Although the unsolicited letter does not always reach a company that has a job opening, it has certain advantages over an answer to an advertisement. It faces little or no competition, and it reaches past the reception desk right to the man with whom you want an interview.

But because it does go to a man who probably isn't looking for an additional employee, the unsolicited letter must be stronger, more forceful and convincing than an answer to an advertisement. It must pack a lot of "sell" in a short space, since you can't count on holding reader interest in a long letter. For this reason the details of your background must be set down in a separate résumé.

An unsolicited letter must avoid an application-blank look and resemble more of the personal letter in tone and appearance. Avoid stating a specific salary. Avoid unessential and unrelated material. Direct your letter and résumé toward a specific job and point up those of your qualities and aptitudes that are essential to the particular type of job you want.

The effective unsolicited letter is interesting, informative, simple, and brief. Since it is basically a sales letter, it should be positive in tone and aimed at the profit motive of the prospective employer. It must attract and hold attention, sell *you,* and impel action on the part of the reader.

Enclosed is a copy of an ad you did *not* run.

I did *not* answer the ad because I do not consider myself a "younger aggressive man"—I am 39 and I have too much business experience to view aggressiveness as the panacea for getting the job done.

On the other hand, I do believe I have the qualifications to more than carry my weight as an administrative assistant to the company president or any other executive in your firm who spends too much of his valuable time with burdensome detail that could be better delegated to a responsible assistant.

I am looking for just such an opportunity to prove myself.

The enclosed résumé of my background and experience will tell you if there is a basis for your further consideration.

Please drop me a line and I will be glad to come in to see you at any time convenient to you.

The start of an unsolicited letter of application has to be particularly strong, because it must entice your prospective employer to read further. Your first sentence must do a big selling job. Here are some sample first paragraphs:

My thorough and varied training in many phases of business management should be of considerable value to you in setting up your new office. Therefore I am sending a résumé of my business background so that you may have it on your desk for consideration when you choose your staff.

May I have fifteen minutes of your time to tell you how I cut the production costs on double-X wheels by 11% for one of your competitors? And how I can do a similar job on some of your production problems?

The company that can profit most from my five years of experience as sales manager at the D.C. Corporation is your company. That was the conclusion I came to after a great deal of study, and as a result I am taking the liberty of sending you this letter.

When you visit New York next month, will you give me a few minutes to tell you how my production experience with the Alpha Company can make me of service to you?

If unfailing loyalty in carrying out company policies, ceaseless devotion to the work assigned me, PLUS twelve years as manager of various departments of the Omega Products Company is sufficient incentive for you to read the attached reference, then please consider this application.

Some other types of effective beginnings are:

1. A tie-in with a person known to the reader—a friend, customer, member of his staff who perhaps suggested that you write.
2. A tie-in with something the firm has done—perhaps the opening of a new branch.

Name-dropping can be overdone, but it does work. Try to mention names known to your prospective employer. These may be previous employers, customers, agencies, or suppliers.

A letter of application may also cover:

Why you are seeking a position
Why you particularly want to work for this company
Why you feel qualified
Why you left your last job—but only if it is a reason that does not reflect unfavorably on you.

In essence, tell why you are qualified for *one* specific job. Don't apply for *any* job.

Dear Mr. Long:
I am a salesman, but not, I think, an ordinary salesman. I like selling and selling likes me. I've liked it since I went to high school and sold ads for the Clinton Bulletin, five years ago.

Yesterday, when I read in the Sun that you were expanding your line, I knew that Maple Products would need more sales—and I resolved to try and convince you to let me make them for you.

At the present time I am employed as a salesman for the Milton Paper Company in Janesville. I have been with the company for two years, since my graduation from Janesville High School. During that period I have increased sales in my territory 48 per cent and earned three raises in salary. However, you can readily understand that my opportunities are limited in this position. I would like to sell a line with a wider sales potential.

I am twenty years of age; I drive my own car and I would be willing to travel anywhere to cover a territory.

My present employers know of my plans, and they will undoubtedly tell you frankly and sincerely what they think of me, if you care to get in touch with them.

May I call you in ten days to arrange for a personal interview? I know that when I speak to you face to face, you will agree that I can be a real asset to your organization.

Yours very truly,

Dear Mr. Cressey:

If you can use intelligent reporting from the South backed by superb photography, please consider my qualifications.

AS A PHOTOGRAPHER:

Three years as industrial and public-relations cameraman for the John Smith Travel Agency. Author of two books on photography and dozens of articles in all the leading photography magazines, all illustrated with my own pictures. Conductor of a syndicated newspaper column on photography. Picture editor of a daily newspaper. Producer of picture stories published in more than a hundred magazines.

AS A REPORTER:

Studied Journalism at the University of Southern California. Worked from reporter to copyreader to assistant city editor of a daily newspaper. Full-time free-lance writer for five years—major features in leading men's magazines, science and mechanic magazines, and a variety of general magazines. I am acquainted with the general needs of business- and trade-publication editors through many years of publicity writing. Recently, I have tried writing business features and found that editors like my work.

My motive in now seeking to work intensively in the business field after a fair degree of success in the highly competitive general publications is probably the same as your own—I think I can make more money, enjoy greater security, and make fuller use of my abilities.

I prefer to work by assignment, but I will feed a stream of material to any editor who can use enough volume from the South to justify my offering complete coverage. For those editors who want a steady correspondent at good rates, I will become a specialist and make intensive study of your readers' problems.

If you think you can use my services, please send me several copies of your publication to help me in slanting my initial contribution.

Sincerely yours,

The résumé

The résumé accompanying your letter will bear the bulk of the factual material. It is a detailed listing of your experience, education, personal qualities, and talents. Make certain you include your full name, address, and telephone number.

Writing a good résumé requires much skill and thought, but the work will be simplified if you use the rough draft prepared at the start. Education and experience should be itemized in detail, with the greatest space and the top position given to the portions most specifically related to the job you are seeking. Mention extracurricular school activities, particularly if they have a relationship to the job you are seeking or indicate your ability to direct and get along with people.

Don't just list titles of jobs you have held, but indicate the nature of the jobs—responsibilities, scope, what you personally accomplished.

If you present your experience chronologically, eliminate the unimportant and the unrelated work. Avoid giving the impression of being a floater who drifts aimlessly from job to job. If temporary jobs are in the list, indicate that they were temporary.

Your final presentation should contain:

1. An explanation of all the experience that applies to the job you're after.

2. Examples of what you have done and proof of the results you have obtained.

3. Education, personal data, personal characteristics appropriate to the job.

Model résumé

JONATHAN B. SAUNDERS
34-35 75th Street, Jackson Heights, N.Y. TWining 1-2543
PURCHASING MANAGER

1961 to date	Assistant Purchasing Manager of the Webster-Rollins Mail Order Company, Long Island City, N.Y. I was called upon to purchase the following types of merchandise:

House Furnishings   Kitchen Goods
Hardware   Electrical Goods

Through intensive market research, I was able to purchase merchandise at the best possible prices during a period in which many of the products were in short supply.

Administered a department of 10 employees and reduced costs by effective utilization of manpower and cost-cutting techniques.

Progressively widened the scope of my position so that my salary was increased from $4,500 to $8,800. Systems established by me were credited with saving the company several hundred thousand dollars by providing complete control of inventories.

1960 to 1961	Public accountant for Ballaban and Norwich, Syracuse, New York.

1958 to 1960   U.S. Army Quartermaster Corps.

1954 to 1958   I was graduated from Syracuse University in 1958 with a B.S. degree in business administration. An accounting major, I also studied business economics, finance, marketing and research.

My summer vacations were spent working for Dey Brothers & Co., Syracuse, N.Y., as stockboy and clerk. During the summer of 1957 I was selected to take part in the store's executive training program.

I am 29, married, and free to go anywhere.

References and letters of recommendation

References are not usually included in a résumé. This is to avoid the nuisance of having your references called too often or called before you have an interview. But if you feel your particular situation calls for references, make certain the people concerned know you are using their names.

A letter of recommendation is valuable only if it is specific, sincere, and somewhat personal in tone. Of course, you can't tell your former boss exactly what to say, but you can show him your application letter and résumé and make tactful suggestions. Remind him of specific facts about your business career: that you cut production costs by 30 per cent; that you saved the firm $100,000 on freight costs; that you increased sales in your territory by $50,000.

Ask that the letter of recommendation be addressed to the prospective employer by name rather than "To whom it may concern." Here are some sample sentences that help make a recommendation a really valuable selling point:

Any sales agency that can profit from imagination plus dollar-producing sales technique will profit by Jim Tuck's services.

He has taken a new product from scratch, planned every stage of its development from package, through presentation, art direction, and media selection. Many of those products are household names today.

Frank Milton will remain a tradition at the C.D. Agency, if only for the outstanding job he did in creating ideas and copy for the X.Y.Z. account.

I believe Morris Saunders to be the largest single influence in creating good employee morale at Hastings.

When you are applying for a job where you are to deal with people—retail clerk, receptionist, waitress—it is sometimes wise to enclose a photograph, one that is a flattering likeness.

After you have finished your letter, your résumé, and your exhibits, test them. Imagine yourself in the position of the person who receives your presentation. Estimate his reaction. Do you get his attention so that he will want to read your letter? Do you hold his interest? Do you convince him that he ought to see you? Do you give him the information he wants to know? Do you sell yourself and your abilities?

Follow-up letters

A good follow-up letter is often the clincher that gets you the job. Such a letter may be sent if you have not heard from your prospect for five or six days. It should add something to what you have said, have a reason for being written, and reminded the reader of your previous letter.

Because I know you have not yet come to a decision regarding the person you plan to hire as Office Manager, I am taking the liberty of sending along this additional memorandum.

Thank you for the friendly reception you gave me last week. I appreciated the opportunity of discussing with you some of the many successful new subscription solicitations I've done for publishers of newspapers and magazines.

Only yesterday the thought occurred to me that I had not stressed my knowledge of the operation of business machines. Although ordinarily a minor phase of office practice, this knowledge has proved most useful in setting up new procedures. On one occasion, I was able to suggest the purchase of a machine and the hiring of one person, where the hiring of three clerks had originally been contemplated.

Even if an application has been turned down, you can still follow up if a spark of possibility remains.

Your letter of June 6th is a model of how to say No and yet leave no hard feelings. I certainly understand the validity of everything you said. However, may I take the liberty of adding a few points that I omitted in my first letter . . .

Letter seeking leads for a job

Dear Mr. Herbert:

You have been so helpful and interested in my career that I am sure you would like to hear of the latest development.

I have left the Smith Company because of its limited size and restricted scope of operation. Of course, I plan to make a connection with a company in the same field, but a bigger and more up-to-date concern than Smith.

Last year alone I saved the company over $100,000 on rerouting and reclassifying their shipments, and I think I could do as much and more for another company.

If news of any openings should come to your attention, I would certainly appreciate your getting in touch with me.

Sincerely,

Help from a third person

One approach to the unsolicited letter is to arrange to have it come from a third person, preferably one well-known in the trade.

Dear Mr. Bingham,

If you are looking for a live-wire young man in your editorial or production department, I'd like to tell you a little about Sid Noble, who for the past two years has done a fine job for us.

As you know, we are dropping advertising, and this means that you or some other publisher can pick up a mighty accurate and smooth-working lad who knows how to bat out copy and follow it through to the finished page. Sid has a keen feeling for layout, knows how to order retouching, has done a lot of paste-up work, and is familiar with all the intermediate steps.

He studied advertising at the University of Pennsylvania, went from school to the Janesville *Bugle*, and then came to us.

In short, he's the kind of fellow who could lighten your work load and make himself a valuable part of your busy organization.

You'll like him. May I send him in for a chat with you?

Very truly yours,

When you get the job

Dear Mr. Sachs:

Thank you for your kind note notifying me of my appointment to your accounting department. I sincerely appreciate the confidence that the appointment reflects, and you may rest assured that I will do everything possible to merit your trust in me.

It is my understanding that I am to act as assistant to Mr. Cummings, the controller, and that my salary is to be $6,200 a year for the first year. Thereafter, my salary is to be reconsidered in the light of the record I have made.

I am looking forward to a long and pleasant association with the Cortland Company, confident that you will be gratified by my work.

Sincerely yours,

Asking for a raise

After you've worked successfully at a job for a while, you will begin to think about a promotion or raise. As soon as the situation comes to a head, you are faced with a dilemma: If I ask and get turned down, will I have to quit? How can I ask for a raise and show I mean it, and yet not be so aggressive as to create antagonism?

The answer is to avoid a threat unless you are prepared to leave. Appeal to fairness and the fact that a raise will help you work better. Avoid such irritating comments as "Joe gets more than I do for the same work" or "I have been doing my work well for a year." Show the extra work you are doing that deserves extra pay. Remember an employer expects you to *push* your salary up, not pull it up after you.

Dear Mr. Cortland,

As you know, I have been working in the shipping department at Continental for more than a year. In that period, the department has lost two men, only one of whom has been replaced.

One of the men who left was the head of the department, Jerry Whalen. Since I have had more training than the rest of the men, I automatically assumed most of his duties. This has entailed more work and responsibility for me, and I have often worked late to catch up on my regular duties.

Needless to say, I enjoy my work and the new responsibility it involves. I think I am doing a good job, and I get the satisfaction that comes from this knowledge.

However, I feel that in view of the added responsibility and work, an adjustment in my pay is indicated.

Would you be kind enough to investigate and see if you don't agree with me?

Respectfully yours,

Resigning

If your job in an organization is not an important one, a verbal resignation is all that is expected. However, if your job holds some responsibility or if you have held a position for a long time, it is a good idea to explain in writing why you are leaving. This provides you with an opportunity to create good will and to leave a pleasant and valuable record behind you.

A letter of resignation should do the following:

1. Give definite notice that you intend to leave at a specific time.

2. Express appreciation for the opportunity, experience, courtesy, and pleasant time you have had. You may modestly mention some of your achievements as a reminder to your employer if you plan to ask later for a letter of recommendation.

3. Explain why you are leaving.

4. Suggest methods of replacement, if it will be difficult for the company to do so.

5. Leave the door open for your employer to call you in and offer a better arrangement.

A letter of resignation should be rather formal, and written "for the record."

Dear Mr. Cortland:

After the June staff meeting, I gave considerable thought to your suggestion that all of us reappraise our work in line with the company's new policy of retrenchment. After serious consideration, I have reached a definite decision to resign from the company, effective September 30th.

You will readily understand my decision in view of my personal financial obligations. I feel that greater opportunities would be available to me in a larger company, where I would be able to widen my experience and seek a position of greater responsibility.

I will miss working for Cortland. My two years with the company have been pleasant and, until our recent difficulties arose, provided a stimulating challenge. I sincerely appreciate the opportunities and cooperation given to me by the directors. I enjoyed working with you, and I regret very much the necessity of leaving. Only the extreme economic pressures placed on me could have brought me to this decision.

I hope that the new methods I introduced into the accounting department and the introduction of bookkeeping machinery have proved that I was worthy of the confidence you placed in me.

I will, of course, help in training the person you select to fill my position. If at any future time a problem should arise, I shall be happy to assist in any way I can.

Respectfully yours,

Employer's response to applicants

Dear Mr. Jones:

We want you to know that we appreciate the time you took yesterday to fill out our forms and provide the examples of your work. Your application for a position with the ABC Corporation is being given consideration by our personnel department.

It usually takes two to three weeks for applications of this kind to be processed before any decision is made regarding employment. Your application will be studied with others being considered for the position during this time.

As soon as any decision is made regarding the filling of the vacancy, you will be notified. In any case, we do appreciate your wanting to join our organization.

Sincerely,

Dear Mr. Carter:

Thank you for calling us yesterday about employment. It was nice of you to think of our company as a place where you would like to work.

At the present time, I am sorry to tell you we can not offer you any encouragement. This is no reflection on your qualification. However, it is just that we do not have an opening now that fits your abilities.

There are, as you know, several companies which are expanding their staffs at this time and I feel sure you will find among them one where your special experience and training can be used effectively.

Very sincerely,

Helpful Sentences

Telling about your experience

During two of my four years at college, I was advertising manager of the college daily paper. In this capacity I increased the advertising revenue by 40 per cent.

Each summer during the past three years I worked in the Milton Furniture Company warehouse, filling orders for. . . .

In high school I was president of the Junior Literary Guild and a member of the Arista Society.

For the past four years I have devoted the greater part of my time to preparing myself for the career to which I think I am best suited—retail merchandising. Next month I will receive my Bachelor's Degree from New York University.

I know that up to this time my training has been entirely academic, but I feel that I could contribute something to your company while I gain in practical experience.

My courses at New York University have taught me the basic elements of merchandising and marketing research. I was elected to the scholastic honorary society in my junior year. During the past two summers I have been employed as a salesman in the Foster Department Store in Janesville.

About salary

I will be glad to discuss the matter of salary with you at a personal interview.

May I suggest that we leave the discussion of salary to a personal interview?

Salary considerations are secondary to the opportunity that this position holds for me. I am certain we can arrive at a satisfactory arrangement.

Selling Yourself

May I show you how I can increase your sales 70 per cent next year?

I will telephone you on Monday to learn when I may show you how these sales formulas can be applied to your business.

I shall phone your secretary on Tuesday to arrange a meeting at your convenience.

I would very much like to talk with you regarding an advertising position in your store. I plan to be in New York during the last two weeks of June. May I have the opportunity of talking to you personally?

References

These men know me and my work from various angles.

May I refer you specifically to the following men and women with whom I have worked on various occasions?

My former employers and those with whom I have done business will vouch for my integrity and good reputation in the trade. May I refer you to the following:

PART II

BUSINESS LETTERS

CHAPTER 17

The Technique of Writing Business Letters

Business letters are the essential means of communication for industry and commerce. In many cases the quality, sincerity, and effectiveness of a company's letters determines its ultimate success or failure. So vitally important is letter writing that many organizations retain professional correspondents to handle business letters and advertising copywriters to prepare circular letters for direct-mail campaigns.

Today, writing business letters has become a fine art that embodies the cross-techniques of psychology, journalism, advertising, public relations, and the graphic arts.

Since business letters represent a company just as salesmen do, their function must go beyond the essentials of presenting information clearly and courteously. They must make friends, build good will, and add to the company's prestige. To accomplish this the letters must sound relaxed and conversational. Unfortunately, too many business letters today still make use of the stilted phrases, hackneyed expressions, and stiff tone of turn-of-the-century business correspondence.

To make your letters effective in terms of today's business world, you should understand and make use of four basic psychological techniques:

1. *Write from the "you" attitude.* Every person is interested primarily in himself and thus responds to a letter written from his point of view. To test the effectiveness of your letter on this point, count the number of *I's* and *you's* in your letter and then compare. A good letter should have a preponderance of *you's* and a minimum of *I's*. But more than this, your letter should have the reader's viewpoint in mind throughout the text.

Compare

I: *I* was happy to hear that my letter of January 5th provided sufficient information for the completion of the order for *us*.

You: Thank *you* for *your* assurance that *you* had sufficient information for the completion of *your* order.

I: *I* want to express *my* sincere thanks for the good word *I* received today from . . .

You: *Your* very kind words . . .

We: *We* make six styles in all sizes, available in cartons of four.

You: *You* may have *your* choice of six styles in all sizes. These are packed in cartons of four for *your* convenience in stocking.

I: *I* cannot quote a rate as *we* have not yet determined a classification for *your* plant.

You: *Your* rate will be fixed as soon as the inspection can provide a classification for *your* plant.

It is axiomatic that one of the most pleasant sounds to the average individual is his own name. To help get the "you" emphasis, some professional correspondents include in the letter the name of the person to whom they write:

Thank you, Mr. Saunders, for bringing our attention to . . .

2. *Accentuate the positive.* Even a letter that has to say No can be written from a positive point of view. Make it an absolute rule never to start or end your letter with a negative. Whenever possible, avoid words with a negative connotation, such as *argument, careless, complaint, disagreeable, error, neglect, unfair.*

Compare:

Positive: Thank you for your order. The merchandise will go out to you as soon as . . .

Negative: We regret to inform you that we will not be able to ship your order until . . .

Positive: It was good of you to send us a check for your order of April 5th. However, your shipment was mailed C.O.D. last Tuesday since our credit department assumed you would want the merchandise as quickly as possible for the holiday trade.

Negative: It is very unfortunate that your payment was received too late to permit us to ship your order.

3. *Make your letters smile.* A business letter should leave a pleasant impression. Get a smile into your letter, a bit of your personality, an atmosphere of good will. A sour letter, piqued attitude, complaining undertone, is comparable to a surly manner in your conversation.

Some phrases have a built-in smile. Here are some friendly phrases that you can and should use freely:

> We shall be glad to . . .
> It is a pleasure . . .
> Thank you . . .
> We appreciate very much . . .
> With our compliments . . .
> You are certainly a good fellow . . .
> Your lovely (kind) letter . . .

Note these beginnings from pleasant letters:

> Thank you for your subscription to ———. Enclosed is a bill at the special low rate now available.

> This is the kind of letter I particularly like to write because it says thanks to a new friend. Thanks for your recent order and the interest in ——— that prompted it. (If you have not already *started* to receive your weekly copies, I want you to know that they will be on their way to you very shortly.)

> I'm sure your confidence in ——— will be more than justified by the issues that will come to you throughout the exciting weeks and months ahead.

4. *Make your copy live.* The reader should *feel* what you say. If possible, create a visual experience. Let the reader see himself doing something—running a machine, telling his friends about his triumphs, selling more accounts, basking in the admiration of his family.

Here's how one writer described a dictionary, and how Orville Reed, a professional letter writer, reinterpreted the same copy.

"This is a big dictionary made to last for years. It tells you what you want to know about any subject. With this dictionary it is no longer necessary for you to search through many encyclopedias to find answers you want to know. Everything is right here. It will be used by every member of the family from the youngest to the oldest."

Of course, the above paragraph gives vital information about the dictionary, but see what happens to this description in the hands of a letter writer who knows how to create excitement with words:

"You'll heft it in your hands and feel the good solid weight of a volume that will last a lifetime! You'll open the big pages and make the exciting discovery that here at last is a volume that tells you just what you want to know about a word or a subject. Never again will you go searching through old dictionaries and encyclopedias—and with this brand-new volume you'll see how wonderfully easy it is to learn and learn and learn . . . yes, every member of your family from school kids to grandmother!"

In a few words this writer makes all other dictionaries appear to be out of date. He does it merely by saying, "Never again will you go searching through old dictionaries and encyclopedias." Notice, also, how he tells that this is a big volume that will withstand rough handling: "You'll heft it in your hands and feel the good solid weight of a volume that will last a lifetime!" He gets his effect with short, active verbs—*last, heft, tell, see, learn*. Notice how he gives added meaning to the word *weight* by using the qualifying adjective *solid*. Observe how he puts "you" into the picture with the phrase *You'll open the big pages and make the exciting discovery* . . .

A really good business letter has a definite character, because it reflects the personality of the company as well as that of the individual. A letter should be spoken—not dictated. It should make use of exactly the same spirit, tone, and language you would use if you were talking across the desk. Imagine that the reader is right there with you.

Seven out of ten letters begin with a "breath-catcher"—a wasted phrase that supposedly helps the writer get into the body of the letter without too much painful thinking. The "breath-catcher" is most often an excuse for writing or a reference to a previous letter. Such a halting start completely fails to use the greatest opportunity of letters—the impact of the first impression.

Avoid such obvious, trite, and irritating expressions as:

Replying to your letter of ...
In reference to our order No. ...
This is to inform you ...
We wish to call your attention to ...
Please be advised that ...
I should like to say that ...

Avoid the phrases that have been worn thin from overuse:

Have you heard about ...
Here it is! The product you have been waiting for ...
No doubt you have ...
We are pleased to announce ...

And of course:

above mentioned	in the near future
according to our records	owing to
as a a matter of fact	so advise us
as the case may be	the above
as per	the party
at an early date	we are writing to tell you
at hand	we beg to advise
at the present writing	we take pleasure
contents noted	we wish to state
due to the fact that	your esteemed favor
in re:	

Wordiness, complexity, and a flat tone are as undesirable as they are frequent in business correspondence. Yet it is not difficult to simplify, strengthen, and add sincerity to your letters. You can achieve effectiveness by following *The 4-S Formula:*

For shortness

Don't repeat phrases from the letter you are answering.
Avoid needless words and information.
Beware of roundabout prepositional phrases, such as *with regard to* and *in reference to.*
Watch out for nouns and adjectives that derive from verbs. Use these words more frequently in their verb form.
Don't qualify your statements with irrelevant if's.

For simplicity

Know your subject so well that you can discuss it naturally and confidently.

Use short words, short sentences, and short paragraphs.

Be compact. Don't separate closely related parts of sentences.

Tie your thoughts together so your reader can follow you from one to another without getting lost.

For strength

Use specific, concrete words.

Use active verbs.

Give answers straightaway; then explain if necessary.

Don't hedge. Avoid expressions like *it appears*.

For sincerity

Be a human being, not an office machine. Use words that connote the personal, such as the names of persons and the personal pronouns *you, he, she, we,* etc.

Admit mistakes openly and sincerely. Don't hide them behind meaningless words.

Don't overwhelm your reader with intensives and emphatics.

Don't be either obsequious or arrogant. Strive to express yourself in a friendly way and with a simple dignity.

CHAPTER 18

The Techniques of Producing Business Letters

Since a business letter represents your company, it is extremely important that it look attractive. Your first purpose is to insure that the letter will be read. An attractive, dignified letterhead, a good quality of white bond paper, neat typing, wide margins, short paragraphs, and uniform spacing all invite interest and create a good impression.

Business letters are typewritten or processed to simulate typewriting on single sheets of bond paper. A special absorbent paper is required for mimeographed letters. In a letter of more than one page, only the first sheet bears the letterhead. The paper size most generally used is 8½ x 11; the envelope should conform in appearance to the paper and measure 4⅛ x 9½. Other sizes of stationery are 7½ x 10, with an envelope 7½ x 3⅞; and memorandum size measuring 5½ x 8½, with a No. 6 envelope, 6½ x 3⅝.

For some purposes a lightly tinted paper and envelope may be used. The letterhead, preferably printed or engraved in black ink, should contain the name of the company, the nature of the business if the name is not self-explanatory, and the address. The telephone number, cable address, and branch offices may also be included. Although a trade-mark or identifying symbol is often used in the letterhead, it is best to avoid too much design and detail.

A business letter is made up of the following six parts:

1. *Heading:* The date only, since the letterhead carries the address.

2. *Inside Address:* The name and address of the person to whom the letter is written.

3. *Salutation:* The forms in general use are—Dear Sir, Dear Madam, Gentlemen, Dear Mr. Jones, My dear Mr. Jones. A colon is always used after the salutation.

April 29, 1968

Mr. Paul D. Neal
Starlight Drive-In Theatre
Lexington, Missouri

Dear Mr. Neal:

A friend of mine stopped in for a chat. "Sit a minute", I said
to him, "while I finish writing this letter to a
customer of mine."

He burst out with..."Ye Gods and little fishes! Are you STILL
writing 'Thank you' letters? This is the age of
get-up--and-go. There's no time for sentiment in
business today. If you'd spend the time you waste
writing 'thank you' letters to go out and get
new business you'd double your volume in no time."

Maybe my friend was right...I don't know... but here's what I said
to him..."I cut my eye teeth in business during
the days when your closest friends were those one
dealt with, day in and day out."

"My enjoyment in business is in dealing with people. If I became
a cold-blooded go-getter maybe we would double our
volume...but tell me, what's the gain?"

"We've grown steadily...we're a good sized outfit...and I'm confident
we'll continue to keep right on growing. But one
thing is for sure...when I stop enjoying my work,
that's when I'll fold my tent and quietly steal away".

So...when we send out a trailer, I STILL want to send along with it
a smile and a 'hello' from

IM/gdt   Irving Mack

January 8, 1968

Mr. Thomas Cortland
Cortland Furniture Co.
Janesville, Ohio

About Simplified Letters

The extreme form of block letter is the Simplified Letter.
In this form, once recommended by the National Office
Management Association, all lines are typewritten flush
left. This applies to the date and the complimentary
close. Because the subject heading, which replaces the
"Dear Mr._____" is cold, modern writers prefer to
use the form which includes the name of the addressee
in the first sentence. In this form, this letter might
begin, "The extreme form of block letter, Mr. Cortland,
is the Simplified Letter." This "dearless" form of letter
is growing in acceptance, for it helps to bring the reader
right into the subject. Because it replaces a routine form
with a personal element, this form sounds much more sincere.
You will be receiving more and more such letters in the
future.

Editor
The Complete Book of Letters

Sylvia K. Mager /hs

THE FORM OF A LETTER

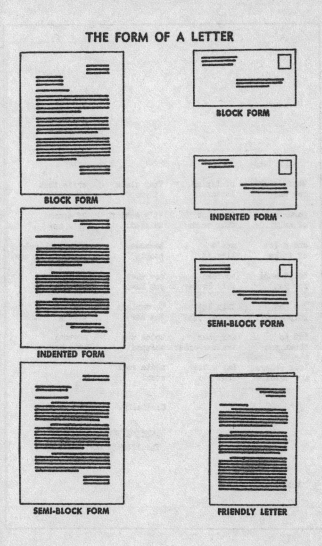

BLOCK FORM

BLOCK FORM

INDENTED FORM

INDENTED FORM

SEMI-BLOCK FORM

SEMI-BLOCK FORM

FRIENDLY LETTER

There's a new way of typing letters. They claim if you write them in short

paragraphs of only three or four words it's easier to read. Of course. it's new

and a lot of folks won't like it because people always object to anything new.

Is it hard for you to read this letter now that you have grasped the idea?

But the purpose of this letter is not just to explain the new idea in typing

but to thank you for your trailer order which was shipped several days ago.

Your orders are welcome! Let's hear from you again real soon!

Cordially.

Irving Mack

for FILMACK CORPORATION

M:NI

Mr. Sidney Noble
Pom Pom Manufacturing Company
700 Sixth Avenue
New York, N.Y. 10025

Thank you, Mr. Noble,

for reminding us that not all letters need
follow the traditional patterns. A short
letter may be placed on a page with a bit
of flare.

This cantilever letter makes a much more
pleasing picture than a small block of type
on a large page. When you want to send a
short note, and no small sized stationery is
available, consider the use of this style to
help make your letter a pleasing picture.

Sincerely,

Editor

N. H. Mager/hs

4. *Body of the Letter:* This is the actual subject matter. It should be well spaced and centered on the page, with left-hand margins of at least an inch and approximately the same for the right-hand margin.

5. *Closing:* The complimentary ending varies in degree of formality according to the tone of the letter. Those in most general use are—Yours truly, Very truly yours, Sincerely, Sincerely yours, Cordially, Very cordially yours, Yours cordially.

6. *Signature:* A business letter is signed by hand in ink, clearly and legibly. Usually the writer's name and title is typed below the signature.

There are three accepted forms for business letters:

The block form. All paragraphs and lines are flush to the left-hand margin. With the exception of the closing, which may be centered or bear to the right, there is no indentation.

The indented form. Each line of the address and paragraph beginnings are indented about five spaces.

The semiblock form. The address is in block form, and the paragraphs are indented.

There are other forms that may be used when a novel effect is desired. These are illustrated among the sample letters given in the following pages. For example, about one in four circular letters eliminates the date. Salutations may be replaced with an announcement set flush to the left.

IS IT TIME
TO GET OUT
OF THE MARKET?

or a memorandum form if the name can be filled in.

For: Mr. N. J. Barton
From: Jonathan Bigley of the Omicron Company

Methods of producing circular letters

Since customarily we think of letters as being individually typewritten and sent singly to the reader, circular letters are more effective if they are written as if this were true.

Except for letters that are individually typed, the closest thing to a personal letter is the individually typed form letter or letter made up of form paragraphs. Since most business situations recur continually, form paragraphs insure effective, efficient, and uniform handling.

The most personal-looking of the letters produced mechanically are those prepared by automatic typewriting. In this process, a perforated master roll is punched as in the old-fashioned player-piano and placed in a special typewriter. This machine automatically types the letters, stopping for fill-ins, such as headings, address, or any desired change in words or paragraphs. The resulting reproduction is exactly like typewriting and has the advantages of minimizing errors and increasing speed. As many as 150 letters may be produced in a day by each machine, and one operator can operate five machines. Some automatic typewriting machines may be set up in tandem to operate from a single roll. Carbon copies are clear and sharp. The whole process results in typed letters done with machine precision and perfection.

Less personal in appearance is the multigraphed letter. The message is set either by hand or machine in a type face resembling typewriter or printing type. Illustrations and signatures may be made on a curved plate of zinc, wood, or rubber. The type and plate are attached to channels in a cylinder. Ink may be applied automatically with a printing roller or the impression may be made through a carbon ribbon. Paper is fed between the cylinder and a rubber roll. Multigraphing machines can print in two or more colors, so that the letterhead and body are imprinted in different colors in a single operation, if so desired. The result is a letter that approximates either a typewritten or printed letter. Names and addresses may be matched and filled in to create the effect of a personal letter.

The flat-bed letter uses metal typewriter type set up to create the impression of actual typewriting, even with occasional highlights to simulate worn type. A wide roll of ribbon is placed over the type, and the printing is done through the ribbon. With matching fill-ins for the inside address, this makes a good facsimile of a personal letter.

Typed fill-ins have a tendency to appear to be just what they are, particularly if special matching type faces are not used. One way to avoid this negative distraction is to make

FRANK FILL-INS

We're blazing your name like this
just to make sure you don't overlook the
TWENTY DOLLAR BILL that you can cash in
on at

Dear Mr. Goodman:

We have typed your name in big
letters so that this message shouldn't
fail to get your attention.

A <u>SAFE</u> INVESTMENT,
MR. MAGER...

MEMO FROM H. H. COSTELLO

In case you missed my recent letter— here is a copy.

The newsletters are free— with your subscription to TIDE. A whole year for only $4.00. Don't miss them — they are vital to your business.

Mail the card and let us start your service immediately! HHC

TIDE - 232 Madison Avenue, New York, New York 10016

the fill-in frankly a fill-in. This may be accomplished by typing the name in a larger type, in a color, or by writing with a special ballpoint pen. Another technique is to use a form letter with a small typewritten memorandum attached.

The printed letter is sometimes used for circular mailings. Although it seldom gives the appearance of a typewritten letter, it permits more leeway in art work, color, and display types.

Many of the advantages of these processes, plus economy in preparation, are offered by offset or multilith letters. The message may be typewritten, handwritten, drawn on a special paper platen, or on a sheet of paper, which is then sent out to be photographed onto a metal platen. The platen is attached to a cylinder, moistened, and inked. In the reproduction process, the moisture attaches to untouched parts of the plate, and ink attaches to portions that have been etched. Since letterheads may be printed in the same operation, there is considerable saving in this process. With some offset equipment, as many as four colors can be run off at the same time.

CHAPTER 19

Sales Letters

Many companies consider every letter that leaves their office a sales letter, since each business letter is an opportunity to sell not only the firm's product but its good will.

Practically everything that can be sold—from smoked hams to swimming pools—is now sold directly by mail. Some companies do all their selling by mail; others depend on letters to develop leads for their salesmen and aid in various phases of their selling operations.

Like a good advertisement, a good sales letter must compel reader attention and interest by enthusiasm, vitality, originality, and a thorough understanding of the specific sales situation. Since a sales letter, more than any other type of letter, has to overcome reader resistance, it must be keyed to the prospect's needs, problems, and interests. To overcome reader resistance, a sales letter usually follows this well-established formula:

1. Arouse interest
2. Describe, explain, and convince
3. Stimulate interest to the point of closing a sale

One school of letter writing describes these elements as a star to arouse interest, a chain to hold interest and convince, and a hook to obtain the desired action.

Another useful outline for a sales letter follows the pattern of creating:

Attention
Interest
Desire
Action

Useful though these formulas are, many successful letters ignore or adapt them and stress sincerity, spontaneity, and credibility.

The techniques of selling by the written word have been the subject of many books. The basic theme of most of these texts was conveyed in one sentence by supersalesman Elmer Wheeler: "Don't sell the steak, sell the sizzle."

The use of a product's secondary appeal has been behind many successful advertising campaigns. But though an emotional appeal to a prospect's desire for prestige, popularity, or comfort is a basic approach, logic must not be sacrificed to emotion in writing effective sales letters.

Long experience has shown the many pitfalls in writing sales letters. Avoid the following: being patronizing or condescending; writing over the head of your reader; using complex, trite, or exaggerated words and phrases; claiming too much for the product and emphasizing too many points in one letter. Understatement is often more effective than wild claims and high pressure. Never assume that your prospect knows about your product or remembers what you said in a previous letter. Also, your letter should aim at creating a mood—an atmosphere conducive to obtaining the results you want. Often the atmosphere alone is almost enough—as in selling perfume.

There is one infallible test of the effectiveness of a sales letter—the number of sales it brings in. As one professional letter writer said: "Make your letter so convincing that the prospect would rather have the product you are selling than the money he must part with to buy it."

The start of a sales letter

Only a few of every hundred circular letters that reach the average executive's desk are read. With these odds against you, it is easy to see why your letter has to have an interesting and exciting beginning.

The most important sentence in a sales letter is the first one since in a large percentage of all letters it is the only sentence that is read. The first sentence has one key function: to attract enough favorable attention to get the reader to continue. A short opening paragraph—indeed, short paragraphs throughout the letter—invite further reading.

Arousing favorable attention requires a pertinent thought to catch the interest of the reader, a thought that can be tied in to the body of your letter without too much explanation. It may be:

1. A striking statement

Would you like an extra $65 each week—in addition to your regular pay?

Honestly, I've got the easiest job in the world!
All I have to do is convince you that you are in line for some husky profits when you take on . . .

We have the answer in CASH for you!

This is a letter to warn you against MONOCLE, a new monthly magazine of political satire.
If, despite this warning and your own better judgment, you return the enclosed card, a free *copy* of this dangerous magazine will find its way into your home. Then you will be really sorry because . . .

Save 42% on the electric bills for
YOUR NEON SIGN! . . . without a penny's cash outlay on your part!

We have stumbled upon a treasure that we would like to share with you.

You may never win a prize for knowing—
What President's hat was held by his defeated rival while the victor read his inaugural address?
What President applied for a patent on a flatboat he invented?
   (It had air chambers for floating over shoals.)

Will YOU Be Ready for the Boom Years Ahead?

The next few years will see the biggest boom this country has ever known. And with it—inflation.
This is still hard for many people to accept. But the fact remains that those who DO prepare for the boom times ahead will reap big dividends for their foresight—and avoid the blunders others will make.

2. An anecdote or joke

A Reader's Digest letter once quoted an ancient Persian poet: "If thou hast two pennies, spend one for bread. With the other buy hyacinths for thy soul."

One time when Lady Astor was making a speech, she admitted: "We women DO talk a lot, but even then we don't tell half we know!"

This is a story of a SUCCESSFUL CHALLENGE . . .

The problem was to develop a simple and effective method of applying the oxidation-reduction technique in castings of copper or nickel-based alloys. Maximum density and freedom from gas porosity had to be insured . . .

A *Let's Have Better Mottoes Association* member who signs himself "Anonymous," and who takes umbrage for reasons not specified, proposes the motto:
"Money can't get you friends but it can bring a better class of enemies."

I'd like to tell you about a teacher who built a fortune of one million dollars in the stock market, yet who never made a salary of more than $6,000 in his life.
How did he do it? Not by any hit and miss method, but by carefully searching for investments with "special" features that others had overlooked. When he found one that satisfied him, he invested some of his savings and waited for it to "work out."
Here's the story . . .

Recently I had the privilege of visiting a community in the San Joaquin Valley of California where a modern miracle has taken place. If you had been with me, I am sure you would have agreed that it was an experience not easily forgotten.

3. A startling fact

$100 grew to $20,000
$100 grew to $17,000
$100 grew to $8,000

That's right! Had you invested a *total of $300* in just three common stock warrants in 1942, your investment would have *grown to $45,000* by 1946.

$10 billion in security values were lost in one week in June!

4. An analogy

There's a firm in Ohio no larger than yours that secured 104 new accounts and made $19,500 in two months from a $5.87 business investment. And did it, mind you, without any special offer of any kind.

Men have much in common besides tonsils.

5. A startling offer

Special Offer to ——— Subscribers Only!
Here's a book we consider so important that we'll send you a copy to read for 5 full days—*entirely at our expense!*

A NEW IDEA—
and I guarantee you'll like it!

HERE IS A SECRET THAT WILL HELP YOU
MAKE MORE MONEY IN 1968 THAN IN ALL
YOUR LIFE BEFORE . . . .

I believe we are in an excellent position to save you some money.

Maybe I can help you better yourself—
by telling you about a magazine that's helping others.

WIN A FREE NEON CHANGEOVER ON YOUR SIGN . . .
IF YOUR OUTDOOR NEON SIGN IS THE OLDEST IN
YOUR BOROUGH!

Invest $500 a Year in These Growth Stocks

Retire with $50,000 in 10 to 15 Years

Here's a bargain in good reading for the whole family that I don't think you'll want to pass up.

If you haven't yet met HORIZON, we invite you now *to see* a magazine made like a quite spectacular illustrated book;

to sample its extraordinary range of contents: arts and ideas from the ancient to the avant-garde, from civilizations familiar and foreign; and

to subscribe on exceptional terms, available for a short time only: *$6 less* than usual.

Dear Reader,

Once or twice in a reading lifetime, a book comes along which is so important, so enthusiastically praised by the experts, and so outstandingly successful that no well-informed person would wish to miss the opportunity of reading it.

We take special pleasure in calling your attention to such a book, which we have the honor of publishing.

6. A gift or free booklet—a "bribe for listening."

Here is your new KOLORITE Guide!

"KOLORITE" is Weber's way of expressing a sincere interest in your office planning problems, Doctor—and so we are pleased to enclose our popular color folio.

Dear Advertising and Sales Promotion Expert:

It took our editors two years to gather the material for this handbook. You get it FREE—by just returning the enclosed card today.

You get over 100 inspiring sales promotion ideas that have paid off brilliantly for industrial advertisers during the past two years.

THE ENCLOSED RESERVATION

—made out in your name entitles you to a FREE copy of the first edition of a new book which shows . . .

A copy of "————," one of the most popular and provocative little business booklets in print, is yours for the asking . . . absolutely free and with no obligation involved. We ask only that you read it carefully.

21 PAGES OF TIMELY IDEAS FOR YOUR BUSINESS

For you . . .

a transparent plastic letter opener-magnifying glass FREE. As a magnifying glass, it will come in handy for the hundred little things you want to look at more closely around the house. And as a letter opener, it is something you will want to keep handy on your desk.

We want you to have this letter opener-magnifying glass for the opportunity it will give us to let you know something about— ———— services and how they save you time, trouble, worry, and money.

The editors of ———— Magazine have just put together a remarkable new booklet entitled "16 Ways to Save Money on Your Phone Bill." It contains valuable information that can help you to *cut your phone bill in half.*

It will take you less than a minute to fill out and return the enclosed postage-paid card entitling you to a free copy of "Forging Ahead in Business." BUT, IT WILL TAKE AT LEAST AN HOUR TO READ THE BOOKLET AND ABSORB ITS CONTENTS.

We are reserving in your name a valuable booklet entitled "———— ————." Your copy will be delivered to you promptly upon receipt of the pull-out card in the window of this letter.

7. The "you are special" approach

It has taken a while, perhaps, to achieve your own measure of success in the world of business. But when you analyze your present position in terms of the progressive steps you have taken, your ambitious cultivation of opportunities, and your overall dedication to your career, you realize, suddenly, you *are* a success.

This letter is for the smartest girl in your office (as part of the inside address).

This letter is addressed to the top man in a closely held corporation. If you're the man we're talking about, you should immediately become familiar with 8 tested ways to increase travel and entertainment expense deductions that are now commanding top-executive attention everywhere.

You are invited to be
an opening night critic . . .
. . . when the curtain goes up on an important and widely
heralded premiere.

My dear wealthy friend:
Any one of these eye-opening money facts may bring thousands
of dollars your way.

Dear Reader:
You have been selected to receive a free copy of Volume I,
Number 1, of SHOW ———, the exciting new magazine of the
performing arts.

Do you realize what an important man you are to Haverford?
You hold the key to success in her Development Program.
You represent the difference between a credible and a distinguished
level of alumni support.

If you're the kind of man this letter was written for, you like the
idea of finding new ways to do things better, and you like saving
money, too.
And if that's the way you like to do business, you very probably
count on some kind of appointment book or desk calendar to help
you keep track of appointments, meetings, dates, and all the other
things you can't afford to forget.

This letter is addressed to the one man in 1,000 who can afford
the best.

There are certain people whom we are glad to welcome as
charge customers . . . and you are one of them.

This is important.
You probably are one of the more than eighty-four million
people in the United States who own life insurance. You own life
insurance because you recognize the obligation you owe to your
loved ones.

You are part of a group of teachers and dealers to whom we
are offering—FREE—an issue of the ——— ——— Plan.

"Dear Sir:"

which starts this letter in lieu of your name doesn't have the personal impact of several other no-name salutations: "Dearest," for instance, or "Greetings."

But what I have to say, and to sell, is nevertheless intended for a man who has a quality of mind and a range of problems and aspirations similar to yours.

A VITAL MESSAGE TO EVERYONE WHO WANTS TO HOLD ON TO HIS MONEY

8. The selection of an individual by definition

In every company there is one man to whom others come when decisions must be made. This letter is addressed to you as the man in your company who carries this responsibility.

To the man who really wants to cut down machine maintenance costs . . .

Because of some distinctly complimentary things ABOUT YOU that we have learned, your name is included among those who should find this letter particularly interesting.

If you were just a name and a street number to us and we knew nothing of your interests, there would be no point at all in asking you to accept what, in the final analysis, amounts to two issues of ——— FREE!

WHY are we writing to *you*?
Because we think you're the sort of person who believes in getting the most out of being alive. Because we think you want the greatest thrill, pleasure, and convenience every second you sit behind the steering wheel of a car!

If you are looking for a way to "Get Rich Quick" by speculating in the stock market, this letter is not intended for you.

9. Asking or offering a favor

May I ask a favor of you—the kind of favor I would not mind doing if I were in your place?

May we take a moment of your time this morning? We should like to have you look around your office, Doctor. A good look, with new eyes. Is your professional home attractive? Is your operating room constructed for maximum convenience with a simple, easy-to-work-in arrangement of space and equipment? Does your reception room induce patient relaxation—or is it coldly clinical? Are your methods and your outlook modern, or do you find yourself practicing with behind-the-times equipment?

Will you help us to help you?

I want to do you a favor. A favor that can put you on the threshold of the greatest *profit*-making opportunities of your lifetime.

10. Asking a question

A question can be an effective way of drawing the reader closer to you. *What do you think, Mr. Brown?* immediately makes Mr. Brown part of your letter.

The question may be used in the opening to create attention, to convince, to emphasize a point, or to get action.

Isn't that right, Mr. Brown?

Don't you agree, Mr. Jones?

What would you do in a situation like this?

Will you please do this for me, Mr. Brown?

A. L. Peters
30 Church Street
New York, N.Y. 10007

Please return this
opinion page.
Thank you.

I hope you will permit us to call you for your advice concerning a publishing suggestion that has been made.

As publishers of J. K. Lasser's famous annual guide, YOUR INCOME TAX, we are aware that many accountants, attorneys, controllers, trust officers and other business advisors use this book to prepare tax returns for clients.

What do you say to a kid who can't walk?

You've seen her, haven't you? She lives down the street, or around the corner on the way to the mailbox.

HOW MUCH PROFIT DO YOU WANT?

How much could you have made (or saved) had you known that the market would turn bearish in February, 1947, and that prices would go much lower?

IS THERE DANGER

In a "Wait-and-See" Policy?

Can you answer these questions:
Are *you* being cheated by social security?
How can you borrow money—and save?
When are honeymoons dangerous?
Can you build your *own* job security?

Are you uncertain about what's going on or unsure about what will happen next?

Why wear a truss?

Did you ever stop to question HOW a certain record is being written in your office and WHY it is written that way?

DO YOU HAVE A DIRTY TOWEL ON YOUR CONSCIENCE?

11. Nostalgia

Nostalgia can be used effectively to convince, to capture attention, or to set an emotional tone. It is an appeal to something in your reader's experience that will arouse his interest.

Remember the dreams we used to dream as youngsters, when we paged eagerly and excitedly through the mail-order catalog?

High adventure, indeed!
That's the feeling we hope you will recapture as you leaf through our catalog pages.

WOULDN'T IT BE WONDERFUL
IF YOU COULD LAUGH
THIS SUMMER
at every customer who walks into your office and gasps:
"It's the heat—it's the humidity—it's unbearable!"
You can have your laugh, because your office will be COM-
FORTABLE . . . THANKS TO A ROOM AIR CONDITIONER.

Is there any music you'd rather hear this evening than your
boy's voice ringing out "Hello, Daddy."

Do you remember the smell of new-mown hay?

Have you ever met someone just once and later wished that
you could get to know him better—have him for a friend, perhaps?

"Why Didn't I Think
of That Myself!"

Dear Doctor:
The title *Doctor* sounds good, doesn't it? You worked hard for
it; you have every right to be proud of it—and it's still kind of
new. You'll probably find some other things new to you in the
months to come as you start to establish yourself in your profession
and build a practice.

May we say "Welcome!"
Going into business is a big step. We know because when we
went into business 34 years ago we had a lot at stake, too. We
weren't too sure then that we'd be around now to write you this
welcome note.
But we are because, like you, we offer a high-quality, dependable product to the most discriminating and hard-to-please buying
audience in the world—the American retailer and businessman.

12. A strong negative thought

On rare occasions a negative approach has been used
successfully, although it is usually fraught with failure. Here
are a few successful examples:

Don't be embarrassed!

Don't risk an infectionl

"A SALESMAN CAN'T INFLUENCE ME" SHE SAID.
Yet her whole life and that of her family is influenced by salesmen.

SHE SAID "I wouldn't have an automatic washer."
"I WOULDN'T EITHER" I answered . . .
1. UNLESS it was fully automatic, no tubs to empty—nothing to clean.
2. UNLESS I wanted to live longer, better, and with less work.
3. UNLESS it was guaranteed five years by a well-known company.
4. UNLESS it would wash curtain, and feather pillows.
5. UNLESS I could starch, dye, bleach, and blue in it.
6. UNLESS my husband was a crank and wanted me to work myself to the bone.
7. UNLESS I was a crank and believed there was no better way of doing anything than the way I did it.

The body of a sales letter

Once you have aroused reader interest by the beginning of your sales letter, you must go on to convince the prospect. This is the job of the body of the letter. Although sales points vary with the product, the basic objectives are to explain what the product can do for the reader and to convince him that your claims are true. If you know and believe in your product thoroughly and sincerely, the body of the sales letter will be the easiest part to write. Before you tackle it, make certain that you know not only your product's virtues but also its faults. Then sell yourself on what you are selling. When the reader finishes a good sales letter, he should feel that the writer really believes in the product he's selling and the company he represents.

Here are some examples of paragraphs that effectively carry the burden of explaining and convincing:

Briefly, ——— cuts down time by enabling a clerical worker to do three jobs at once:
   Posting to customer's statement, ledger card, and sales register, all in one operation.
   Wage statement on employee's check or cash pay slip, on

earnings-record card, and on pay-roll summary sheet, all in one operation.

Accounts-payable check, remittance advice, journal entry, all in one operation.

You've Seen It Yourself . . .

The wholesome fun *your* youngster has whenever an issue of ———— arrives.

You've seen how he enjoys the page after page of stories . . . pictures . . . games . . . riddles . . . jokes . . . news and good comics that are in every issue of this first complete newspaper for children.

You've watched how eagerly he follows the sport tips from the experts . . . the latest scientific findings . . . the do-it-yourself experiments.

You've noticed how he learns about hobbies . . . different occupations . . . pet care . . . musical instruments . . . good books and culture from other lands.

Yes, by bringing ———— into your home, you're giving your youngster a great deal of wholesome, educational pleasure.

When you look over the enclosed Reply-O-Letter samples, note how easy they make it for your customers and prospects to say "Yes!"

There's nothing to sign—no postage to pay—and the card *stays* with the letter until the receiver is ready to act.

The address automatically becomes the "signature"—that's part of the magic of Reply-O-Letter.

You immediately sense the value of having the reply card *with* the letter. That way it can't be misplaced. It is always at the receiver's fingertips, ready to be rushed on its way back to you.

Stated simply—Make It Easy for People to Act and You Get Better Results!

The secret's in the scale. Now typewriter margins can be set *before* paper is inserted in the machine. Now your typists can center headings with ease and perfection. Absolutely no "margin math" is ever needed. Nor is it necessary to move the typewriter carriage.

With the perfect positioning scale there's no fumbling . . . no figuring . . . no time-wasting retypes . . . no inaccuracies, because your typists will be able to center letters and headings correctly the very first time.

Creating credibility

Today's customer is a skeptic who wants everything proved to him. As a result sales letters make a special effort to prove their point. This may be done by any of the following devices.

1. The guarantee

But that's not all we offer. If for some reason the prepared material doesn't cover your particular situation, our advertising department will be glad to apply its skill and experience to *your* promotional problems. There is no charge for this personalized advertising service. It is one of the many extra services we have set up for you, and it is available at all times. This guarantee is backed by one of the world's largest insurance companies.

2. Free sample

Will you please tell us the name of the person in your organization who is responsible for the methods you use in writing, routing, and supervising office and factory records?

We'd like to mail him a special portfolio of manufacturing forms. This portfolio is a handy filing folder containing . . .

Several samples of ——— are enclosed. Look at them, try them, test them. We're sure you'll like them.

3. Free trial

Read this book at my risk and expense. Don't send a penny now. Just your permission to send it on to you to read for ten (10) whole days.

If at the end of the 10 days, you feel that ——— is not the answer to your financial problems, return it and no questions asked. If, however, you wouldn't part with it for love or money (and we don't believe you will), just send $3 in any convenient form and the book is yours to keep, to own, and to use as a ready reference.

The ——— has to be seen to be believed. Without seeing it, you can't realize how many applications it will have to your particular office routine. Without seeing it, you can't appreciate how easy it is to use and how economical it is to operate. You have to see it—and we want to show it to you. Like its many satisfied users (General Motors, Continental Can, and Du Pont, among others), we know that you won't do without it once you have seen what it can do for you.

4. Testimonials

"I do not usually write testimonial letters," says Mrs. Hugh Kerr of Cincinnati, Ohio, "but I do want to thank you for Lawn Care and to report the astounding results from the use of Scott's Seed and Turf Builder. This is my first experience with Scott's and I am delighted."

We just received a report from a satisfied owner . . .

Read what others say who are sorry now that they did not start sooner. Our many satisfied users are our best advertisement. For example, Mrs. Fluelleh writes . . .

Mr. and Mrs. Edward Heyman, of Sachsonville, Illinois, were driving around the city one evening.

"We saw a lawn," wrote Mr. Heyman, "that was in a class by itself. Neither unusual heat nor almost complete lack of rain appeared to have affected it. I made bold to go to the house and ask for an explanation. The owner replied tersely, 'Scott's Seed and Turf Builder.' That seemed to him to tell all."

5. Reputable user or sponsor

The value of ——— is acclaimed by the country's most progressive dealers in gift merchandise. Join the more than 16,400 subscribers who attest to the value of this magazine by reading it month after month.

The Upsilon Co., of St. Louis, has carried subscriptions for 30 or more of their men for years. And their history has been one of continually increasing sales volume.

S. T. Coleridge's of Janesville, Ohio, started years ago with a handful of subscriptions. Now they provide ———— for 47 of their men . . . and in the meantime have grown to be one of the most successful houses in that area.

A. B. D. carries 41 subscriptions for the salesmen in their branch offices on the West Coast. They've been doing this as a "group subscriber" since 1932.

6. Statistics of acceptance

More than 10,000 sales managers have found these books active sales aids to the men on the road. Wouldn't it be a good investment to get ———— for all your salesmen to help them plan for more effective selling and better results?

Over sixteen million owners attest to the fact that Ronson is truly The World's Greatest Lighter.

7. Reference to the receiver's experience:

When you received this letter, you felt something inside the envelope. You consciously or unconsciously asked yourself, "What can this be?" So—you opened it.

8. Reference to the writer's experience:

If I could arrange for you to meet, in person, the Editorial Staff of ————————, you'd be as impressed as I was this afternoon. I have just come from an editorial meeting. I sat there fascinated, watching these men and women judging material received from our representatives who cover the markets and news centers.

9. Tests of the product in use

Here are a few examples of its durable qualities:
Ran a month on wearing-apparel unit without padding or flannel.
Formerly changed padding, flannel, and cover every week.

Ran 27 days, 243 hours, 16,250 shirts—on a swing bosom press.
Ran 25 days on collar press, 21 days on sleeve press, 23 days
on bosom press, 17 days on body press—actual working time.

10. The reason why

Because of quality production, we are able to offer you these
forms made on the best-grade Bristol board at the following low
prices.

11. Offer of comparison

The unusual thing about the special services that you get is
the fact that they cost you no more. Compare prices: ———
costs far *less* when you consider the extra wear (not tear!) you
get from all your washables!

12. The case history

We had *two* calls this morning for young ladies to stay in
homes where they can *earn* their room and board . . . and we
have not run an ad for places in many weeks. The time of year is
now approaching when people are making their plans for fall
and winter.

13. Description of the raw material

Here are a few interesting facts about the last issue you have
received:
To produce it for you, our 16 traveling editors consulted more
than 200 plants, interviewed more than 300 key men in industry,
and covered over 8,000 miles!

Ending the letter

The last part of a sales letter is the clincher, the extra
deciding point that will turn the reader into a customer.
This may be a special bargain offer, a time limitation, or
merely a summary of your previous arguments. If a letter
deals with several points, it is wise to recapitulate before
you make your final appeal. Here are a few endings that
have been used successfully:

1. Limited-time or limited-quantity offer

THIS OFFER WILL POSITIVELY BE WITHDRAWN NOVEMBER 29, 1968

Do this today. Mail the postage-free card in the window of this letter. Get it in the mail now so that these THREE GREAT HOLIDAY BONUSES can be yours without a penny's cash outlay! Don't wait—put your best foot forward for the Holiday Bonuses. You'll be glad you did. Because only a limited number of these new aids is available, it's impossible for me to send more than one to each teacher. So please do not order more than one for yourself. As soon as more become available, I'll see to it that you get as many as you need. There's no obligation for this helpful service, of course.

This unusual offer must necessarily be LIMITED.

You may now enroll in ——————— for the low fee of $1.00. Your ONE DOLLAR brings you every feature of my complete course, training, and service.

2. Time urgency

Time is growing short, so send today for your free-of-charge booklet and folder. There's no obligation for them or for any further information you may require. Just mail the attached card now.

Now is the time to lay in your spring supplies. Use the enclosed order blank to tell us your needs. We'll do the rest. Send no money until you get the invoice. Specify later shipment if you like. Do it now while you have the urge. You'll thank us many times this coming year for suggesting it.

But do it today—the croup season is here . . . now!

3. Premiums, special services, or combination offers

A special offer should be made to stand out. This can be accomplished by using indentation, a contrasting ink, a different type face, etc.

Our director wants so much for you to have the benefits of this course now that she has arranged a special gift for you if you enroll promptly.

Fill out the enclosed order form. Drop it in the mail before Saturday, May 5th—and we will send you your own personal copy of this lavishly illustrated annual.

4. Increase in price

The low prices, effective till December 31st, are listed below. You'll notice they give you a 10 per cent saving if you send your check with your order.

5. Personal pride

Be the first in your community to have one of these new lawn mowers . . .

6. Making response easier

This may be accomplished by enclosing stamped or business-reply cards or envelopes, permitting telephone response, or requiring no cash at the time of ordering.

A self-addressed envelope that requires no postage is enclosed for your convenience. You may use the back of this letter for your reply. We will appreciate it if you will let us hear from you soon.

Naturally, the brochures won't cost you a penny. And there's no obligation, either. So you'll have them that much sooner, please send us the card right now.

The above card requires neither postage nor signature. Just drop it in the mail and you will receive full information about the plan *and* the very useful tax facts booklet.

Jot your name on the card above right now—then drop it in the mail. I'll see that you get this timely, helpful information—without any cost or obligation on your part.

7. Salesman's call

Call me today for a free demonstration. We will send a representative at your convenience.

You will hear from our nearest division office in a few days . . .

8. Buy at retail stores

Get a bottle of ————————— from your favorite grocer today and discover how it brings out the hidden flavor of all good foods.

Thorough as this folder may be, you can't really see the full value of ————————— until you see it "in the flesh." Our representative at your neighborhood A. B. C. store will be happy to show you his display . . .

For the convenience of people living in your area we maintain an office located at . . .

9. Delays and apologies

If your dealer happens to be temporarily sold out, due to the ever-increasing public demand, leave an order with him because it will pay you to wait for a genuine Ronson lighter.

The unprecedented demand for our booklet during the past few months has exhausted our supply. We are taking the liberty of enclosing a leaflet . . .

Some closings irritate. Avoid the following:

Don't pass this up . . .
And oblige . . .
Trusting this will be satisfactory . . .
Just sign on the dotted line.
Beg to remain . . .
Don't miss this opportunity.
Yours while they last.
You'll be sorry if you don't order now.

Sample sales letters

Dear Mr. Smithers:

I wonder if you know John Smith. John's a dandy fellow. He's a type. Everybody knows him and everybody likes him. He thinks the world of his family, and people admire him for it.

I caught him the other day just as he was driving away from home. The folks were out to wave him "good by." He keeps his car in fine shape, and you could see the whole family was proud of it.

Well, here was my proposition to John. I said:

"John, you're in a hurry to get away—just hand me 20c and I'll leave some papers here with Mrs. Smith. You look them over tonight when you get home. They outline a darn good bet that you'll want to take me up on."

John tossed me 20c and rode away as I yelled after him:

"So long, see you later! You'll get your 20c back if you're not satisfied."

When Smith got home that night he found my little note, which has been copied and is attached hereto.

Yours very truly,

Dear John:

You gave me 20c this morning.

Here's how it was working for you all day long: If you had met with a fatal accident in that car of yours, the 20c would have been converted into $30,000.00 cash for Mrs. Smith.

And that isn't all! It sounds too good to be true, John, but just take two minutes to read the attached leaflet carefully and you'll find exactly how that small sum of 20c protected the Smith family throughout the entire day. Then ask Mrs. Smith to show you the F.&C. Policy I left. It covered every move you made today, whether you were in the car or not.

As you read the leaflet, John, take particular notice of this: PRIVATE conveyances (that means your own car or any other PRIVATE auto or vehicle) come in for the large DOUBLE BENEFITS.

That's where this proposition beats any other you ever saw. As I say, just read the leaflet carefully.

Now I can't be around at your garage door every morning, John, but if I could, isn't it a fact that you would gladly put up 20c and ask me to leave the $30,000 stake in Mrs. Smith's hands? Well, here's an easier plan: send me a check for $69.80 and the proposition stands for 364 days more.

You know, it's a peculiar thing but the fellow who owns a car usually spends more to insure the CAR against smash-up than he does to insure HIMSELF against the very same thing. And still *he* is very *likely to be in the car* when trouble comes.

Which is worth more to your family, John—*you* or the *car?*

Yours,

P.S. I guess I don't need to tell you about the F.&C. The company has been doing business for almost 50 years, has assets of 27 millions, and has paid over 90 millions in claims.

"YOU DON'T HAVE A CHINAMAN'S CHANCE . . ."

When I was a boy this was a favorite expression used to describe something that had no chance of succeeding.

It wasn't until I was grown that I learned why a Chinaman didn't have a chance. He lived as his ancestors had lived before him. What was good enough for them was good enough for him.

IN THIS COUNTRY WE LIVE BETTER THAN OUR PARENTS. BETTER THAN OUR GRANDPARENTS. AND WE WANT OUR CHILDREN TO LIVE BETTER THAN OURSELVES. WE WANT THEM TO HAVE A BETTER EDUCATION, THE MODERN CONVENIENCES THAT WE DID NOT HAVE. That is the reason we have progressed more in 200 years than some nations have in 2,000. We have better plumbing, better medical care, better food preparation, better heating and air conditioning, better mechanical and labor-saving devices.

BEING PROGRESS-MINDED HAS CAUSED US NOT ONLY TO INVENT BUT ALSO TO ACCEPT THE TELEPHONE, RADIO, STEAM ENGINES, TELEVISION, AND ANY NUMBER OF HOUSEHOLD GADGETS AND EQUIPMENT TO MAKE THE WORK OF THE HOUSEWIFE EASIER.

An automatic washer such as the Laundromat could not get very far without the acceptance of the housewife. Why does she like it?

BECAUSE . . .
> IT WASHES CLEAN
> IT RINSES THREE TIMES
> DAMP DRIES
> SHUTS OFF
WON'T YOU SEE IT TODAY AT EITHER OF OUR STORES?

Dear Baby:

Ever since you arrived, everybody has been telling you how adorable you are . . . and you certainly are that. But has anyone had the nerve to tell you what an awful nuisance you can be to Mother until you learn your proper "bathroom" manners?

We'll just bet that no one has, but we think you ought to know . . . and now that you do know, you probably feel embarrassed and want to help Mother all you can.

So, just between us, we're going to do something for you! As soon as you get home from the hospital, we're going to have one of our salesmen call at your home to take away your soiled baby clothes and "those things you fasten with a safety pin." Next day he'll bring them back clean and snowy white. He's going to do that every day for two weeks. And just because it's you, he's not going to charge Mother or Daddy one penny for all this service. Nobody can say then that you're a nuisance to Mother, can they?

Yours,

P.S. Just have Daddy fill in the card or phone 7247 and tell us when you're going home.

SHE TOLD ME ABOUT HER HUSBAND

This woman took me in her confidence . . . she confessed things that most women are ashamed to admit.

"We paid rent for eleven years before my husband could see that we had only rent receipts to show for our money. Then it was a job to convince him that we needed our own furniture. Today both house and furniture are *paid for*.

"We did without an automobile for years . . . Just because we couldn't make up our mind.

"And when we bought our first washing machine, it was a used one and ten dollars seemed like a lot of money to pay for it. But it was a lifesaver.

"NOW, today, twenty years later, after the children are all grown and I want an up-to-date automatic washer, it's still the same old story. . . . THE SAME OLD EXCUSES . . .
"FEAR OF GOING IN DEBT"
"WE MIGHT MOVE"
"INTEREST RATES ARE TOO HIGH"
"PRICES ARE COMING DOWN"
"NEW MODELS ARE COMING"
"IF I COULD SPEND WHAT THE WASHER COSTS TO MAKE HIS WORK LIGHTER, I WOULD CERTAINLY DO SO. YOU WOULD THINK HE'D DO THE SAME FOR ME, WOULDN'T YOU."

This is the true story of what one woman told me. A wife hardly ever admits these things about her husband. *Why did she tell me?*
Here's why . . . She was sick and tired of having to fight for every little bit of progress made in her family.

I am sure that your wife would never have reason to say or think these things about you, but be on the safe side—*call me today* and tell me to deliver that *wifesaver*. If she thinks you are wonderful now, she will think you were sent from heaven when she sees our truck before your house!

ONLY 9½% OF YOUR LAWN COST IS SEED

When you add up the cost of labor, topsoil, fertilizer, grading, etc., you've got 90½% of the total lawn expense. But the seed, that remaining 9½%, may be the greatest determining factor in the results you get.

Odd, isn't it, that people will go bargain hunting for lawn seed in view of the above facts? We don't recommend skimping anywhere along the line, but when it comes to seed, you definitely shouldn't. The so-called bargains don't materialize. After all, it's a lawn you want—not just a package of seed.

The seed you select becomes your lawn. A poorly conceived mixture, no matter if you think you've got a bargain, can't produce a beautiful, enduring lawn. You can't fool Mother Nature—she brings forth exactly what you sow.

Scott's is the finest blend of the proper grasses. Year after year it is America's first choice. Scott has experimented with dozens and dozens of blends, with the so-called miracle grasses, with the widely heralded discoveries, the lawn panaceas. Consistently the Scott blend beats them by a wide margin.

When you use the best you pay fewer dollars for the lawn. You get the grasses you want. You avoid the weeds and unwanted varieties of grass found in cheaper mixtures. In fact, you take the only short cut to lawn beauty. Scott's Lawn Seed is, in the end, the real bargain. Sow it yourself and recommend it confidently to your friends and neighbors.

Cordially yours,

Dear Miss Smith:

"We'll start you at $340 a month."

That is what an employer told one of our graduates when we sent her for an interview this week.

How would *you* like to have an interesting secretarial position in a modern business office at a starting salary of $340 per month?

Many of our young lady students start at the above salary; some at more, others at a little less. The starting salary depends largely on the course one selects, the skill one develops, and individual personality factors.

In attending MDC, you are assured of an opportunity at the *better* positions. This old, established institution has been training young women and men for preferred office positions since 1902. Many employers always call us first—and we are not able to fill nearly all the calls we receive.

You can take a secretarial course at MDC with the assurance of an opportunity at the *better* positions when you have finished. Won't you please let us hear from you? Simply call us at 2-5778, collect, or write for any further information you may desire. It will be a pleasure to co-operate with you and your parents.

Yours truly,

Hi there!

You know MISS OTIS? She's the buyer in JUNIOR DRESSES, where I TOIL. Smart! She knows every SOURCE in the market. And the way she keeps merchandise moving, you'd think she was a TRAFFIC COP or something. But she *used* to have a DICKENS of a time with STOCK CONTROL!

One season she'd order LOW . . . and the young-in-size would stampede the place. Next time, she'd throw most of her OPEN-TO-BUY into some really JAUNTY numbers. And they'd HANG there . . . and HANG THERE! And the MERCHANDISE MGR. didn't like it a bit—I mean you could TELL!

And that's how it went till one BRIGHT day a WISE OLD BUYER told her all about this AIR EXPRESS. How it keeps inventories DOWN . . . sales UP . . . customers EVER so happy. WELL, what a difference THAT made! If you want to know why—just take a peek at this little folder on the right. You'll SEE.

Seems more and more buyers ARE seeing the HUGE advantages of AIR EXPRESS these days. I know it's done WONDERS for JUNIOR DRESSES. Now when our racks get the DEPOPULATED look, MISS OTIS just puts a call through to the market . . . specifies AIR EXPRESS . . . and we're in business again. She LOVES that perfectly CO-ORDINATED air-ground service to just about everywhere. And, believe me, SHIPPING certainly appreciates those AIR EXPRESS extras, like door-to-door DELIVERY . . . generous VALUATION coverage . . . and RECEIPTS at each end of the trip. And all at absolutely NO extra charge.

And, say--there's nothing, but NOTHING, like AIR EXPRESS for slimming down your LOST-SALES record. Just ask MISS OTIS.

Love (that AIR EXPRESS),
Margie

Are you a classic-car enthusiast? You may or may not be, but you are probably aware of this very popular hobby shared by many people all over the country.

There are still many old relics maintained in good running condition. Polished brass fittings and shiny paint make these cars appear brand-new and efficient.

But as enthusiastic as these hobbyists are, none of them would think of using these obsolete machines when they have to travel efficiently and in a reasonable amount of time.

So it is with other machinery, equipment, or systems. You as an Egry Register user have indicated your keen interest in office efficiency and protection. As a progressive person you must realize that Egry constantly strives to improve its products and services. Naturally, through this constant effort we have been able to offer our customers a constantly improved product.

While your present machine may still be giving good service, it is obsolete because of new developments in design and operation. Obsolescence inevitably results in new equipment purchases only when another investment in the equipment pays for itself. We know this to be true in the new Egry Elite Tru-Pak, which incorporates all improvements possible in appearance and mechanical operation. It is the product of many years of research and engineering.

A brand new Elite Egry register, with your machine as a trade-in, will cost you only _____.

Cordially,

Would you like to cut office overhead costs . . .

By producing TWO typewritten records in the time an operator now needs to finish ONE?

By having any regular typewriter equipped to swing into action as a high-speed "biller" whenever peak loads require it—without altering that machine's readiness for regular work?

These and other improvements are practical possibilities—when paper work is analyzed with a view to fitting the most efficient methods and latest devices of simplification to one's specific form-writing and -handling requirements.

They are made possible by an exclusive principle of feeding continuous forms in typewriters and other business machines. Standard Register's method for feeding, aligning, and registering forms continuously and automatically is ingeniously simple.

It's the basis of complete "methods improvements," which in actual installations have increased the production of typed records per operator hour—depending on circumstances—from 30% to 100% or even 150% or more!

Enclosed is a folder describing the Registrator Platen principle.

Would you like to see an actual demonstration of continuous operation with no interruptions? There is no obligation. Just call our Representative, Mr. ———————, The Standard Register Company Sales Office, ————————————, ————— ———————————, telephone ———————————.

Cordially yours,

Dear Mr. Cortland:

The enclosed copy of a letter from a former student, Mr. J. W. Robel, is a typical example of how MDC graduates advance to *executive* positions. You are urged to read the letter carefully; also, to read the enclosed folder, which will tell you more about how you can make your high-school education pay you big dividends and the opportunities that will await you as a graduate of MDC.

A copy of our beautiful prospectus, *Your Tomorrow*, will be mailed to you promptly with our compliments, if you will kindly fill out and return the enclosed postage-free post card. Why not fill out and return the card *today*?

The prospectus tells *more* about the many advantages offered by MDC, and includes an outline of our different courses, the cost of tuition, scholarships, etc. It also tells about the many interesting opportunities that will await you, as a graduate of MDC, in business, industry, or civil service.

A cordial invitation is also extended to you and your parents to pay us a personal visit, so that you may see our school in action and ask any questions that may occur to you. If it is not convenient for you to come to see us, we shall be glad to have our Registrar call at your home to explain to you and your parents our courses, methods, terms, living accommodations, placement service, etc., without obligation.

Again, congratulations on your approaching graduation from high school. I am looking forward to seeing you or hearing from you. With every good wish,

Yours truly,

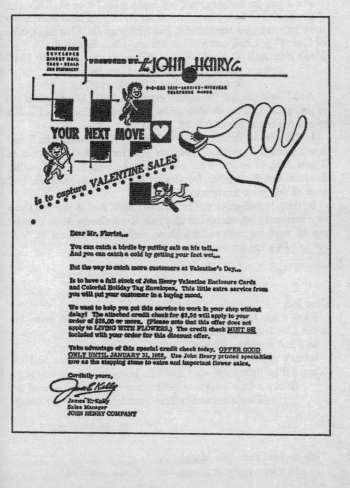

PRODUCED BY: the **JOHN HENRY** Co.

YOUR NEXT MOVE ♥

is to capture **VALENTINE SALES**

Dear Mr. Florist...

You can catch a birdie by putting salt on his tail...
And you can catch a cold by getting your feet wet...

But the way to catch more customers at Valentine's Day...

Is to have a full stock of John Henry Valentine Enclosure Cards and Colorful Holiday Tag Envelopes. This little extra service from you will put your customer in a buying mood.

We want to help you put this service to work in your shop without delay! The attached credit check for $2.50 will apply to your order of $25.00 or more. (Please note that this offer does not apply to LIVING WITH FLOWERS.) The credit check MUST BE included with your order for this discount offer.

Take advantage of this special credit check today. OFFER GOOD ONLY UNTIL JANUARY 31, 1958. Use John Henry printed specialties now as the stepping stone to extra and important flower sales.

Cordially yours,

James E. Kelly
Sales Manager
JOHN HENRY COMPANY

Dear Mrs. Alton:

> Roses are red,
> Kahn's is gay,
> Look what's ahead—
> ST. VALENTINE'S DAY!

Yes, this store of ours is full of bright ideas just now—happy new ways to lend Sir Cupid a helping hand!

For a gift, for instance, that will make a big hit on the 14th, and then proceed to be a year-round reminder of your fond thoughtfulness, let us suggest our colorful, beautifully made "King and Queen of Hearts" pajamas, patterned in red-and-black face cards.

Men's sizes A, B, C, D: $5.00   Women's sizes 32 to 40: $5.00

Boys' sizes 4 to 12: $3.50 ... 13 to 20: $3.98

Boxer shorts, sizes 30 to 44: $1.50

And here's another "Valentine Special": Lady Manhattan shirts in red pima broadcloth with white heart embroidered on the left side of the collar. Sizes 10 to 16. $5.95.

In fact, in all departments of all three Kahn stores you'll find novel, amusing, practical, welcome gifts for all the Valentines in Texas! And, of course, a complete mid-season collection of quality fashions and furnishings for the well-dressed men, women, and boys of this great community!

So drop in and enjoy our latest lively look! And if you can't pay us a personal visit, remember that your Kahn Charga-Plate account can be used for mail and telephone orders—not only for St. Valentine's Day but for every day in the year.

Cordially yours,

Dear Joe,

I lost a sale last week because someone I know didn't know I'm in the Life Insurance business.

So I had my picture taken!

I don't expect all of Janesville to rush to the phone and say "Tom, I'll be right over"—but this I do hope,   *(photograph*

> When a Life Insurance need arises   *pasted to*
> Please remember Tom Saunders   *the letter)*

Sincerely yours,

It's renewal time, Mr. Mager ...
... so take a moment please, and O.K. the attached.

Dear Former Subscriber:

Do you *really* want us to destroy the plate pictured above, formerly used to address your subscription copies of ——————?

You did not renew, but there is a blunt finality in destroying this symbol of what I hoped was a friendly relationship between us.

Each of these little plates represents real people to us, not merely names on a list. You see, we get many letters from readers about their problems and interests; others we see in person. Through these thousands of contacts we have come to think of our subscribers as people we know. I cannot be complacent about the loss of even one subscriber.

Stop us from cancelling your subscription. There's still time. Just enclose this card in an envelope with your payment and mail it right away.

> Charles Mason
> TIME. The Weekly Magazine

P.S. There is no need to return this card if you've already sent in your payment.

Just a note, Mr. Tompkins . . .
  to let you know that your subscription to
  The *Times* is up for renewal—expires with
  the next issue, in fact.

Obtaining information

FOR YOUR
CIRCULATION MANAGER

We consider this the most important letter we shall be sending you this year. It's important because we are asking you to send us your subscription rates for the 1967–68 season so that we may list your correct subscription price in 97,500 agents' price lists and in 1,500,000 subscriber booklets.

So please fill out and return to us the enclosed Rate Sheet just as soon as possible. We shall appreciate an early reply as we plan to issue our catalogs much earlier this year.

Now you can be sure
that everything you plant
will grow—and grow—and grow

Why is it that some people have so much good luck with growing things? How come your neighbor can plant most anything and see it flourish—and apparently without much effort—while your own hard work often brings indifferent results?

Successful plant growth depends on proper food and enough water. Water isn't much of a problem. But knowing what plant food is necessary and how much can make the difference between success and failure.

EEESY GROW Fertilizer Packets solve the plant feeding problem. With this new *measured* feeding development, controlled release of fertilizer *guarantees adequate plant nutrition* for 5 years.

You fertilize with EEESY GROW just once. Minute holes in the plastic package release just the right amount of nutrient, not too much to cause burning and not so little that the plant starves. The result is perfect plant feeding and luxuriant growth *for the next five years.* Fertilize with EEESY GROW and water your plants regularly. You'll soon have the green thumb reputation that comes with 100% success with growing things.

You'll have less plant disease or insect damage when you use EEESY GROW. Healthy plants resist disease and insect pests. EEESY GROW insures plant vigor to ward off most common perils to health growth.

This is the practical way to fertilize. You can grow a perfect tree, for example, with 31 cents worth of EEESY GROW a year. Or keep a rose bush living in luxury for 8 cents a year. And there's no work to it. Put the fertilizer packet close to the roots, cover it and forget it. That's all there is to green-thumb growing with EEESY GROW.

Anytime (right now for instance) is a good time to start. Order a box of EEESY GROW today. $2.98 postpaid, and see how magnificently your plants respond. It's guaranteed to satisfy. If you don't see startling results in 60 days return the unused balance for a full refund of your purchase price, no questions asked.

This is how to be sure your plants will grow—and grow—and grow.

Sincerely,

The Digest of Investment Advice
Att: Mr. A. L. Peters
New York, N. Y.

MR...

This is a miniature of the envelope that used to bring the INVESTMENT Dealers' DIGEST to you.

Sorry we can't mail a copy of the DIGEST to you now. You see, your subscription expired and your renewal hasn't come in as yet.

But you can still get the current and future issues by merely returning your renewal instructions now. Just shoot this back to us in the enclosed no-stamp envelope.

To make sure you don't miss any of the important issues ahead, ACT NOW !

M. S. Barbiere

Renew my subscription for 1 year at $22 :
2 years at $41 ; 3 years at $59 .

( ) *Remittance Enclosed   ( ) Bill me

*No need to enclose check with your renewal. If you do, thus eliminating bookkeeping expenses, we will extend your subscription one additional month

CHAPTER 20

Turning Inquiries Into Sales

In all too many companies, the occasional inquiries from prospective customers are treated casually. Yet a large factor in business-letter writing should be the turning of these inquiries into sales.

An inquiry received by a business firm is a ready-made opportunity to create good will and promote sales. Responses should be prompt, courteous, friendly, and a complete answer to the questions asked. If your response must be delayed, send a note acknowledging the inquiry and explaining your delay.

An examination of the inquiries that come into your office will usually indicate a pattern that can make use of uniform answers. Where inquiries vary, form paragraphs can be prepared to meet each of the questions commonly asked.

The usual parts of a letter responding to an inquiry are:

1. An acknowledgment or statement that the inquiry is being answered.

2. A detailed response to the questions, or explanation why a refusal is necessary.

3. Additional information that may be helpful.

4. An offer of further help if necessary.

One important and frequent problem is inducing the reader to examine carefully enclosures included with the letter. Samples of successful responses to inquiries are shown in the following pages.

Dear Sir:

It is a real pleasure to send you the information requested, and we appreciate your thinking of Leitz in connection with your photographic requirements. As you look over the enclosed literature, note how each piece of equipment dovetails into an over-all system, the Leica System of Photography. Note also the quality, beauty of design, and simplicity of operation.

The Leica is the most versatile camera made for black-and-white and color. There isn't a photographic task it cannot master. Whether it's an action shot or portrait, a wide panorama or a close-up of an insect's head, the Leica WILL GET IT! Photography under poor light? Photography under difficult conditions? Leica high-speed lenses or Leica flash makes it easy for you.

The Leica camera, its lenses and accessories, hold the envied position of world leadership. It is manufactured by Ernest Leitz, Wetzlar (in West Germany), who for over 100 years has produced optical instruments of high precision.

We hope to welcome you soon into the great and ever growing Leica Family. Visit the Leica dealer in your locality and see the many exclusive features that make it the finest photographic instrument available. Meanwhile, for any further details use the handy form we are enclosing in the window of this letter. It needs no postage, no addressing—just drop it in the mail.

Cordially,

Dear Mr. Jones:

Thank you for your interest in UNITED Business and Investment Reports. Enclosed is the latest issue of our weekly UNITED Bulletin.

By reading it, you will get the best possible idea of its completeness; its condensed, quick-reference form; the valuable information it contains; the definite, helpful recommendations it gives.

But the chief—the exclusive—feature of UNITED Reports is the unique method that underlies all information presented and every forecast made. This is the UNITED Opinion Method of forecasting, fully described in the enclosed folder. It assures greater accuracy and dependability, and gives you in one Report the combined judgments and opinions of all leading authorities.

As a subscriber, you would be privileged to request Special Reports on any stocks or bonds. This is a very valuable feature of our Service—and it is included without extra charge. In many cases, the profits secured through just one Special Report have more than paid for the entire cost of the Service.

UNITED Service—through the UNITED Opinion Method—has been exceptionally successful in interpreting current trends and selecting profitable stocks. As a result, UNITED is today serving more individual investors than any other investment advisory service.

A Service with the exclusive features, the "profit-building" record of UNITED, has special value under today's conditions. You can test it for six months, at a cost of only $35, and on a Refund Guarantee basis. Read the enclosed application form—then start your test of UNITED Service by returning the form today.

Cordially yours,

Dear Mr. Cortland:

When the mailman stopped at our front door today, the most welcome bit of mail that he left us (next to the equipment orders, of course!) was your inquiry about _____ equipment.

We like to hear from someone like you because we are in the equipment business; but even more important as far as you are concerned is that your letter indicates an intelligent approach to your entry into the dental profession.

You are using sound judgment in examining and evaluating for yourself the merits of the equipment you are considering purchasing. Since *you* will use the equipment, *you* should rightly be the judge of what will serve your purpose best.

Our catalog pages tell the story of _____ equipment. The reading of that story should prove interesting and worth-while. All the experience of more than a half-century has been condensed into a few short pages.

Thank you so much for your letter. It may represent the best six-cent investment you ever made.

We sincerely hope so!

Cordially,

Helpful Opening Paragraphs

The enclosed booklet will give you the information you asked for in your July 7th postcard.

The book you requested is on its way to you.

Thank you very much indeed for your planning form of September 10th and the sketch of your proposed new clinic.

The enclosed office layout has been drawn by our Planning Department to allow the best possible use of available space. . . . However, if these plans do not meet your full requirements, Dr. Doe, please let us know and we will try again.

The booklet you requested is enclosed. It answers the questions most commonly asked about. However, we know that this small booklet couldn't possibly contain all the interesting and important facts about this amazing new service. So, if you have any further questions, please feel free to write. You'll get a prompt reply.

Thank you for your letter of September 14th, and the interest expressed in our ——————.

We are certain you will agree that here is a good investment in working comfort. No longer is there any need to tolerate the dentist's long-accepted occupational hazard—fatigue.

Thank you for your request for our booklet *Cash or Sympathy*, which we are pleased to enclose. This booklet is fascinating to read, but before you turn to it we want to pay you a friendly little visit in the form of this letter.

When your letter came in requesting the 1967 Spring Catalog, our mailing department hastened to forward your copy immediately. You see, we try to give the best of service and satisfaction in everything we do.

We're glad to know from your recent inquiry that you are interested in learning about ————.

I enjoyed hearing from you and am real pleased that you are interested in having my recipe for making pie the Spry way . . .

How nice it is to know that you are interested in cooking with ————.

A warm sun is shining here again today, and in a few hours the streets and parks will be filled with people relaxing in the warmth of an Arizona winter.

Thanks a lot for your request for information about ————. The enclosed circular will probably give you most of the information you want.

Getting the enclosure read

Turn right now to the enclosed folder. First, look at those eight photographs on page three. See how good a detective you are! See whether you find that same woman as she looked before and after taking the DuBarry Success Course.

In the enclosed folder you will see pictured the five new models of _____.

We believe this booklet should be helpful to you because in it we have answered the questions most people ask us about _____.

In the booklet, on page five, you will find a detailed list of _____.

Just one more thing before you read our booklet.

CHAPTER 21

Follow-up Letters

After you have mailed a sales letter, seen a prospect, or made a sales call, you will find some prospects have not been entirely sold. A follow-up letter to complete the sale is required.

For this reason many sales campaigns are designed to include a series of letters. This is particularly true in selling expensive items, which may require and warrant the cost of a series of letters. Follow-up letters are also sent to steady and one-shot customers who are good prospects for more sales of the same or different products.

Two conflicting problems confront the writer of follow-up letters. The letters must have some continuity and relationship to previous letters—yet they must be sufficiently different so that the contents are not obviously "old news." A series of sales letters sent to the same prospects should vary in the selling points emphasized. If they appear too similar, later letters in the series will go unread, perhaps unopened. Changing the size and style of the letter and the envelope tends to increase the chances of your letter's being read if you are mailing to strangers; mantaining a uniform style tends to build up your relationship with established customers.

A follow-up letter should have a reason for being sent beyond the fact that it is one of a series. It may tell about:

1. A special offer, a limited supply.
2. An additional sales point.
3. A new circular, booklet, or memorandum presenting an additional viewpoint.
4. The ease of ordering.
5. Your thanks to the reader for a previous order or for showing interest or special courtesy.

6. Or it may be merely a simple remainder, a check on the receipt of previous correspondence.

After a sales call

Dear Mr. Saunders:

I want to thank you personally for the courtesy you showed to our Mr. Jones when he paid you a call in regard to the purchase of a burial estate in _____ Memorial Park. We know and we want you to know that the opportunity offered is unique.

To our knowledge no beneficiary ever refused to accept a life-insurance check. In the same way, a purchase of a burial lot in advance of actual need in _____ Memorial Park will never cause you regret.

During the past year more than 200 families have selected and purchased, in advance of need, their family burial lot in a section under development.

We are now opening an additional section, known as Section "L," and by making an immediate selection you are afforded an unusual opportunity—both as to choice of location and low price.

I suggest that when Mr. Jones next calls at your home you make this all-important decision and select a location from his map, taking advantage of a situation that may never be offered again. The prices right now are from 33⅓ to 50% less than they will be when the section is completely finished.

Our experience proves that this method of purchase increases the value of your life insurance, and we assure you that Mr. Jones's visit is occasioned by our sincere desire to provide this definite need at a time when the purchase will be a definite benefit to your en-entire family.

> Very truly yours,

P.S. It may be of interest to you to know that more than three thousand families have already purchased here—because _____ Memorial Park provides the finest at the least cost.

Thanks a lot, Mr. Moon!

I certainly appreciate the friendliness and interest you and Mr. Wetzel showed me yesterday.

During the course of the day I make so many calls on "tough" purchasing agents and sales managers, that a pleasant reception goes a long way.

I sincerely hope that I can be of service in keeping your customers sold on _____.

Again—many thanks!

Sincerely,

Dear Mr. Sampson:

You were out the other day when our Mr. Jones called. He has told us about the friendly interview he had with your assistant, Mr. Finn, and he asked that we write you and confirm matters brought up in the interview.

I am sure that Mr. Jones has gone over our various products with you and Mr. Finn on other calls, so I will not repeat the information in this letter. I know that you are busy and I do not want to take up too much of your time, but there is one point that I would like to bring to your attention. That point is the service we are equipped to give.

In the early days of our business—which, by the way, was over twenty-five years ago—we learned that it wasn't enough just to furnish quality floor treatment and maintenance products. No matter how good the products, they will not prove satisfactory unless they are applied properly. Therefore, all our products are sold with a guarantee that one of our trained floor-maintenance engineers will be on the job to supervise the application of the materials. All our representatives are schooled and trained in correct floor-maintenance procedure. Mr. Jones, for example, has been with us for over ten years, and he has had experience working with all types of floors. He is one of our most conscientious representatives and whenever he promises you anything, you can be sure that it will be done.

All floors present individual problems that cannot be solved by merely purchasing so many gallons of this or that product. We follow through to see that the floors are put in perfect condition when our materials are being used. When you work with Mr. Jones, I am sure you will agree with me that he is a competent and conscientious floor-maintenance engineer.

You can place your order for Vestal products with the assurance of complete satisfaction both as to quality of products and proper supervision.

Yours very truly,

After a visit from the prospect

Dear Miss Whitelaw:

I appreciate your coming to see us today and regret that I did not have an opportunity to discuss with you our school, courses, and employment service. However, I am sure Mr. Worth told you about the advantages offered by MDC and the great demand for our graduates.

Naturally, you want to attend a well-known school that enjoys an outstanding reputation among employers. MDC has been training young women like yourself here in Janesville since 1902, and we have graduates in practically every office of any size throughout this entire area.

A copy of our illustrated prospectus, *Your Tomorrow,* has been mailed to you. It contains information that should be interesting and helpful to you. For your future's sake, we trust you will take time to give it careful reading.

Many other young women have virtually assured their "Tomorrow" by registering or starting secretarial courses with us this month. It is to *your* interest to get started on your course as *soon* as you can.

The demand of MDC graduates is several times the supply. Last Monday we sent a young lady to apply at a legal firm for a secretarial position. When one of the partners asked the other what he thought about employing the young lady, he replied, "If Mr. _____ recommends her, that's good enough for me." She was then told to report on Tuesday morning at a starting salary of $425 per month. That is what really counts, isn't it?

Finally, you can take a secretarial course at MDC with the assurance of an opportunity at the *better* positions when you have finished. Won't you please let us hear from you? Simply call us at 2-5778 or write for any further information you may desire. It will be a pleasure to cooperate with you to the fullest.

Yours truely,

A Special Arrangement to Help You
Start *Your* Success Course *at Once*

Dear Friend:

Your name came up this morning when I was talking with Miss Delafield, and when she learned that you had not yet enrolled, she asked me to write you at once. For she wants you to know that if it's a matter of money, she has some good news for you.

Originally, all our students paid their tuition in advance. But many business girls, teachers, and others asked if they could pay in two installments. We were glad to arrange this, and if it would be more convenient—you, too, may take advantage of this plan.

Instead of sending $19.75 now, you may, if you prefer, send $10.50 with your application and $10.50 in one mouth. The first two weeks' lessons and the handsome Travel Case of DuBarry Preparations will be sent right away, making it possible for you to start on the same basis as those sending the full tuition.

If you could read some of the letters that are pouring in from students of our Home Success Course, you would not want to lose an hour in getting started yourself. For the results are so real and they can come so soon.

For example, Miss B_____ writes from a small city in up-state New York: "What your course has done for me in just one week has amazed me." And Mrs. K_____ writes from Connecticut: "I would not go back to the person I was two weeks ago for all the world."

Hundreds write to tell how they have streamlined their figures, won the compliments of friends for their new graceful slenderness and improved skin, hair styling, and make-up.

With so many students enthusiastic about the practical value of this course, and with payments arranged for your convenience, surely there is no reason now to delay any longer. Use the application enclosed to take advantage of the special two-payment plan.

Miss Delafield hopes you will send it by return mail, so that she may plan for you the personal beauty program that can mean so much to your happiness and well-being.

Yours sincerely,

After a sale

Thanks for your request—
and here is your copy of _____, the NEW Coleman book, which tells you how to have *more fun outdoors.*

Whether you go on family picnics, week-end outings, auto vacations, camping, hunting or fishing trips, you are sure to find many ideas and suggestions that will help you get more fun from your outings.

Thanking for an order

Usual "Thank You"
letter omitted . . .

> at the suggestion
> of the Society for
> the Suppression of
> long "thank you"
> letters!
> Sincerely,
>
> Irving Mack

P.S. They tell me people don't read lengthy letters anyway . . .
and the chances are, you don't need to be reminded that we
appreciate this order.

After a sales letter

Dear Mr. Blank:

Since a letter is less of an interruption than a phone call, I'm
taking this means to ask if you will do me a favor.

Would you review the brief proposal I mailed you last week and
let me know frankly how effective it was?

We don't want to persist beyond the point of good salesmanship.
An expression from you as to whether we may fit into your plans
this year will be warmly appreciated.

Cordially yours,

Dear Mr. Seberts:

WILL YOU PLEASE DO ME A FAVOR?

Tell me whether you received our literature?

(A) Whether it gave you the information you desired?

(B) Whether you are still interested in attending MDC?

(C) Whether you have made other plans?

(D) Whether you have any problems, financial or otherwise?

If the latter applies in your case, write us as you would a friend
—or come to see us personally. I am sure we can *help* you, and it
will be a pleasure to do so.

If you have changed your plans or made other arrangements, we
shall be glad to take your name off our list and not send further
letters and literature.

There is a self-addressed, postage-free envelope enclosed, and you may use the back of this letter for your reply. May we hear from you soon? Thanks, in advance, for your cooperation.

Yours truly,

Gentlemen:

About 10 days ago we sent you a _____ Sample Kit. Since then we have heard nothing from you and are beginning to wonder whether you received these samples. Please let us know by return mail, because if you did not receive your kit we will send another.

Perhaps the package is lying around your office as yet unopened or perhaps you haven't had the time to try your samples. If this is true, I wish you would do me a personal favor and spend about two minutes right now, examining the contents of this interesting kit.

First off, in the tan folder you will find working samples of the _____ drawing board. It's real fun playing with these samples and bringing up the "magiclike" patterns simply by applying the Developer No. 6 with a brush or pen. In the pink folder you will find samples of _____, the drawing board that enables you to put both light and dark tones of shading, in addition to solid blacks and high-light whites, right in the original drawing!

Your big thrill, of course, is in the green folder. There you will find samples of the sensational new _____ drawing board. Now you can produce *graduated* tones! You get actual combination and high-light halftone effects right in your original drawing, and a complete range of tones from a high-light dot to a solid black!

Every _____ product is a money-saver for you. Your fields are unlimited, and the originality and unique effects you can inject into your art work are second only to the tremendous savings in production costs.

If you kit has not arrived—please let me know at once. If it has, I'll appreciate it if you will drop me a line and tell me what you think of it.

Very truly yours,

Gentlemen:

Last week we sent you our prices for your inspection tags.

Since we have not heard from you in the meantime, I thought you might like to be reminded of them. Naturally, we would like to make your tags for you.

If, for any reason, the order has been placed elsewhere, will you please let us know? We would appreciate any information you'd care to give us.

A stamped and addressed envelope is enclosed for your convenience.

Cordially,

P.S. If you're real busy, just jot a note in the margin of this letter, please.

Have you Received YOUR Copy of Our
Booklet "What You Can Do—What
You Can't Do As an Apparel Man"?
IT'S FREE!

To give you the help you need to save precious time and money, to show you step-by-step how to handle the problems confronting you every day in business, I would like to send you a copy of—

WHAT YOU CAN DO—WHAT YOU CAN'T DO
As an Apparel Man

—a graphic survey just compiled by John Harmon Doe, member of the New York State and a Washington D.C. bar, an outstanding attorney in problems of the apparel industry, and a former chief attorney for the Securities and Exchange Commission. This invaluable booklet lists and clarifies for you a host of difficult situations and problems.

Look at some of the subjects analyzed in the pages of this helpful booklet—

how recent SEC and FTC decisions are being interpreted
how to protect a brand name
how to handle problems of employee seniority
how far a landlord can go
how much you can alter or rebuild
how to protect patents and designs
how to deal with government agencies
how to deal with "outside" tailors
when and to what extent you must pay overtime
AND HOW to deal with many other problems vital
to your business.

This booklet is not for sale. It is prepared solely for the use and benefit of our subscribers, but we shall be glad to send you a copy without charge if you will fill in and return the enclosed card.

The publication and distribution of this time- and money-saving booklet is a part of the service that we render nationally to subscribers of _____. We are glad to extend it to you as a prospective subscriber.

To the large majority of manufacturers, wholesalers, and retailers who read _____ every week, it is more than just an interpretative newsweekly bringing them timely information of the women's apparel industry.

It is designed to help you buy and sell more goods at a lower cost. It is written simply and vividly—not sketchy reports, not flash bulletins, not mere conversation . . . but hard, unbiased, reliable facts and the definite steps for you to take so by knowing *what* to do and *when* and *how* to do it you can be ahead of your competitors.

Yours truly,

Gentlemen:

All right, we're "naïve."

I sent you a letter last week. I sent the same letter to a number of other book publishers. One of them called us naïve.

Perhaps that is what you are thinking.

Because a book printer who has earned an enviable reputation for quality asks to be judged on price—he's naïve.

Because a printer, whose books are regularly included in the Institute of Graphic Arts selection of the fifty best printed books of the year, thinks he can underquote the careless corner-cutters, he's naïve.

Because when prices are jumping and book publishers' profits are vanishing, a printer offers low prices instead of getting his cut while the getting is good, he's naïve.

All right, then we're naïve. If you could see our plant, study our reputation and financial position, talk to our customers, realize the steady and profitable business we have built, you might think that it is better to be naïve than to be smart.

We want to print fifty additional books this year. We want to use some idle equipment, and we want to use it on books. We want to print and manufacture just one book for you. We predict that we can beat your regular printer on price and deliver comparable or better quality and service. Our favorable position here in Zenith, our knowledge of the business and our long years of successful operation, our efficient plant and the current fact of some idle equipment, all combine to make our costs low.

If that's naïveté, I think you ought to take advantage of it. May we quote on just one book?

Very truly yours,

IT'S STILL YOUR MOVE

A year's a long time to remember a letter, but you may recall that at about this time in 1967 I wrote asking if you would return an enclosed postcard questionnaire concerning Practice Filing Equipment.

Just recently, as I was rechecking the replies, I noticed that no card was returned by you . . . so it's still your move.

The purpose of the card (I've enclosed it again) is to correct and bring our mailing list up-to-date so that we may send our many free services to users only. If I do not receive your card by the end of the year, I will have to assume that you're no longer using the practice equipment.

Your name, therefore, will be taken off the mailing list, and we regretfully will have to discontinue sending you our *Free* services, including Q & A letters and the certificate plan.

Naturally, we'd like to send you this material for as long as you wish. And the same goes for your fellow teachers. I'll be doubly grateful, if you'd not only return the postpaid card now, but list on it the names of teachers you know who are also using Practice Filing Sets.

Cordially yours,

Dear Neighbor:

Did you miss the opportunity to earn a ten-per-cent return on a dollar when it was offered to you last year? If you did, here's your chance to earn ten per cent—plus.

So many people were disappointed last year through missing the 60-day deadline that we are repeating the offer this year.

We've opened a savings account for you here at the Bergen Central Savings and Loan Association. Enclosed is your temporary passbook showing the dollar we have credited to your account. The dollar is yours if you just add ten dollars or more to it within the next sixty days.

Your savings here will earn 5 per cent each year, and every member's account is insured, up to $10,000, by the Bergen Central Savings and Loan Insurance Corporation. Savings made by the tenth of any month will earn dividends from the first of that month.

If you find it inconvenient to call at either of our two offices,

we'll be glad to open your account for savings by mail. All you
have to do is write your name and address on the top of this ten-
porary passbook and mail it to us with your check or money
order for your first deposit.

You'll find it pleasant and profitable to save here.

Sincerely,

Sales letters in a series

> USE FACT-POWER
> TO GENERATE SALES-POWER
> ONLY FACTS CAN TELL YOU . . .
> *WHO* TO SELL—PROFITABLY

You know it's true. All the selling time, talent, and energy in the
world aren't worth a hoot unless they're directed at the right
people.

They are the ones your salesmen have to see and sell—the people
with the need to use, the power to buy, and the ability to pay
for your products and services. To keep *them* in your "sales
sights," you need a system that flashes their identity and enables
you to take timely action.

Kardex Visible Sales Production Control *is* that system, because it constantly keeps these vital facts at your fingertips . . .

Who is being sold—*now*
Who is being inadequately covered
Who has stopped buying—*and why*
Annual sales potential of each account
What-percentage of that potential *you* are getting
Which accounts are profitable—which are not

Like other sales executives in leading organizations, you, too,
can locate your sales targets quickly, easily, and accurately with
Kardex Visible Sales Production Control.

Now is the time . . . the absolutely right time . . . to learn more
about fact-powered Kardex Visible. Use the card above to get
the whole story in a 24-page descriptive booklet—yours without
cost or obligation.

Sincerely,

And here's an important point! There's no time lost figuring sales-to-quota percentages. You figure them automatically with the Graph-A-Matic Computing Chart—exclusive with Kardex.

USE FACT-POWER
TO GENERATE SALES-POWER
ONLY FACTS CAN TELL YOU . . . *WHEN* TO SELL—PROFITABLY

When to sell may be right now on some of your accounts . . . a week from now on others . . . a month from now on still others.

The facts that tell you *when* go off like an alarm if you use the Kardex Visible Sales Production Control System.

Then you know—

When . . . calls were made last—and *result* of each
When . . . sales were made last—and *amount* of each
When . . . old accounts stopped buying—and *why*
When . . . new prospects should be called on—and *where*
When . . . new accounts were added—and by *whom*

Then you act fast—synchronizing your salesmen's time and efforts so they reach the right people in just the right time to sell.

Your salesmen have the competitive urge. Now they'll get the competitive jump—time and time again with Kardex Visible Sales Production Control.

This whole Kardex story is waiting for you in a really valuable 24-page handbook—yours without cost or obligation. *Now's the time to initial the card and drop it in the mail to get your free copy.*

Sincerely,

And don't forget that Kardex "exclusive"—the Graph-A-Matic Computing Chart that enables you to figure automatically sales-to-quota percentages with stop-watch accuracy.

USE FACT-POWER
TO GENERATE SALES-POWER
ONLY FACTS CAN TELL YOU . . . *WHERE* TO SELL—PROFITABLY

Steering your salesmen to the pay-off points today takes more than a sense of direction. It takes specific knowledge based on facts.

When your facts are in sight, so are your sales. That's why you need a system that signals them visibly. And Kardex Visible Sales Production *is* that system because it shows you in a flash—

Where . . . your biggest markets are concentrated
Where . . . sales are rising—or falling off
Where . . . competition is getting the jump
Where . . . you can cut your selling costs
Where . . . to aim more aggressive promotion
Where . . . to schedule extra calls

Sales executives using Kardex Visible Sales Production Control also find they get visibly better sales *cost* control.

So act now to get the complete Kardex story—including details on the amazing Graph-A-Matic Chart that automatically enables you to compute sales-to-quota percentages.

No charge for this 24-page handbook. No obligation, either, Just fill in the card and drop it in the mail—today.

Sincerely,

Sales promotion letter

Managers
All Book Stores
United States of America
Dear Nice People:

I enclose for you a copy of the cover to my book *THE PRESI-DENT I ALMOST WAS*. I'm sorry I couldn't send the book as well but I am just a poor Presidential loser from the 1968 election.

All my neighbors and relatives who borrowed my copy to read say it is going to be a best seller. So I am writing you to ask a little favor. Please put me on the counter beside your cash register and maybe we can all make money together.

In my gratitude I might do something for *you* in 1972 when I hope to become both First Lady and President of the United States. If you are interested I have open right now Postmaster General, Secretary of State, and Ambassador to England. What is your pleasure?

Your friendly,
Mrs. Yetta Bronstein
THE BEST PARTY

Dear Mr. Mager:

You will remember that I wrote you recently asking for your candid opinion of the samples we made for you.

Very sincerely I was anxious to get a frank reply. I hope the fact that I have not heard from you means that you are among the 98 per cent of our patrons who are thoroughly pleased. Perhaps you have been in touch with our sales representative. If so, I have not yet heard of it.

The purpose of this letter is merely to repeat that we want you to be thoroughly satisfied with our work. If there is anything about the samples that fails to please you, won't you take them to the shop and discuss them with John Timothy, our production manager. Whatever can be done to improve them will be done, of course, without further expense to you. If you would prefer to send them directly to me with your comments, or write me about them, please do so.

Yours very truly,

Helpful Starting Sentences

You have the answer to a question that is puzzling us.

When I examined the list of dealers whose sales hadn't increased during the last year, your name was on the list.

One day last week I got to looking at sales figures for March. Naturally I was (happy to see) (surprised to notice) that your sales of _____ (had hit a new peak) (had dropped).

Yesterday my secretary placed your inquiry of last March on my desk with the notation: "You haven't heard from Mr. Jones."

Have you tried the sample of _____, Mr. Jones?

Have you had an opportunity to test the trial shipment of _____ we sent you?

About a month ago, we sent you _____.
Did my circular about _____ reach you promptly?

This letter contains some mighty important information, which I am sure you will be glad to have.

```
                    FEBRUARY
        (This ) S M T W T F S
        ( is  )       1 2 3 4 5
        ( the )   6  7  8  9 10 11 12
        (Date!)  13 14 15 16 17 (18) 19
                 20 21 22 23 24 25 26
                 27 28
```

You see, the cost of _____ _____ training has already been materially increased. Men who contact us now for the first time must pay the new, higher rate. BUT —NOT YOU!

It is fine news that you are joining us as a _____ subscriber.

If you have not already started to receive your weekly copies, I want you to know that they will be on their way to you very shortly.

Now that you have had an opportunity to familiarize yourself with our _____ we are interested in learning your opinion of it—and if you wish to continue receiving it on a regular basis.

Did you receive our letter offering you a $2.00 rebate on your one-year renewal to _____?

In view of your interest in the _____ service expressed in your letter of November 10th, and in view of the important juncture that now appears ahead, you may like to have me outline the fundamental outlook for you.

Three weeks ago I sent you a letter with a stock-market chart outlining four reasons why stock-market action was taking on the characteristics of a "Bull Market."

Mr. Smith says you were mighty nice to him when he called on you yesterday.

SPEAK UP! How did you like your sample copy of _____

We have sent to you a complimentary copy of _____
_____ so that you can see for yourself how the many
important departments in this service can help you in your business. This newsweekly will keep you informed about many things
of vital importance and will be sent to you each week for only
23c.

Have you reserved your *FREE Advance Copy* of
"1969 SURVEY: THE PLAN FOR SELLING
COMMERCIAL REFRIGERATION"

Requests are pouring in, so if you have not as yet mailed in your
questionnaire, please do so now while we are still accepting them.
A duplicate copy of the questionnaire has been placed in the
window of this letter. It will entitle you to a *free,* first-press copy
of the 1969 Survey, immediately upon publication.

CHAPTER 22

Good-Will Letters

An important type of sales letter is the good-will letter, whose purpose is to sell the good reputation and friendliness of a company. It aims to build good will in the customer-company relationship, hold present customers and obtain new ones, revive inactive accounts, and invite customers to buy more and varied products. The underlying purpose of all good-will letters is to create customers by making friends.

Good-will letters may make capital of a particular event, or situations may be created to make a letter appropriate. They are sent to anyone of importance to the firm: customers, personnel, sources of supply, etc.

Insurance men traditionally send birthday greetings to their clients. Alert salesmen watch for opportunities to send customers notes of congratulation. A large order is an excuse for a thank-you letter. A new customer may receive a note of welcome, an inactive customer a letter of reminder (perhaps a reminder that there has been no price increase). Holidays; the opening of a new department, outlet, or branch offices; new products; a change in personnel all provide opportunities for good-will letters. The credit department may send a letter of appreciation to those who pay their bills promptly. The sales department may write to wish a customer success in a new venture. A family new to the neighborhood is often sent a welcome note, a booklet about the neighborhood, a coupon redeemable at a retail store, or a gift of one of the company's products.

On the following pages are tested samples of successful good-will letters.

Welcome to newcomers

Dear Neighbor:

We're glad you chose Dallas for your new home and sincerely hope you'll enjoy living here.

There will be so many interesting things to do while establishing your home—new places to go, new friends to make. As the oldest retail store in Dallas, we are anxious to greet you and make you welcome in any of the three Kahn stores most conveniently located for you.

For over 82 years, the discriminating residents of Dallas have relied on E. M. Kahn's to bring them a wide choice of fine merchandise at sensible prices. Just take a look at the famous names shown at the right . . . names you've come to know because they represent QUALITY. You'll find a full stock men's wear at all three stores and everything for men, women, and boys at the Main Store and at our beautiful new Wynnewood-Oak Cliff Store.

Come in, neighbor, browse around and say hello to our friendly, courteous salespeople, who are eager to serve you.

To make your shopping even more enjoyable, we offer you —as one of a selected group of our new neighbors—the convenience of a Kahn's Charge Account.

As a Kahn's Charge Customer, you will receive notices of sales and special events before they are advertised in the newspapers. Whether you make your selections at the store or order by mail or phone, you simply say "Charge It."

Of course, your Kahn's Charga-Plate will allow you to charge at all three of our stores. If you would like to have this charge privilege extended to other members of your family, just indicate it on the reply form. Right now, while you're thinking about it, pull out the handy, post-free form enclosed above and mail it back to us. Your Kahn's Charga-Plate will be sent to you promptly.

Cordially yours,

WELCOME! We're mighty happy to have you with us!

As a special "guest" of the Around the World Program, we know you are going to enjoy this first "Magic Carpet Tour" of a foreign land—as well as this beautiful, large-size wall map.

This "introductory" gift will start you and your family on a thrilling new adventure.

Parker's Welcome You!

We feel sure you will enjoy your residence in the Quad-Cities. You are cordially invited to pay us a visit to become familiar with Davenport's Fine Store, where only merchandise of perfect quality from this country's finest manufacturers is featured.

We have for your convenience, two types of accounts, a Thirty Day Account for your regular daily needs and a Budget Account for those larger purchases.

Please fill in and return the enclosed application in our postage-free envelope, to arrange for a Parker's Charge Account.

It is our hope that this message will convey to you something of the friendliness that is traditional at Parker's.

It will be a pleasure to serve you.

Cordially yours,

Invitation to open an account

Dear Mrs. Crosby:

Yours—and just in time for Christmas, too. That's what makes our brand-new "C.A.B." so EXTRA welcome!

Yes, Kahn's smart, modern "Continuous Budget Account," which gives you six months to pay with no down payment, is yours, all yours, in every nook and corner of these three thrilling gift stores of ours—yours the moment you make your request.

Then rush in to see the biggest, most beautiful, most varied, most inspirational holiday collection we've ever assembled for the happy men, women, and boys of this community. In fact, to give you some idea in advance of our 1967 treasures, we've already mailed you a list of nearly one hundred of our choicest Christmas suggestions—in a size you can readily slip into your pocket or purse for handy reference.

So be with us soon—often—early! The staff will do everything possible to aid you. And remember, your Kahn Charga-Plate with our well known Divided Payment Plan or our new "C.B.A." is your key to pleasant, accurate service. In brief, we're yours for a most joyful Christmas!

Cordially, as always

Christmas
1968
P.S. Our always-welcome gift bonds are here to help solve your gift-giving problems.

Looking through our records the other day, we notice that many of your neighbors are enjoying the convenience of a Dey's Continuous Credit Account. And because we are anxious to help make your shopping just as pleasant and easy . . .

> We would like to open a
> D. C. C. Account
> in your name.

Thanks for opening an account

Thank you for opening a charge account with us. In doing so, you have placed us under the present obligation of seeing that your complete satisfaction with every purchase merits your continued good will.

Our showing of men's clothing is comprehensive and includes the best creative work of America's foremost designers.

Reputable brand names that guarantee your satisfatcion include Society Brand, Varsity Town, Surretwill, and Fashion Guild clothes, as exclusives in Minneapolis. Other reputable brands such as Nunn-Bush shoes, Interwoven socks, Wilson Brothers haberdashery, Mallory hats, and McGregor sportswear, will also be found here. We are very eager to have you get better acquainted with our store, our stock, and our personnel. You may be sure we will try to serve you intelligently and well at every opportunity. Won't you make it a point to come in frequently?

> Cordially yours,

Thanks for prompt payment

In the daily course of work my attention is directed to many accounts, but seldom to those in good standing. I decided, therefore, to devote some of my time to customers such as you.

Speaking personally as well as for Parker's, I appreciate your consistent promptness in paying your account. You make my work easier and more enjoyable. For that reason I want to sincerely thank you.

If at any time some problem arises in connection with your shopping in our store, please do not hesitate to call on me. I shall be most happy to see that everything possible is done to make your associations at Parker's pleasant and agreeable.

> Cordially yours,

Usual "Thank You"
letter omitted...

> at the suggestion
> of the Society for
> the Suppression of
> long "thank you"
> letters!
>
> Sincerely,
>
> *Irving Mack*
> Irving Mack

P.S. - They tell me people don't read
lengthy letters anyway ... and the
chances are, you don't need to be
reminded that we appreciate this order.

Thanks for any occasion

I've been wished a Merry Christmas, a Happy New Year, a Happy Birthday, and what have you . . . But this morning one of my customers wished me a "Happy Spring Season."

It's a good thought . . . so I'm stealing his idea by passing it along to you, and wishing you a "Happy Spring Season." But I'm going to carry it a bit farther, and wish you not only a "Happy Spring Season" but good Spring business, and a pleasant Summer Season as well.

With all of my well-wishing, I almost overlooked thanking you for your trailer order, which has already been shipped. So, once again . . . please consider yourself heartily thanked!

Welcome to a new customer

STOP ME IF YOU'VE
HEARD THIS STORY!

They tell of a young chap who walked into a telephone booth and called a certain number, and if I recall right, this is the way the conversation went:

Is this Mrs. Smith?

Yes.

I understand you had an ad in the paper yesterday for a chauffeur. Is the job filled yet?

Yes.

Is your new chauffeur satisfactory?

Yes.

Thank you. Good-by.

The drugstore clerk, who was rather curious, asked the chap if he was applying for the job. "No," he answered, "I have the job, and I'm just checking up to find out if I'm satisfactory."

That's exactly the reason we are writing you today—because we want to know whether the trailer we sent you recently was satisfactory.

We of Filmack are not content just to sell you a trailer, collect our money, and forget all about it. So if anything about the trailer wasn't just exactly to your liking, we are right here ready to make good.

Sincerely,

P.S.—And don't forget, we are eagerly looking forward to serving you again—and here's hoping it will be real soon.

"Our photographer took a picture of my desk!"

Yes, Mr. Mack is away on a well-deserved vacation.
Our office comic sent him the card that you see
illustrated above...but don't believe it...it isn't true!

All of his correspondence is being answered daily, with
the exception, of course, of a few letters that only he
can answer...and all the young Macks are following thru
seeing to it that all orders are filled promptly.

Just because the boss isn't here to thank you, doesn't
mean we aren't appreciative of your business...so thanks
for your recent order which is appreciated by all of us
at Filmack, including

Vi Dane

Vi Dane
Mr. Mack's Gal Friday

P.S. - Oh yes...I forgot to mention that your trailer
was shipped several days ago!

ONE OF THE REAL JOYS OF YULETIDE IS THE OPPORTUNITY TO PUT ASIDE THE ROUTINE AND CUSTOMS OF EVERY DAY BUSINESS AND IN REAL SINCERITY WISH OUR FRIENDS OF GASNER'S RESTAURANT A VERY MERRY CHRISTMAS AND A HAPPY NEW YEAR.

DURING THIS SEASON OF THE YEAR IT IS APPROPRIATE TO EXTEND OUR THANKS FOR YOUR GENEROUS PATRONAGE. WE BOAST NOT OF THE CUSTOMERS WHO COME IN BUT ESPECIALLY YOU FINE FOLKS WHO COME BACK ... AGAIN OUR SINCERE THANKS.

FOR YOUR INFORMATION IF YOU ARE PLANNING A CHRISTMAS PARTY OR THEY ARE MAKING PLANS FOR A GATHER-ING FROM YOUR OFFICES, PLEASE GIVE GASNER'S RESTAURANT YOUR SERIOUS CONSIDERATION. WE CAN HANDLE PARTIES OF 10 TO 200! HOWEVER, TIME IS FLYING AND WOULD SUGGEST AN IMMEDIATE PHONE CALL FOR RESERVATIONS.

GASNER'S RESTAURANT
75 DUANE STREET
SEotor 2-0879

Dear Miss Freeman:

Although I should like very much to do so, it is impossible for me to shake hands with every one of the thousands of New Yorker guests and tell them personally how much I appreciate their patronage.

But I do want you to know that we are glad you visited us. I hope you were comfortable and that you found our service so satisfactory that we may know you as a "regular New Yorker."

Since we are eager to plan our services to the guest's liking, I should appreciate any suggestions you care to submit on the enclosed form. Please tell me about any ideas that would make this hotel a more enjoyable home for you on your next visit. You may be sure they will receive our earnest attention. An envelope that requires no postage is enclosed for your convenience.

On your next visit to New York, please give us another opportunity to serve you.

Cordially yours,

Dear Mr. Saunders:

Even though I did say it the other day here in the store when you made your purchase, I want to say it once again . . .

"Thank you!"

I want you to know that I sincerely appreciate your patronage. And remember . . . now that the sale has been made, Maurice Weiner just *begins* to serve you.

I won't feel that the sale is "closed" until you receive full wearing service and lasting satisfaction from your purchase . . . until you honestly feel that you have received full value for every dollar spent!

It is my earnest hope that our business relations may long continue.

Very sincerely yours,

Offering additional services

Dear Mr. Harvey:

Many an auto dealer considers that his service department, like taxes, is a necessary evil. He likes to forget about the sale almost as soon as it is made.

Frankly, we don't feel that way about it and never did. We feel it's a vital part of our job to help you keep your car running smoothly . . . safely . . . economically.

That can be done by regular attention, by skillful servicing, by checking trouble before it starts. That's why we urge you to let only factory-trained men service your car regularly.

It's to your advantage . . . they know your automobile as they know their ABC's!

Cordially yours,

Dear Mr. Noble:

"Those boys are O.K." —That's what we like to hear you say about us.

If you come in and we do a lot of things for you and you don't spend a dime, we want you to know we're almost as pleased as if you shot the works.

We don't say "just as pleased"—that wouldn't be quite true.

It's human nature to want to make a sale—but we shall be glad to see you, even though all you need is some helpful service that won't cost you a penny.

We look on our business as a long-pull proposition. If we treat people right they'll treat us right and we'll do business with them when they're ready.

If you'll make it a habit to drop in on us whenever your car needs attention—even if it's only water for the battery, air for the tires—we'll appreciate it and try to show you we're more in-interested in you as a business friend than in what you spend.

Sincerely yours,

HAPPY BIRTHDAY TO YOU!

HAPPY BIRTHDAY TO YOU!

Well, maybe it isn't your birthday, Mr. Cram . . . but have you forgotten? . . . it's your car's birthday!

Yes, just one year ago we delivered that smart, sparkling new automobile to you. We hope it's given you a year of driving enjoyment and comfort . . . and that it will continue to do so.

It seems fitting that today, on your car's first birthday, we should say "Thank you" once again for buying it from us. And because we are still just as much interested in your car's performance as we were the day you bought it—we have a birthday surprise for you!

If you will drive in within thirty days, we'll give your car a thorough factory-specified 20-point lubrication . . . FREE!

It won't cost you a cent. Just bring this letter along. We'll be looking forward to seeing you roll into our driveway soon.

Cordially yours,

Reminder of past service

TO THE ONE
INTERESTED IN
"FINISHING" WORK

SUBJECT: The Stock We Didn't Spoil

Gentlemen:

A customer of ours suggested that we send this letter to you. We had taken him through our plant and he had watched a die-cutting and finishing job in process.

Among other things, he was very much impressed with our minimum of spoilage. On the job in question, we had run more than 80,000 sheets with a total spoilage of just 26 sheets—and of these 26, we had salvaged portions of some of the sheets equal to about half of this tiny spoilage.

This is an everyday affair in our plant, but our customer was so impressed by the lengths to which we ordinarily go to minimize spoilage that he felt it was an item we might have overlooked in our sales story.

Sure, it costs a little more for us to be this careful, but time and time again we've proved that the few pennies per thousand that represent the additional cost of this careful handling don't amount to anywhere near the extra billing that you as a printer get out of jobs finished by BARRETT.

In other words—you can and do sell the portion of your job that would customarily be allowed as spoilage in finishing. This extra billing that you get on your job sometimes amounts to a worth-while portion of the total finishing cost! Just another of those "hidden values" that we sometimes forget to tell you about—but are there working for you all the time. Please bear this in mind the next time you have an order for die-cutting or finishing of any kind, and let us actually show you what we mean.

Yours very truly,

HAPPY BIRTHDAY!

to your BOSTONIANS . . .

OUR RECORDS SHOW THAT YOU LAST PURCHASED
BOSTONIANS HERE ON MAY 26, 1968.

We sincerely hope that these shoes have given the genuine
solid comfort and performance you'd expect from fine shoes like
Bostonians. So here are GREETINGS to your Bostonians, with
a fresh new pair of laces to dress them up for the occasion.

I'll bet that the way we delivered a recent shipment for you
caused little or no comment. There were no headaches, no long-
distance phone calls or telegrams.

It was delivered as it should be—QUICKLY, SAFELY, and
ON TIME.

Lifschultz Service lets you relax in the knowledge that your
merchandise will arrive *on schedule* in *good shape.*

Here is the service you can depend on with Lifschultz:

TO AND FROM CHICAGO—2nd MORNING DELIVERY
TO AND FROM MILWAUKEE—3rd MORNING DELIVERY

And you get this *EXPRESS SERVICE at freight rates!*

Everything about Lifschultz Service is designed to help you.
Over-all control covers your merchandise every minute—through
trained employees whose job it is to keep their eyes on your
merchandise even while in transit.

Just pull out the card at the top of this letter and mail it.
It's all addressed and needs no postage. It will bring you complete details on how Lifschultz Service can help YOU.

Cordially yours,

P. S. Ask us about our Special PACKAGE RATES on small shipments—considerably lower than truck, rail, or express!

Thanks for long standing customers

Dear John,

During the past 60 days I compiled an inventory of those on
whom I could depend during many years with the James Company.
Your name stood out on the list as one who not only liked to help
people, but who was imbued with real good will.

For timely assistance when our company needed it most I thank
you. For steadfast loyalty in time of difficulty as well as good times

you have my gratitude, for your efforts added greatly to the success of my associates and me on countless occasions.

I wish you many more years of pleasant and profitable associations with the Miran Company. I'm sure you'll apply the same keen business sense and tactful perseverance for which you are noted.

The best of everything.

Sincerely,

Thanks for customer interest

Dear Mr. Mager:

I want you to know that we are grateful for your interest in our recent program.

The constructive thought, time, and effort you gave to this problem is particularly commendable and is deeply appreciated.

You may be assured that if I can be of any assistance, I will make every effort to work with your organization.

Sincerely yours,

Dear Mr. Samson:

I was positively delighted with your note which came in yesterday's mail concerning our new project.

It is the encouragement of good people like yourself that makes the week's problems more bearable.

Please keep up your keen interest in our work. Indeed, I would be sad indeed if it were not for the periodic encouragement from good souls who make us feel we are not totally unheard.

Very sincerely,

Thanks to a vendor

Dear Mr. Jameson:

The invaluable service rendered by you and the staff of the Leader Company and your outstanding activities during the year can not be overestimated.

I want you to know how deeply appreciative I am for the cooperation and many courtesies we received, and how much they help us carry on our work.

In the New Year, I shall look forward to a continuance of our cordial relationship, and I want to extend to you my very best wishes for your every success.

Sincerely,

CUSTOMER'S CHARGE ACCOUNT REPORT SHEET
Attention of
ALDEN S. FIELDS, *Credit Manager*

LYTTON'S
235 South State Street, Chicago, Illinois
Stores in CHICAGO, EVANSTON, OAK PARK, GARY and JOLIET

O. K., Mr. Fields:
I'll gladly cooperate by answering your questions below.

1 We, at Lytton's, greatly value the friendship of our customers. For this reason, please tell us if all your relations with us have been completely satisfactory to you?
   ( ) Yes   ( ) No

Comments:

2. Although you have not used your charge account recently, we hope that you will do so again soon. Just check here to have your charge account kept ready for your use whenever you wish ( )

Your Name _____

Address _____

City and State _____

(Please mail in enclosed reply envelope. No stamp required.)

YOU'VE GOT ME WORRIED, MY FRIEND!

If you had a friend that
Suddenly stopped seeing you
For no apparent reason
You'd be worried
Too...wouldn't you?

You've got me stumped...
Once you were a good
Customer, but now we hardly
Hear from you...I wonder why...
Is there a reason?

You've got me wondering...
Honestly...we try to give
Good service...and make the
Kind of trailers that sell
Tickets at the BOX OFFICE...We
Try to do a good job...
But maybe we slipped up somewhere
With you.....did we?

It will certainly make me happy
If you'll give me...
The "low-down" and tell me
Why...you are no longer sending
Us your special trailer business...

Just write it on this letter...
Or if there is no special
Reason...just say that
And send it in...Will you?

I'd certainly appreciate...
Hearing from you again...The space on
The right is for your answer
So reach for a pencil...Now
...Won't you?

Irving Mack

M:rf

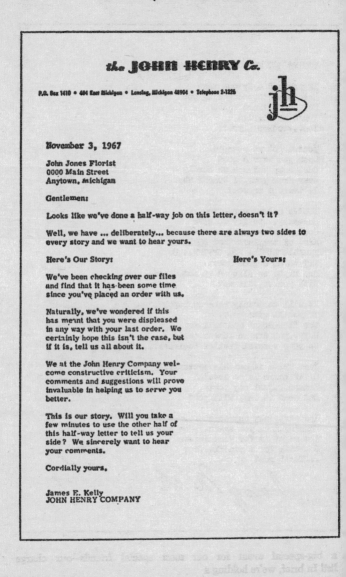

the **JOHN HENRY** *Co.*

P.O. Box 1410 • 404 East Michigan • Lansing, Michigan 48904 • Telephone 2-1226

November 3, 1967

John Jones Florist
0000 Main Street
Anytown, Michigan

Gentlemen:

Looks like we've done a half-way job on this letter, doesn't it?

Well, we have ... deliberately... because there are always two sides to
every story and we want to hear yours.

Here's Our Story: Here's Yours:

We've been checking over our files
and find that it has been some time
since you've placed an order with us.

Naturally, we've wondered if this
has meant that you were displeased
in any way with your last order. We
certainly hope this isn't the case, but
if it is, tell us all about it.

We at the John Henry Company welcome constructive criticism. Your
comments and suggestions will prove
invaluable in helping us to serve you
better.

This is our story. Will you take a
few minutes to use the other half of
this half-way letter to tell us your
side? We sincerely want to hear
your comments.

Cordially yours,

James E. Kelly
JOHN HENRY COMPANY

Dear Mr. Saunders:

For your continuous generous support and assistance and understanding in our many problems last year, we take our hat off to the Simplex Company.

During the year, the Martin Company has been given extremely courteous and cooperative service. Among other things you have made possible a continuous flow of production in very difficult times.

For this, as well as other past courtesies, we wish to thank you and the members of your staff, and we look forward to a continuance of this very cordial relationship.

With every good wish to you and your organization for 1969,

Sincerely,

Customer revival letters

KISSES AND ORDERS . . .

You don't see any connection?

Well—isn't it true that the harder they are to get the more we appreciate them?

No foolin'—when we fail to hear from you about once in every so often, we miss you.

Like most live showmen, you probably are continually trying out new stunts to pep up the box-office receipts.

There's nothing like a good special-announcement trailer to help you put these stunts over big.

As I figure it, another ought to be due right about now. How about it—am I right?

—So let's hear from you again real soon, because we're rarin' to be of service to you.

Sincerely,

Dear Mr. and Mrs. Walker:

What could have happened? Where have you been? Why haven't you called upon the handy E. M. Kahn Charga-Plate account you opened some time ago?

Won't you tell us why? Right away? On the card enclosed? We really want to know! And while you're at it, do let us know if you wish to have your Kahn Charga-Plate account kept open?

Meanwhile, we've something pretty nice to let you in on! Yes, a big-special event for our most special friends—our charge list! In brief, we're holding a

PRIVATE SALE BEGINNING TODAY FOR OUR
PREFERRED CHARGE ACCOUNT CUSTOMERS

as exciting as any in our history! just look at the features!

FOR MEN: Reductions up to 20% on groups of Society
Brand, Stein Bloch, and Roger Belmont suits,
sports coats, slacks; and on all Freeman Master
Fitter and Bootmaker Guild sport shoes and
brown and black calf oxfords. Groups of straw
hats reduced 25%. Also $5.00 white broadcloth
shirts at $3.95, or 3 for $11.00; $1.50 broad-
cloth boxer shorts at $1.19, or 6 for $7.00; $3.95
to $15.00 sport shirts at $3.15 to $11.85; and
similar reductions on pajamas, etc., etc.

FOR BOYS: Reductions up to 25% on groups of short-sleeve
shirts; summer pajamas from age 2; junior and
cadet slacks and summer suits.

FOR WOMEN: Discounts up to 40% on dresses in the season's
most popular cottons, sheers, prints, and shan-
tungs. Also new Stroock's Adeline Fleece coats
in charcoal, gold, red wine, star blue, and Paris
pink at the very special price of $69.95.

So hurry in! Be here early, long, often. Say "charge it" again
and again—to enjoy each and every savings opportunity! But
first—this moment—let's have that card! No postage needed—
just a few kind words! We'll be grateful, indeed, to hear from
you.

Cordially yours,

Dear Mr. Johnson:

You, as a Kings Highway Savings Bank depositor, are the
most important part of this bank. It is, therefore, a matter of
concern to us when we note that your account has not been used
for some time.

Up until now your visits here to use your account were the
only means we had of measuring whether you were pleased with
our services.

Now, however, with this easy-to-answer letter you can tell
us if you are taking advantage of the bank's many other facilities
... or anything else you might want to tell us!

Would you say we have lived up to the standards you expect?
Would you say we have served you well?

Perhaps you haven't used your account lately because you
have moved or because you have misplaced your passbook.
(We'll gladly issue a new one!) Whatever the reason, please tell

us on the confidential form in the window above. No postage stamp is needed, and you don't even have to sign your name. Your suggestions and criticisms are always welcome. Your reply is earnestly requested, and we will be grateful.

Sincerely,

Dear Mr. Saunders:

We've been proud to consider you one of our satisfied customers, and trust that you will still answer the roll-call with a Yes even though you have not used your charge account recently.

If you have simply not been in the market, this is merely to express our appreciation for your trade and to remind you that we are anxious to serve you again whenever you are ready.

If, however, you were in any way not pleased with our services or products, please let me know at once so that the matter can be adjusted promptly.

We hope you will be in to see us soon.

Yours very truly,

(Picture of a sad-eyed bloodhound at top of printed letter.)
WORRIED!

Worried as a pup that has lost his best friend.

It's been over 60 days since you last visited our Service Department, and we're wondering what's happened to you.

Your car may be running sweet and smooth . . . but 60 days without a lubrication is too long. Regular lubrication maintenance is the way to keep your car purring like a kitten. Regular service by the boys here in our Service Department is the best way to *Keep Your Car Up And Your Costs Down.*

Offering you a better service for your car is our business. You will find our service facilities complete. Anything you need from a squirt of oil to a complete motor overhaul you can get quickly and conveniently here . . . and we guarantee our service to you.

Drive in today for an expert lubrication by Al and Bob. These men are specialists. When they lubricate your car you will feel a real smooth-riding difference in your driving.

Cordially,

Old Friends are like
the "tick-tick-ticking"
of a clock

Filmack Corporation
1327 S. Wabash Ave.
Chicago, Illinois 60605

Dear Customer:

The remark, "I'd stand on my head to hear from you again" may be just a flip phrase to some people...

But if acrobatics will help me to find out why I haven't heard from you lately...here I am...UPSIDE DOWN!

Seriously, whether we write upside down or the regular way, all we're trying to say is...we miss hearing from you! I do hope there's nothing wrong, because we certainly would like to serve you again.

So let this be a little reminder that when you need any special trailers to send the order to

[signature]

For FILMACK CORPORATION

M:u4

You get so accustomed to hearing the ticking of a clock that you rarely notice it—until it stops.

Our business relations with our patrons are much the same as the ticking of the clock—we look upon them as friends and assume that everything is running along smoothly and to their complete satisfaction.

Of course, we strive to keep our service at a high peak of efficiency that will give satisfaction to our patrons.

But once in a while, like the stopping of a clock, we find that a customer and friend has ceased dealing with us.

Evidently the clock has stopped in your case, because we have not had the pleasure of serving you during the last thirty days.

And as we handle not only tires, but batteries and other merchandise that are purchased daily, we would like to see your name more constantly on our books.

Your good will means a great deal to us. Will you please stop in, drop me a line, or phone me an let me know why the clock has stopped? Are we at fault?

Sincerely,

Dear Scott Customer:

I like to give our old friends a preview of the season before the curtain goes up. Because of your past loyalty to Scott's, we consider you in this category.

Last fall we told everyone we could about the distressing situation in Kentucky Bluegrass. Elsewhere you will read that we consider Bluegrass to have the same relationship to the lawn world as steel to the national economy.

Since that warning in September, the situation has become worse. The severe drought cut so deeply into production that supplies of good seed are at an all-time low and the price is at a correspondingly high level.

But regardless of price, there is no substitute for Kentucky Bluegrass, nothing that duplicates its many assets. So when you eliminate it from top-quality lawn mixture, or lower the percentage, you make that mixture less desirable.

It is with some pride and also with some temerity that we announce that Scott's Lawn Seed is unchanged as to formula. It makes the finest lawn that can be produced. We are not willing to lower quality, yet we agree that the price is terrible. We can't help it, that's for sure—and even at the price we doubt if our supply, much under last year's consumption, will last through the spring.

We're starting the season with our heads high because we have something that few, if any, others can boast of—the best there is, regardless of scarcity. There's no compromise with quality at a price we are simply compelled to ask. That is the pre-season message. We wanted you to get it before the rest.

> Cordially yours,

Dear Mr. Cortland:

Are we right about your name, initials, address? Are we wrong—have we done anything that could keep you from us? Have you your Charga-Plate—or is it lost, misplaced? What do you think of _____, the neighborhood store we built for your delight and convenience?

Won't you tell us these things—this very moment—on the card enclosed. Help us put our records straight in good time for Easter '69! Help us make _____ the ideal suburban shopping center we constantly have in mind!

> Very sincerely,

Dear Mr. Holland:

You have been missed since we moved from our old location at Nicollet and 6th Street to our new quarters at 38 South 6th Street, four doors down toward Hennepin. We are in a new modern air-conditioned store, where every stitch of merchandise is brand-new.

We are bound and determined to have a quality store for people who buy quality merchandise. Men's suits, overcoats, and topcoats occupy our beautiful new second floor. The first floor accommodates our men's furnishings, shoes, and sportswear.

Losing old customers is too much like losing old friends. Although a great deal of effort is made to bring in new customers, nothing makes us so happy and pleased as to have an inactive account revived.

You will find in our new set-up such highly regarded names as Society Brand, Varsity Town, and Fashion Guild in clothing, Arrow and Wilson Brothers furnishings, Mallory hats, and Nunn-Bush shoes, together with Interwoven socks, McGregor sportswear, and numerous other standard brands.

A person is judged by the company he keeps; we like to be judged by the patrons we keep. To accomplish this we try to have the brands you like at a price you like and a congenial staff to serve you.

We do hope we will have opportunities to serve you now that the fall season is here.

Cordially yours,

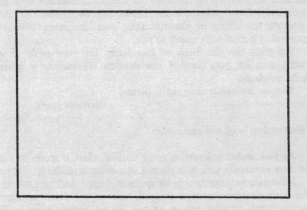

Above is a picture of the boss . . . he turned as white as this sheet when he found out you hadn't ordered any trailers from us for a long, long time.

You see, we've had the pleasure of making trailers for your theater many, many times (with satisfaction, we thought!), so he naturally worries when we don't hear from you.

What's kept you away from us for so long? Won't you take a second or two and scribble a line down below telling us what the trouble is?

Anxiously,

Write here . . .

Dear Mr. Fields:

Just a few lines to say "hello" across the miles and to tell you of our desire to be of further service to you.

This week we decided to check over our customer files. We discovered that during the past ninety days we have not had the pleasure of filling an order for you for our _____ Inhalant for bronchial asthma.

It may be that you have purchased directly through your own

druggist, which is what we prefer you to do, or perhaps you do not require the use of our product any longer.

In any event, we would be very happy to hear if you are using our ———— Inhalant and, if so, the name of the druggist from whom you purchase. If you will do us this little favor, we will include a FREE 7¾ cc bottle of our ———— Inhalant with your next order for a one-ounce size bottle. You may order this direct through this office or through your own drugstore, whichever procedure is most satisfactory to you.

You may use the back of this letter for your reply if you wish, and for your further convenience we enclose a postage paid envelope.

May we have your early reply, please!

Cordially yours,

Welcoming back old customers

As you probably know, a great deal of effort is made to bring in new customers and, to a degree, our effort is justified.

However, nothing makes us quite so happy and pleased as to have an inactive account revived, and so we want to express appreciation at your return to our list of active accounts. We hope that you will find every satisfaction with our merchandise and service.

Reputable brand names that guarantee your satisfaction include Society Brand, Varsity Town, and Clipper Craft clothes, Dalton and Barbiseo hats, Nunn-Bush shoes, as exclusives in Minneapolis. Other reputable brand such as Arrow shirts, Interwoven socks, Wilson Brothers haberdashery, McGregor sportswear, etc., will also be found here.

We hope that you will find it convenient to drop in frequently and take a look at what we have to offer. We will enjoy seeing you and give you everything we have in the way of service.

Cordially and sincerely yours,

Dear Mr. Saunders:

When Enoch Williams, that genial service manager of ours, walked into my office this morning wearing a wide grin, I knew it spelled g-o-o-d n-e-w-s.

And when he told me you had stopped in for service—well, I couldn't help smiling, too. Your friendship and patronage mean a lot to us, and it's a real pleasure to serve you again.

You can be confident that your car received the efficient care and attention you wanted it to have—and more! For you'll find our skilled mechanics, using the latest equipment, gave your car that "extra something" that keeps it running as smoothly as the day it rolled out of the factory.

Thanks again for driving in. We hope you will call upon us regularly to keep your car in A-1 shape.

Cordially yours,

Holiday letters

WISHING MR. CORTLAND A VERY MERRY CHRISTMAS AND 365 DAYS OF GOOD DRIVING

As we ride through life at the wheel of the car called Business, we pass many good friends and customers without expressing our true feeling of appreciation for their patronage.

Then that grand old man St. Nick takes the wheel at Christmas time and gives us the opportunity to say the things we should have said all year long.

Thanks a lot for your business. We appreciate it sincerely and wish you . . .

A very Merry Christmas,

Dear Mrs. Saunders:

"MERRY CHRISTMAS"

What a wealth of meaning there is in those two words! They stand for joy, good feeling, good fellowship. To me, they will never grow old or trite.

Some men have thought of fancier ways of saying these words. I've seen some tricky greetings and some beautifully written sentiments. But I believe that if I lived to be a hundred, I'd still stick to the sincere old-fashioned greeting . . . "Merry Christmas."

I wanted to extend that greeting to you in this letter, since I cannot greet you face to face with a warm handshake. I want you to know that we're all mighty grateful for the privilege we've had of serving you.

I hope the year coming to a close was a good year for you and that 1968 will be even better. You can count upon our 100 per cent cooperation to help make it so.

Cordially yours,

Dear Mr. Townley:

In a few hours clocks all over the world will strike out 1967 and ring in the New Year.

As we of Mullen & Bluett look back on this year just passed, we are grateful indeed for your friendly patronage and for the privilege of numbering you among our good customers.

So with warm personal regards I send to you from our entire organization a sincere wish for much new happiness, health, and prosperity throughout the coming New Year.

Most cordially yours,

Congratulations

Dear Mr. Cortland:

Because we take a personal interest in all the things that are important to Miami, we are taking this opportunity to congratulate you on your approaching marriage to Miss Margaret Saunders.

Many young married people come to Burdine's for advice and help in planning their new homes. In fact, they've been coming for two generations! We have several convenient plans that help them pay out of their income and keep money in the bank.

We hope you will come in and bring the future Mrs. Cortland. If you are interested in joining our family of "pet" customers, you have merely to say so.

Please feel that you are always welcome at Burdine's—whether you come to buy or to browse around the store and "just look."

Cordially yours,

Gentlemen:

We were just trying to think of a new way of saying congratulations and best wishes. Just something a little extra special . . . that's how we feel about the opening of your new shop.

Perhaps you know that we are sort of the "grandpappy" of the enclosure-card business. We have been in business thirty-four years, but there is nary a creak in our bones nor a falter in our stride.

No doubt you are teeming with new ideas and ambition. Well, the John Henry Company may be old in years, but in ideas it is just as young as ever. We have been the leader in our field for years, and we are still seeking higher levels.

Our line is an extensive one . . . enclosure cards, tags, stickers, blotters, stationery, and envelopes . . . everything to make your new shop complete and ready to serve any customers.

We will be happy to send you one of our #41 catalogues upon request along with a price list.

Again our congratulations and best wishes on your new venture.

May we hear from you soon?

Sincerely,

Apologies

Dear Mr. Adams:

An after-dinner speaker here recently remarked facetiously that the only trouble he could find with our hotel was the fact that it didn't have rubber walls, since some of his audience was obliged to hear him over the air.

Oddly enough, that remark contained more truth than humor. When I was informed that we were unable to give you a room promptly on your recent visit to the _____ I felt that I must write and apologize. While we naturally welcome the great amount of business that brought about this delay, we sincerely regret the inconvenience it must have caused you. I hope you will overlook it and appreciate our predicament.

And may I suggest that on your next visit you let me know in advance, so that I may have the pleasure of looking after your accommodations myself. Please write me personally; and if there is any special service or attention that would make your visit more enjoyable, by all means let me know and I shall be happy to arrange it.

Cordially at your service,

Helpful Starters

I certainly appreciate . . .

Thank you for . . .

Your very nice gesture . . .

It was good of you, Mr. Smith . . .

We were indeed happy (proud) (glad) . . .

We were sincerely (honestly) (very) sorry to hear about your loss (fire) (misfortune).

Congratulations on the fine job you did . . .

As soon as I saw this week's sales report, I wanted to say congratulations on the fine increase you made . . .

We want to make sure that everything moves along to your satisfaction.

We'd like to do something to help you build bigger profits.

We ought to know each other better, and I think this will be a step in the right direction.

It will always be our aim to . . .

It make us feel glad to . . .

CHAPTER 23

Credit Letters

Since most modern business is done on a credit basis, credit letters play an important role in business-letter writing. Credit correspondence includes the following types of letters: applications for credit, requests for credit information, responses to credit-information requests, letters granting credit, and letters denying credit.

Credit is granted only after the necessary information has been received and satisfactory arrangements have been made with the debtor. The problems presented by such credit correspondence fall into four groups: 1. Obtaining accurate and adequate credit information. 2. Giving credit information that is truthful and accurate, but does not alienate a present customer. 3. Refusing credit tactfully without alienating a customer. 4. Granting credit so that it will be accepted and used.

Credit information is given and accepted on a confidential basis, but no letter should be written that cannot be justified.

In applying for credit, a brief letter is sent before the first order or with the initial order.

Applying for credit

Gentlemen:

We plan to place several orders with your company in the next few months, and we would like to have an account opened on your books.

You will find us listed in the trade credit books and Dun and Bradstreet. If you require any additional information, please let us know.

Very truly yours,

Gentlemen:

For several months we have been purchasing merchandise from you on a C.O.D. basis. We would like to have a charge account opened at this time for our mutual convenience.

Please let us know what information and references you require, and your usual credit terms.

Very truly yours,

Asking for credit information

Unless you are rated by a recognized credit agency, the company from whom you solicit credit will usually respond by sending a form requesting specific information about the condition of your business and the names of companies with whom you do business. This letter takes the following form:

1. An expression of pleasure at the request for credit.
2. An explanation of why information is necessary.
3. A request for specific information: credit references, bank references, financial statements, or the filling out of a credit questionnaire.
4. An assurance that the information will be considered confidential.
5. Some good-will build-up.

Dear Mr. Saunders:

We are happy to welcome the Saunders Company as one of our credit customers. Your account has been opened, but we would like to have some information to complete our records.

Will you be good enough to fill out the enclosed form and furnish us with the names of three other firms with whom you do business?

We hope the opening of your account will be the beginning of a long and happy association with us.

Very sincerely yours,

Dear Mr. Jones:

Thank you for your order dated June 14th. It is being processed in accordance with your wishes.

Since this is your first order, we are enclosing a form application so that a line of credit can be opened for you. Please fill out the enclosed form and return it to us as soon as possible, so that there will be no delay in your shipment.

We are pleased to have the opportunity of adding your name to our list of accounts.

Very sincerely yours,

Gentlemen:

Thank you for your Order #5609 for 50,000 tags. We are glad to have it.

However, we find that the information available through regular trade channels is not complete enough to establish your company's credit. We realize that a thorough credit investigation would probably indicate that your company is in good shape financially, but investigations of that kind consume both time and money.

Since you want the tags as soon as possible, I thought you might like to send us a check for $100.00 to avoid the delay that would be caused by our making a credit investigation. Or, if more convenient, send $50.00 and we will ship them "Balance due—C.O.D."

We will enter your order as soon as we receive your check. If you prefer not to send a check, please give ten or twelve credit references and your latest financial statement, if you have one.

Yours truly,

Sending credit information

Gentlemen:

Thank you for your courtesy in shipping our order of June 14th. As you requested, we are returning your credit-information blank and a list of business references.

If you should require additional information, please call on me.

Yours very truly,

Gentlemen:

I am happy to send along your credit form and the list of three firms with whom we do business, as you requested.

Please be good enough to complete your credit check as quickly as possible, since we are awaiting shipment of our order. If credit cannot be granted within the next five days, we will accept this shipment C.O.D. to expedite delivery.

Very truly yours,

Making inquiries

The letter asking for information or a business favor should be tactful, short and to the point, clear and complete. If a number of questions are asked, it is best to number and list them, since this minimizes the chances of any points being overlooked.

If the information is to be considered confidential, explain the use you plan to make of it and give assurance that it will be kept confidential.

Letters asking for credit information from others are usually form letters and include:

1. An indication that you have been referred to them.
2. A request for information.
3. Assurance that it will be held in confidence.
4. An expression of appreciation.
5. A questionnaire that usually asks:

Length of time the company under question has been doing business with the company queried

Terms
Credit limit
Amount now due
Amount past due
Highest recent credit
Manner of payment
Payment experience

Dear Sir:

The Omicron Company of Janesville, Ohio, has given us your name as a credit reference. We shall appreciate any information you are able to offer in this connection. It will not be necessary to write us a letter; simply answer the questions listed on the reverse side of this inquiry and return it to us in the stamped envelope enclosed for your convenience.

You have our assurance that your reply will be held in strict confidence.

Very truly yours,

Dear Sir:

Mr. Thomas Chatterton has referred us to you as his employer. We shall appreciate your letting us have the benefit of your knowledge of this employee.

It will not be necessary to write us a letter; simply answer the questions listed below and return this letter to us in the stamped envelope enclosed for your convenience.

You have our assurance that your reply will be held in strict confidence.

Very truly yours,

Employed at present?_____How long employed_____

Position or capacity?_____

Average monthly income?_____

Are prospects for continued employment favorable?_____

If no longer with you, what were reasons for discontinuance?

_____

Character_____ Ability_____ Age_____

Reputation in community_____

Present address_____ Other remarks_____

Date_____ Signed_____

Gentlemen:

We have received an application for a line of credit from the Cortland Furniture Co., of Janesville, Ohio. They gave your company as a credit reference.

Will you be good enough to give us the following information:

Have your credit relations with this company been satisfactory in the past?

What is the extent to which credit has been granted by you?

What information do you have regarding their reputation?

Your cooperation will be very much appreciated, and of course, anything you tell us will be kept in strictest confidence.

Very truly yours,

Sample credit questionnaires:

Reputation_____

How long have you dealt with him?_____

Highest credit given on: Charge account_____

Highest credit given on: Installment credit_____

Amount owing at present: Now due_____

Amount owing at present: Past due_____

Prompt in meeting obligations?_____

Present address_____

Present remarks_____

Date_____ Signed_____

How long have you known?_____ Age_____

Married or single_____

Character_____ Reputation in community_____

Occupation_____ Name of employer_____

Is employment steady_____ Estimated monthly income $_____

Amount owing you: Now due $_____Past due $_____
Prompt in meeting obligations_____
Present address_____
Remarks_____
Date_____   Signed_____

Responding to a request for credit information

Gentlemen:

The Cortland Furniture Co., of Janesville, Ohio, has been on our books for seven years. Their record of payments has been entirely satisfactory during this period. Their custom is to discount bills within ten days. Their purchases average over $5,000 a month during the height of the season.

Mr. Thomas Cortland, president of the company, is highly regarded in this area, and we are happy to provide a reference for him.

Sincerely yours,

Gentlemen:

Although we have had some dealings with the A.B.D. Corporation, our relationship has not been sufficient to justify our vouching for them.

We have made four small shipments to this company during the past three years, and payments have been satisfactory. The firm has a good reputation in the trade, but we have no first-hand knowledge of their credit standing.

I regret that I cannot furnish you with more helpful information.

Very sincerely yours,

Gentlemen:

We regret that we cannot give you a satisfactory reference for the A.B.D. Corporation. During the three years we have been doing business with this company, our experience has not been satisfactory.

Our normal credit terms are 30 days net, but their account has been from 30 to 90 days in arrears during most of the time we have been doing business. Their present balance of $127.50 includes purchases made as long ago as four months.

This information is, of course, given to you in confidence in an effort to be helpful.

Very sincerely yours,

Granting credit

Letters granting credit should include:

1. An expression of pleasure at opening the account.
2. Explanation of credit procedures.
3. An offer of help or service.

Dear Mr. Noble:

It is a great pleasure to present the G_____ Credit Card you recently requested. We hope—and believe—it will immediately earn a place among your most important cards and that you'll carry it with you wherever you drive.

You'll find many advantages in making consistent use of your G_____ Credit Card. It provides a permanent record of your expenditures for gasoline and oil—and of gasoline taxes for deduction on your income-tax return. It eliminates the need for carrying large amounts of cash for buying gasoline and oil on trips. And in addition to automotive products and services, you can use your Credit Card for purchases of G_____ Aviation and Marine products. If you heat your home with oil, your card may be used to establish credit for deliveries of _____. We sincerely believe that regular use of your G_____ Credit Card is your assurance of getting the finest petroleum products obtainable.

The enclosed folder tells you many other facts of interest about your new Credit Card. We hope you'll take a moment to read it now, so that your G_____ Credit Card will serve you to the full extent for which it is intended.

> Very truly yours,

MORE CREDIT TO YOU . . . .

Your exceptionally fine credit record affords us the opportunity to extend you ADDITIONAL CREDIT—WITHOUT QUESTION —WITHOUT DELAY.

As a well-established Buffalo resident, you are familiar with Kleinhans and probably have had occasion to visit our store. Since we are anxious to make your Kleinhans shopping even more convenient and pleasant,

WE HAVE OPENED A
KLEINHANS CHARGE ACCOUNT
IN YOUR NAME.

As a Kleinhans Charge Customer, you will receive advance

notice of our sales and special offerings. Your Kleinhans Charge Account gives you the liberal privilege of 90 days to pay bills.

There is no charge for this extra convenience—no red tape of any kind. Simply say "Charge it" when you make your selections at Kleinhans, or when you order by mail or phone. It's as easy as that!

In addition, the Kleinhans Credit Card, which we will issue in your name, is a recognized credit reference throughout Western New York.

We'd like to make sure that we have your name and address entered correctly. Simply check the post-paid card enclosed above and drop it in the mail. Also check whether we should send your Kleinhans Charge Card or whether you'd prefer to pick it up yourself the next time you're in the store. Just ask for Mrs. Howard in the Charge Account office on the second floor.

Cordially yours,

Denying credit

Letters refusing credit should include:

1. An expression of pleasure at the request.
2. Suggestion that sales be made on a cash basis and an expression of regret at not being able to open a credit account.
3. A good-will and selling build-up.

Dear Customer:

Your confidence in us, as displayed through your application for a charge account, is appreciated.

We wanted to open a regular charge account for you, but we were unable to secure sufficient satisfactory information.

Since we are most anxious to have you as a customer, we suggest that you make use of our convenient merchandise coupon account.

With these coupon books you can buy anything in the entire store just as if you were purchasing with cash; and you pay for these books on easy monthly terms.

A card issued in your name is inserted at the top of this letter. Simply present it at our credit office on the fifth floor and all details concerning your coupon account will be explained to you promptly.

We look forward to the pleasure of serving you.

Yours very truly,

CHAPTER 24

Collection Letters

The object of collection letters is to get the money without losing the customer. They are usually written in a series, each successive letter stronger in tone than its predecessor, and sent out at intervals varying with the type of credit risk involved. A poor credit risk will be dealt with sooner and more frequently than a good credit risk. A poor risk may receive four letters over a two-month period, a good credit risk five or six letters over a six-month span.

In writing a collection letter, keep the debtor in mind. Visualize his situation, and remember that in most cases he is sensitive about his inability to pay and would like to pay his bills on time. Adopt the "you" attitude and avoid the negative, belligerent, approach. Don't bluff or beg for money. It is important to be firm, definite, insistent, and persistent. Be tactful, courteous, factual, and friendly even when forceful. Since collection letters occasionally entail legal problems, don't make unwarranted threats. Consult an attorney before threatening legal action. An open letter or postcard should never contain any message that might prove embarrassing or defamatory to the recipient.

A collection letter is made up of the following parts:

1. A statement of the amount involved. (A bill may be enclosed.)
2. Arguments for payment.
3. An appeal for payment or a demand for payment by a certain date.
4. A sales talk, if appropriate.

The most common arguments for payment are:

Routine: We have already asked twice for payment. The amount is too small to warrant all this expense and bother.

End of a period: We are closing our books for the fiscal year. We are being audited.

Fair play: What would you do in my place? We shipped to you promptly, isn't it only fair that you . . .

Cooperation: Credit is extended as a courtesy to our customers.

Pride: We would not wish to place you on our delinquent list.

Credit loss: We would not want to have to report you to the trade credit association.

Cut off supply: We will not be able to ship to you unless . . .

Legal action: We will be forced to turn your account over for collection unless your check is received.

After the first or second letter, each further letter in the series should specify a date by which payment is expected. The first collection letter usually follows an invoice and several statements that may have reminders typed on them or a sticker with a reminder message. It is usually a "calling to your attention" letter. Thereafter, the letters become more insistent. Here is a typical series of appeals:

1. Your account is past due.
2. Account was overlooked.
3. May we ask if there is something wrong?
4. Appeal to fair play.
5. Appeal for maintenance of good credit.
6. Threat of posting with credit agencies.
7. Threat of legal action.
8. Resort to legal action.
9. Lawyer's letter threatening suit.
10. Serving of summons.

Telegrams are effective to indicate the urgency of making payment by a certain date.

Here are some sample collection letters:

Just a Little Reminder . . .
that the following bill (s) has been overlooked for payment:

Date of Invoice	Invoice #	Amount

Enclosed is a duplicate invoice for each bill to assist you in checking your records. If I can be of further service, just say the word.

Thank you for your cooperation.

Cordially,

Just a Reminder

A past due amount is included in the balance on the enclosed statement.

Your prompt remittance will be appreciated.

Thanks.

If you have already mailed your check please disregard this notice.

Please Note that your account, as shown on the attached statement, is past due.

May we have your remittance by return mail? . . . . *Thanks!*

PAYMENT of your account is solicited in the same courteous manner as your patronage. Both are necessary to our success. We are glad that you have availed yourself of the convenience of a G—— charge account. All we ask in return is your cooperation. Won't you please forward payment * * * **PROMPTLY** * * *

Thank You

Gentlemen:

We believe that the invoice covered by the enclosed statement for $_____ must have escaped your attention.

Since the item is one for which payment is due, we would appreciate it very much if you would send us your check. Please let us know if payment is being withheld for some special reason.

Thank you for your attention to this matter.

Very truly yours,

Gentlemen:

Three of the nicest words in the English language are "Please" and "Thank you." It would "please" us very much if you would "please" pin your check for $_____ to this letter and return it in the attached self-addressed envelope. It is now past our 30-day terms.

If you have done so already, "please" disregard this letter. In either case, it will be a pleasure to say "thank you."

Cordially,

Dear Mr. Johnson:

There are many pleasures in serving our good customers, but there are some problems, too.

It is always a problem to know whether a customer has forgotten to send a check and would like to be reminded, or if payment is being temporarily delayed for some reason not known to us.

If we have not received your check for the amount listed because you have overlooked it, we are sure you would like us to call it to your attention so that you might send us your check now.

Since part of the account is several weeks past due, your remittance at this time will be very much appreciated.

Sincerely yours,

Please!
You know . . .

—how hard it is to ask for money
—and say just enough to get it
—without offending.

Your check for the balance below may be on its way. If not, we know you will want to send it now.

In either case—thank you.

Sincerely,

Balance due $_____

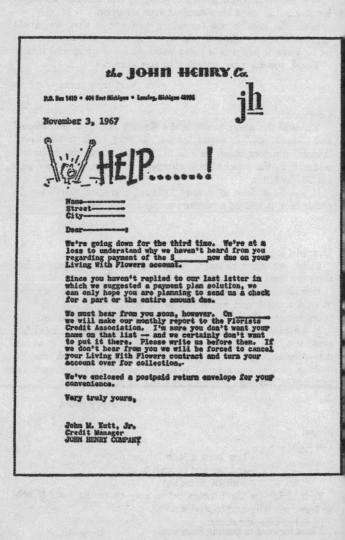

the **JOHN HENRY** Co.

P.O. Box 1419 • 404 East Michigan • Lansing, Michigan 48905

November 3, 1967

HELP......!

Name----------
Street----------
City----------

Dear----------:

We're going down for the third time. We're at a
loss to understand why we haven't heard from you
regarding payment of the $_____ now due on your
Living With Flowers account.

Since you haven't replied to our last letter in
which we suggested a payment plan solution, we
can only hope you are planning to send us a check
for a part or the entire amount due.

We must hear from you soon, however. On _____
we will make our monthly report to the Florists
Credit Association. I'm sure you don't want your
name on that list -- and we certainly don't want
to put it there. Please write us before then. If
we don't hear from you we will be forced to cancel
your Living With Flowers contract and turn your
account over for collection.

We've enclosed a postpaid return envelope for your
convenience.

Very truly yours,

John M. Kutt, Jr.
Credit Manager
JOHN HENRY COMPANY

Dear Mr. Johnson:

All of us overlook a bill now and then . . . it arrives during a busy day and gets misplaced or put aside during the rush.

Because we're sure you've "just forgotten," we know you won't mind this friendly reminder of the $_____ due on your account.

It isn't a very old or large account, so why not send us your check today? We've enclosed a postage-paid return envelope for your convenience.

If your check is already on the way to us, may we suggest you toss this letter into the nearest wastebasket, use our return envelope for some list additions (which we hope you're contemplating) . . . and accept our sincere apologies for an unnecessary reminder.

Cordially,

Dear Mr. Johnson:

I know from your credit rating that you are not neglecting your account with Cortland because of lack of funds.

What's more probable is that you just haven't realized that this item is now several months past due.

I am sure you are as anxious as we are to get this off our books. A statement of your account is enclosed. May I count on having your check now? I'm very anxious to scratch your name off this "past due account" list of subscribers.

Thank you.

Very sincerely yours,

Refusing shipment

I wish I didn't have to write this letter.

But I am afraid I must.

We just can't ship the order we received from you this week because your account has fallen behind the credit terms we set up for you in our original agreement.

A check from you in the amount of _____ will solve the problem. It will make me happier because it will permit me to make the sale. And we will fill your order on double rush.

I look forward to hearing from you.

Very sincerely,

Acknowledging past payment

It was good to see your check for _____ in this morning's mail. This brings your account almost up-to-date.

A small balance, _____, remains on your account. Please try to get this cleaned up before the end of the month.

Thank you.

When a difficult account is paid up

The check received today brings your account up-to-date.

We do appreciate the effort you have made to pay the past-due balance and want to assure you that your credit is now open for the full amount of $15,000.

If, in the course of our writing to you, we have sometimes seemed severe or demanding, I hope you will understand that we, too, are under pressure to keep collections on a current basis, if we are to keep credit costs down and to maintain our low price schedule.

Rest assured that we consider you a favored customer with whom we hope to continue a long and happy business relationship.

Very sincerely,

As you can understand, most of the letters I write are concerned with collecting money. Sometimes they are not the pleasantest reading in the morning mail.

That is why it is a particular pleasure to write a letter saying "Thank you" for bringing your account to a current basis. We appreciate your sending the recent check that removes you from our collection system and sincerely hope to have you as one of our "regular customers" in the years ahead.

Dear Mr. Doe:

May I offer a helping hand?

Because I've had no reply to my letter of May 20th regarding payment of your account, I have begun to wonder if perhaps some temporary difficulty has delayed your check. If such is the case, will you take a minute to consider a proposal that I hope will offer you a practical solution to the payment of the $_____ due on your account.

We propose: that, upon receipt of your approval, we divide the amount due at this time into monthly, semi-monthly, or

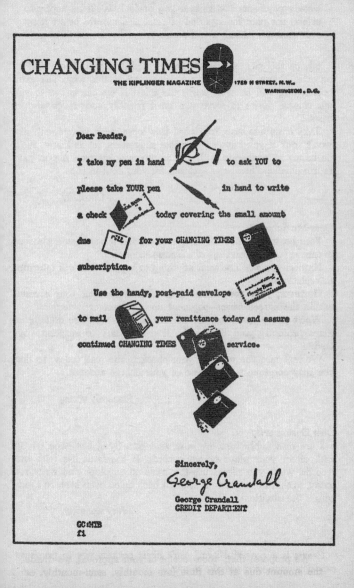

CHANGING TIMES

THE KIPLINGER MAGAZINE   1729 N STREET, N.W.,
WASHINGTON, D.C.

Dear Reader,

I take my pen in hand   to ask YOU to

please take YOUR pen   in hand to write

a check   today covering the small amount

due   for your CHANGING TIMES

subscription.

    Use the handy, post-paid envelope

to mail   your remittance today and assure

continued CHANGING TIMES   service.

                    Sincerely,

                    George Crandall

                    George Crandall
                    CREDIT DEPARTMENT

GC:MB
fl

weekly payments (whichever you prefer). We'll be happy to extend the plan for a period of _____ months or set it up over a shorter period, if you desire.

I hope this suggestion will prove helpful to you. There will be no extra charge for handling your account in this way. The extra bookkeeping will be well worth the effort if we can prove to you our sincere desire to serve you on a friendly and understanding basis.

Take a minute now to return this letter with your comments, won't you? If you have an alternate suggestion, let us know. We'll be happy to cooperate with you in any way we can. A post-paid return envelope has been enclosed for your convenience.

Cordially,

Dear Mr. Johnson:

Your business is sincerely appreciated, and it has been a pleasure to extend you the privilege of a charge account.

Naturally, we do not want anything to happen that will interrupt this relationship.

However, your cooperation is needed in keeping your account within the agreed terms—payment upon receipt of statement.

Won't you please send us your check covering these delinquent items promptly, and thus make it unnecessary to suspend your credit.

We feel sure you will put your check in the mail today, so that you may continue to enjoy use of your charge account.

Sincerely yours,

Dear Customer:

I am reasonably sure, by now, that something has gone wrong with either your plans or our records. If the fault lies with our records, won't you please use the enclosed envelope and write me today, so that I can get your account back on an even keel. In short, here is the situation:

Very sincerely,

Dear Mr. Wheeler:

Credit is a powerful word, isn't it? It permits you to purchase products upon your promise to pay.

"Let George do it"

THERE'S always the fellow who says— *"Let George do it."* Every time they count on him, he isn't there. He ducks the draft, dodges taxes, *Never pays a bill* 'til the sheriff comes. He never gets much out of life.

Please don't be a *"Let Goerge do it"* Guy.

Pitch in and send along *your check* today.

DUN

is an ugly word,
meaning wasted bills and letters and work.

DONE

is a beautiful word,
meaning things we've accomplished.

DUES

are the cause of the one, and the means
to the other.

PLEASE send in your *DUES*, and let it be *DONE*,
instead of *DUN*.

This Bill ...

costs as much as a
whole glass of milk
we could give to an
undernourished
youngster.

Help us avoid such
waste by *paying
your dues now!*

You have no doubt found your _____ credit card a worthwhile convenience, and we have been glad to extend you this courtesy. However, in order to do so it is necessary that we have immediate payment, because a large percentage of the amount owed represents state and federal taxes, which we must pay each month, regardless of when we receive payment.

We want to continue serving you without interruption, but we must temporarily suspend credit unless we receive your remittance promptly. Please send us your check today and keep your credit good.

Sincerely yours,

Dear Sir:

Any person who keeps his account with a company paid up feels a certain satisfaction. He feels that he is a privileged person who is always welcome. But if he lets his account lag, there is a temptation to go elsewhere for his needs.

We want your business, and we want you to feel that you are the privileged customer you really are. You will receive continued good service in exchange for prompt payment.

Just pin a check to this letter and mail it now.

Sincerely yours,

P.S. If you cannot remit at once, we must reluctantly ask that you pay cash for current purchases until your account is in proper shape.

Dear Mr. Doe:

We want a check of some kind!

Either a real check or a pencil check alongside one of the items listed below. We would like to know just where we stand. So please check up on your bankbook today and drop a real check into the mails tomorrow. Or check one of the items below and drop this letter into the nearest mailbox tonight—using the enclosed stamped envelope:

( ) I am sending check herewith.
( ) Here is part of your bill to show you that my heart is in the right place.
( ) I'll try to pay each month from now on in the same amount as the enclosed check.
( ) I think I can pay this on the _____, so I am enclosing a postdated check.
( ) Here is all of it—SHUT UP!

Very truly yours,

October 23, 1968

Dear ———:

Roses are red,

Violets are blue,

Send us a check

And we'll love you.

Unless your check is already en route, we will expect one by return mail. Our records show your September balance — due October 20 — remains unpaid.

Life is much sweeter when bills are paid when due. As you know, we permit the deduction from the balance as shown on your current statement of the last 60 days billing plus any returns in transit for which you have shipping receipts.

Sincerely,

Maurice

Maurice W. Salomon
Vice President
Circulation Director

Account
Dealer
Date Due
Amount Due

As a matter of convenience to you, we notified you several days ago that the first installment on your account fell due on the above date. Unfortunately your remittance has not been received.

It is possible that you may be having some difficulties in arranging payment in accordance with your agreement, but surely you will appreciate the importance of letting us know the reason for the delay. We are anxious to help you complete your purchase, but the responsibility for making the payments rests entirely with you. If personal contact by our representative is required, we must make a collection charge to partly offset this extra expense.

We know from experience that when one falls behind in payment, it is doubly difficult to catch up. Won't you please make arrangements for immediate payment of the installment which is now past due, and assure us that future installments will be met promptly as agreed?

Very truly yours,

Dear Customer:

You may always depend upon our fullest cooperation. May we have yours also?

Because of the condition of your account, it is now necessary that you send your remittance in full or lay aside your credit card and make current purchases for cash.

Why not attend to this account now, while you have this letter before you? The amount needed to bring your account up-to-date is shown above.

Sincerely yours,

Dear Sir:

Enclosed you will find our August statement of your account, showing a long-past-due balance of $46.80. For your convenience, we are enclosing an itemized tape with a copy of each open invoice.

In spite of our regular monthly reminders, you have failed to pay these charges or to offer any explanation for your nonpayment. At this time we request that you send us your check in full to clear this past-due balance. If there is any reason for your nonpayment, kindly let us know without further delay.

Please give this matter your immediate attention and direct your reply to the attention of the undersigned.

Very truly yours,

Dear Sir:

We are concerned that you have not answered our recent letter about your account, because we value your patronage highly and want to number you as one of our good credit customers.

The nature of our products is such that it does not permit us to extend credit very far in excess of our regular terms of payment upon receipt of statement. For this reason it is important that you mail us your check today in the enclosed business reply envelope.

If you are not in a position now to send us a remittance in full, then we must reluctantly request that you return our credit card, pay as much as you can, and tell us when the balance may be expected.

Sincerely yours,

Dear Customer:

This is your last opportunity to place your account in a satisfactory condition.

Since we have been considerate of you, we feel sure that you will want to do the fair thing and arrange immediate payment. We are anxious to spare you any unpleasantness that might arise from further delay in settlement, but the decision rests entirely with you.

Surely you will send at least a partial payment at once and avoid other measures to collect.

Sincerely yours,

Gentlemen:

Registered mail is being used for this letter because something has gone wrong; somehow you must have missed our previous communications.

Now I learn that your name is to be marked "uncollected" on our credit records. You ordered a subscription some months ago but it was never paid, and is about to be cancelled for non-payment with the next issue.

Of course your name does not belong on any list of uncollected accounts—but auditors will be auditors. And they point out that our various letters have already cost us almost the amount of the bill.

Very truly yours,

Dear Mr. Smith:

Fifteen days have passed since payment of $_____ was due on your account.

If the payment plan we mutually agreed upon fails to solve the problem of collecting this account, we must decide upon a firmer step—turning the full amount due over to the Blank Credit Association for collection. We don't want to do this. I'm sure you don't want us to do it. Why not keep your payment plan currently up to date by sending us a check for $_____ by return mail and eliminating the necessity of having someone call on you personally for collection of the full amount due?

We will take no steps before _____ 19____. Please send us your check before that time and preserve your credit rating. You'll be glad you did.

Very truly yours,

Dear Sir:

Because of the unsatisfactory condition of your account, as indicated above, it has become necessary to revoke the credit privilege heretofore granted to you.

You are requested to immediately return the credit card, and you are hereby notified that the further use of this card for the purpose of securing _____ products on credit will be without authority of the company.

Yours very truly,

Dear Sir:

Thank you for returning your credit card.

Would you now give your delinquent balance shown above serious consideration?

If your financial condition has not improved sufficiently to allow payment in full, please give us another substantial payment by _____.

Sincerely yours,

Dear Mr. Johnson:

I am writing you this personal letter as one friend to another in a final effort to have you amicably adjust your account.

The attached statement of your account was just handed me with the following brief memorandum:

"Account seriously past due. Have written several letters with no response. Suggest placing with attorneys immediately."

When your account was opened, our credit investigation indicated first, through ability and willingness to pay, you had established yourself as a good credit risk. This is an enviable reputation for a person in any walk of life—one of which he may rightfully be proud.

Judging by the confidence expressed by your references, I believe that you are as deserving of credit today as you were when the account was opened. I also believe that you are sincerely concerned about the serious effect your present delay is having upon your good record.

Should you make it necessary for us to place your account with our attorneys for collection, *your* credit rating will suffer. Once your credit is gone, you will find it difficult to regain, and you will have nobody to blame but yourself. Every man makes his own credit reputation.

If you cannot pay in full immediately, then let us have as much as you can spare and a series of postdated checks, or a definite promise for the balance. If you cannot pay anything right now, please write me a full explanation on the back of this letter and indicate when you will be able to pay. You can be sure we will meet you more than halfway on any reasonable proposal. It is imperative, however, that your remittance or reply reach me *by return mail*. You can use the attached self-addressed envelope, which is marked for my personal attention.

I want to save you the added expense of attorney action. Just *do your part*, and I will be most willing to do mine.

Sincerely,

Dear Mr. Johnson:

It is always with the greatest reluctance that we resort to legal action in procuring settlement of an unpaid account.

However, the circumstances surrounding your indebtedness appear to leave us no further choice. The claim will be referred to our attorneys if a satisfactory settlement has not been arranged within seven days.

It is now up to you.

Sincerely yours,

Dear Mr. Johnson:

Only a wire will stop it now.

We have sent many friendly requests for payment, but for some reason you have not cooperated.

Today we placed your account for the amount shown above in

the hands of our attorneys. The only way you can stop the sure, swift, and costly proceedings of legal action is to wire us *right now*.

Sincerely yours,

When payment is received

Dear Mr. Roe:

Thank you very much for your recent remittance. It has enabled us to reinstate your account.

Credit has been reinstated with the understanding that future charges will be paid according to terms calling for settlement in full upon receipt of statement. These terms were outlined on your original application and are shown on the reverse side of your credit card.

Your cooperation will be appreciated and will help us maintain your account properly.

Cordially yours,

Dear Sir:

Your business and your prompt payments on your credit-card account are very much appreciated.

The last several payments have been in round figures, which haven't permitted balancing your account through any particular period. It has been our experience that confusion is likely to occur when this isn't done because of the relative frequency of purchases and similarity of amounts in a credit-card account.

We are anxious, of course, to avoid anything that might give rise to a misunderstanding with our customers at some future time. Therefore, we hope you will find it convenient to remit, at least every second or third month, in an amount that will balance through some particular monthly statement.

Will you make your next check for the exact amount of the statement? Thank you.

Sincerely yours,

Dear Mr. Noble:

Thanks for your payment of $_____, which leaves a balance of $_____.

Undoubtedly something has prevented your payment in full, but we feel sure you will send an additional remittance next week to bring the account in line. If this is impossible, please jot a note at the bottom of this letter explaining your circumstances and notifying us when we may expect another check.

Your cooperation will be appreciated.

Sincerely yours,

Dear Mr. Saunders:

Your last payment was sincerely appreciated. We have been expecting to hear from you again, and we hoped you would find it convenient to reduce your balance of $_____.

We feel sure that you desire to handle this account satisfactorily, and we want to cooperate with you during your period of financial stress. Your payments, however, should come forward at regular intervals—not more than 30 days apart.

If you cannot pay in full, how about another payment on account?

Sincerely yours,

P.S. The enclosed return envelope is for your convenience in mailing a check. Should you find it impossible to forward remittance at this time, please return your credit card, to be held until your account is paid.

In response to suggested payment plans

Account
Date Due
Amount $

Dear Mr. Rogers:

Arrangements to extend payments on your contract have been completed in accordance with your request. The due date and the amount of your next installment are shown above.

May we remind you that this extension does not change the expiration date of your automobile insurance. In order that you may plan for its renewal at the proper time, we suggest you examine the policy.

It is a pleasure to be of service by making this change in the terms of payment for your convenience.

Very truly yours,

Dear Mr. James:

We were pleased to hear form you regarding your account. The plan you have outlined for the payment of the $_____ due is completely satisfactory to us and has already been put into effect.

Your name is no longer on our "collection list." We have put your file under "payment plan" in our bookkeeping department, where it will receive special attention. You will, of course, receive no more notices from us regarding payment of your account, since we feel you responded to our payment-plan offer in good faith and will soon have the amount due completely paid.

As a special service we have enclosed _____ post-paid return envelopes—one for each of the $_____ payments you have agreed to make during the next _____ months. Under the flap of each envelope you'll find a notation of the payment due.

If we can be of any further service to you, please do not hesitate to let us know.

Cordially,

Dear Mr. Wheeler:

We were pleased to reinstate your credit within a short time after it had been suspended. This was done, however, with the understanding that you would pay your account promptly in the future.

As we explained to you at that time, a large percentage of the price of petroleum products represents state and federal taxes, which we are required to pay promptly, regardless of whether our good customers have paid us. Naturally, payment reasonably close to our terms is necessary.

These terms, as shown on the original application and on the reverse side of your credit card, are payment upon receipt of statement.

We want to avoid marking your account "Permanently C.O.D.," so please let us have your check immediately. Hereafter, please arrange for payment of future invoices when received; otherwise we shall have to request the return of your credit card.

Sincerely yours,

Special situations

Dear Mr. Jones:

We are concerned to learn from your recent letter that you are unemployed. No doubt it is but a temporary condition, and we are sure you will soon be at work again.

Under these circumstances, we are glad to help and are quite willing to carry the balance until your financial condition improves. A notation to this effect has been made on our records so that the delinquency in your account will not reflect permanently on your credit standing with us.

In return, will you please let us know from time to time how you are progressing?

Sincerely yours,

Dear Mr. Smith:

We are glad to help you by extending sufficient time on your account to carry you over the period of financial stress.

In fairness to both of us, we ask that you please keep us informed of your situation so we can determine just what treatment your case deserves.

Perhaps you have found employment and are now in a position to settle the account. If not, we should appreciate your writing us whether or not it will be possible under your present financial condition for you to make small monthly installment payments. This would enable you to clear this balance within a reasonable time.

Please let us hear from you.

Cordially yours,

Dear Mr. Doe:

Have you recovered from your recent illness?

You will recall that we granted you additional time due to the condition of your health. We hope you are well again and are in a position to remit now.

May we please hear from you?

Sincerely yours,

Dear Mr. Taylor:

The more you buy with your credit card, the better we like it.

However, we've found that people who employ their cards only for personal use average a certain amount each month. Lately your purchases have been above that average, and we would appreciate it if you'd tell us why.

If your card is being used primarily for commercial purposes (even though some personal purchases may be made), we would like to include it with our commercial accounts. A separate record of commercial accounts is kept, for which we use a different numbering system. Will you please give us this information by checking the proper space below?

We'll be happy to send a new credit card with a commercial number if your case calls for it. A business reply envelope is enclosed for your convenience.

Thanks!

Dear Mr. Parks:

Your statement attached shows a credit balance.

This credit was brought about by:

( ) Paying for _____ account twice.

( ) Payment received and credited to your account without information regarding charges being paid.

( ) Payment credited to your account, which does not show any balance outstanding.

Please indicate below what disposition you want made of this credit balance and return this letter in the enclosed business reply envelope.

                                                    Cordially,

( ) The credit will be absorbed by future purchases.

( ) Refund the amount.

( ) The credit balance is not correct for the following reason: _____

                    Signed _____

CHAPTER 25

Claims and Adjustments

Making complaints

In writing a claim letter, it is well to keep in mind that even in the most efficient business organization some things go wrong occasionally. So write firmly but politely with the assumption that the error will be cheerfully corrected. Avoid exaggerated statements, unnecessary threats, and loss of temper. Be clear, to the point, fair, and courteous. If you have prepared a letter while you were angry or indignant, put it aside for a day and then read it over before you mail it.

In general, the higher the official you write to, the quicker and more satisfactory the response.

A claim letter should include:

1. A clear explanation of what is wrong.
2. An explanation of the inconvenience caused.
3. A statement of the steps necessary to rectify the situation.
4. A request to have the matter attended to promptly by appealing to fair play or pride, or if necessary, by threatening loss of business or legal action.

Gentlemen:

On June 3 we placed our Order #725 with you for seven dozen No. 4B2 bolts and one gross of No. 2578 togglebolts.

Although your salesman assured us of three-week delivery on small orders, it is now six weeks since the order was placed.

Some of these bolts are required by a customer to complete a shipment of furniture to South America. Your delay is causing great loss to him and the loss of considerable good will to us.

Please do everything possible to see that this order is shipped to reach us no later than Monday, July 15th.

Very truly yours,

Gentlemen:

Your statement of July 1st, with the notation that prices on No. 4762 chairs have been increased 15 per cent, has just come to my attention. Our purchases last month on this item amounted to $1,205 at the old price and $1,380 at the billed price.

No formal notice of price change on this item was ever sent to us, and we featured it in our summer catalog at a price based on your last quotation. Orders from this catalog mailing are now coming in, and we find that costs based on your new prices are out of line with the selling price.

You can readily appreciate the unfairness of the situation in which we now find ourselves.

We have always considered you one of our most ethical suppliers. Our purchases from you totaled over $100,000 last year. You will agree, I am sure, that a sudden price increase under these circumstances would place an unwarranted burden on us.

Under the circumstances, we trust that you will continue to make shipments on the basis of the last price until our new catalog is issued in September, and will make an adjustment in the prices charged for our June purchases.

Very truly yours,

Gentlemen:

Your shipment of Windsor rocking chairs arrived today, with four maple chairs broken.

We reported the damage to the express company when the shipment arrived, but at the moment they are disclaiming responsibility because of the fragile nature of the merchandise.

Will you please rush replacement on the four chairs and take the necessary steps to collect for the damage from the express company? The shipment carried the number 4B76423.

If any further information is required, please wire us.

Very truly yours,

Letter of complaint

Dear Mr. President,

Fair is fair.

When I bought a television set from Seeds last February, I depended primarily on the good name of Monarch which appeared on the set. Of course, the one-year warranty was also a big factor.

Since last February my set has been in service just about 25 percent of the time. The warranty expires next month and I am still not satisfied with the reception I am getting. My neighbors, with similar sets, get all stations but I can tune-in on only two.

Of course, the service company does make repairs under the service guarantee. But it hardly seems right that I should have the set only part of the time, that I must go to the trouble of sending it out almost every month, and that I must look forward to having a troublesome set after the year's warranty is over. Apparently I got a lemon.

Under the circumstances, don't you think it would be proper to replace my Monarch set with a new one, sparing me all the troubles and your company all the service costs?

Don't you agree?

Very truly yours,

Making adjustments

Keeping an old customer is just as important as gaining a new one. Answering claim letters—particularly when the claim is not justified—is a difficult problem. Most people are honest and believe the claims they make. Answering them requires promptness, courtesy, tact, friendliness, and sympathy. The first reaction in answering a claim letter is often a feeling that the complaint is not justified. This must be overcome by getting the "no" out of your mind before you start to answer. In making adjustments, the "you" attitude and the "positive attitude" are particularly important.

Not: This will acknowledge your complaint about the _____ recorder shipped to you on December 10th. The recorder was shipped in a factory-sealed carton that had been inspected before being sealed. Under the circumstances, I believe your claim for damages must be made to the express company that handled the shipment.

But: I can readily understand your disappointment in not being able to use your _____ recorder over the Christmas holidays.

         As you may have noted, the recorder was shipped to you in the original carton, inspected and sealed by the _____ Company before shipment to us. I have checked the inspection number on the instrument sent you, and it has been verified by the manufacturer.

Under the circumstances, I believe you will have no difficulty in collecting from the express company that handled the shipment. I have already informed the company of the damage, and I am forwarding a claim form with this letter. The express-company adjuster will visit you within a few days after you file the claim.

If there is anything further we can do to be of help, please feel free to call on us.

Not: If you had read the instructions carefully, you would have seen that the master screw must be loosened before the apparatus can be disassembled.

But: On the instruction sheet you will note a reference to the master screw. This must be loosened before the apparatus can be disassembled. Once this is done, you should have no difficulty in changing the working parts.

Not: You were dissatisfied . . .
But: You were not entirely satisfied . . .

Not: We cannot supply this merchandise for 30 days, due to a shutdown in our Milwaukee plant last month.
But: Delivery can be made by the end of next month, since production has already begun at our Milwaukee plant.

Every complaint received by a company is an opportunity to make a friend as well as an opportunity to save a customer. Even in making compensation for a fault, it is important (1) to keep the customer happy; (2) to avoid giving the impression your product and services are often subject to complaint; (3) to avoid showing reluctance.

A good adjustment letter leaves a pleasant aftertaste—whether it says Yes or No or compromises. It should be natural in tone and should sound like a letter written personally to the particular customer, not a form letter.

If the letter must say No, it may use any of these approaches:

1. Appeal to sense of fair play.
2. Show the disastrous effect if this policy were universally adopted.

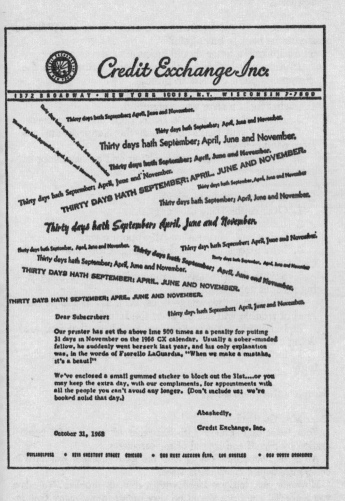

Credit Exchange Inc.

1372 BROADWAY • NEW YORK 10018, N.Y. WISCONSIN 7-7800

Thirty days hath September; April, June and November.

Thirty days hath September; April, June and November.

Thirty days hath September; April, June and November.

Thirty days hath September; April, June and November.

Thirty days hath September; April, June and November.

Thirty days hath September; April, June and November.

THIRTY DAYS HATH SEPTEMBER: APRIL, JUNE AND NOVEMBER.

Thirty days hath September; April, June and November.

Thirty days hath September; April, June and November.

Thirty days hath September; April, June and November.

Thirty days hath September; April, June and November. Thirty days hath September; April, June and November. Thirty days hath September; April, June and November.

Thirty days hath September; April, June and November. Thirty days hath September; April, June and November.

THIRTY DAYS HATH SEPTEMBER: APRIL, JUNE AND NOVEMBER.

THIRTY DAYS HATH SEPTEMBER: APRIL, JUNE AND NOVEMBER.

Thirty days hath September; April, June and November

Dear Subscriber:

Our printer has set the above line 500 times as a penalty for putting
31 days in November on the 1968 CX calendar. Usually a sober-minded
fellow, he suddenly went berserk last year, and his only explanation
was, in the words of Fiorello LaGuardia, "When we make a mistake,
it's a beaut!"

We've enclosed a small gummed sticker to block out the 31st....or you
may keep the extra day, with our compliments, for appointments with
all the people you can't avoid any longer. (Don't include us; we're
booked solid that day.)

Abashedly,

Credit Exchange, Inc.

October 31, 1968

PHILADELPHIA • 9311 CHESTNUT STREET CHICAGO • 208 WEST JACKSON BLVD. LOS ANGELES • 660 SOUTH BROADWAY

3. Explain the impossibility of conforming with the request.

The test for a good answer to a claim letter is "Will your customer be back to buy again?"

The adjustment letter should include:

1. Acknowledgment of the complaint written with the customer's point of view in mind.

2. Explanation of the cause of the error or what led to the belief that an error was committed.

3. Explanation of what is being done about the claim.

4. A good-will build-up to sell the company and restore confidence.

5. An offer of further cooperation and an assurance of satisfaction.

Here are some pitfalls to avoid:

1. Overemphasizing the complaint.

2. Indicating the company was negligent.

3. Indicating "surprise" or "disappointment."

4. Minimizing the fault by saying errors are "bound to occur."

5. Saying "that it never happened before" or suggesting it could not be avoided.

6. Giving negative suggestions, such as "We hope this kind of trouble will not occur in the future."

7. Indicating your motives are selfish or that you are doing a big favor.

8. Indicating you are making the adjustment grudgingly.

Sample adjustment letters

Dear Mrs. Cortland:

Your letter of February 14th has received very careful consideration by myself and several of my associates.

All of us sympathize keenly with the local problem you have in competing with a major chain store.

However, we, too, are faced with a difficult problem. To allow you a special low price would be very unfair to our many customers, several of whom face problems similar to yours.

In recent years we have absorbed several increases in labor costs in order to maintain our present price structure without taking anything away from the quality of our line. Our present margin over actual manufacturing cost is the smallest we have had in 37 years in business. It would be unfair not only to our other customers but to ourselves if we offered a price reduction at this time.

Because of our long business relationship, we very much want to find some way of helping you. Therefore, I am asking our sales-promotion manager, Sidney Milton, to visit you in Janesville next week. He has in mind a cooperative promotion plan that may well be more helpful than any price reduction we could possibly offer.

I sincerely hope that we can be of real service.

Very cordially,

Dear Mrs. Saunders:

Thank you for your letter telling us about the incident on the No. 37 bus last Friday. It is only through letters like yours that we can learn about the occasional slip-ups in our policy of continuous courtesy and service.

The facts in your letter are being investigated by our personnel office, and proper steps will certainly be taken not only to discipline the persons responsible but also to make certain that the chances of a similar incident's occurring are eliminated.

Sincerely yours,

Dear Mrs. Noble:

The mails are carrying a new "Annie" doll to you special delivery, so that you can have it for your daughter's birthday.

We regret very much that the doll came to you in damaged condition. All the dolls are inspected at the factory before they are packed in cartons. However, on rare occasions a package gets unusually rough treatment in shipping and some damage results. Your new "Annie" received extra cushioning to avoid any possibility of breakage.

Will you be good enough to return the damaged doll to us by parcel post addressed with the enclosed label, which also carries the proper postage? A damage report, filled out in accordance with the facts described in your letter, is also enclosed. We would like you to sign it and return it in the business reply envelope for our insurance record.

I am sure your daughter will be thrilled with "Annie" and that the doll will bring her many hours of joy.

Your very truly,

Dear Mrs. Milton:

I know just how you must have felt when the first films taken with your new camera came back out of focus. It is a real disappointment when a good shot goes wrong.

Because I wanted to make certain that I was doing the right thing, I took your letter to our technical department as soon as I received it. They examined the films carefully and feel certain the trouble lies in your lens adjustment.

Rather than ask you to return the camera to us, they suggest that you take it to a local dealer, Joseph Binger & Sons, at 128 Elm Street, in your city. I am dropping a note to him, requesting that he make any adjustment necessary and bill us for his services.

After he has made the proper adjustment, I am sure you will find your camera everything you hope for.

Sincerely,

Dear Sir:

Thank you for sending your check in payment of your November bill. Please accept our sincere apologies for writing to you as we did.

Our collection letters proceed automatically in a series, and occasionally a payment crosses a letter in the mails. This is apparently what happened in your case.

Your check has been properly credited, and your account is now marked paid in full.

Very sincerely yours,

Dear Sir:

Your lighter has been received and will be replaced in good operating condition and returned to you at no charge.

We are returning your 10c in stamps, since we never charge for the repair of a Zippo, regardless of its age or condition.

Very sincerely,

Dear Mr. Noble:

As soon as your letter telling us about the poor results you have had with our camera came to my desk, I took it over to the technical department. Naturally, we feel badly when a customer is not completely satisfied with one of our products, and we try to do two things:

1. Keep our customer happy.

2. Make certain we avoid the same difficulty arising at a future time.

Mr. John Linson, our production engineer, examined the negatives and the prints you enclosed. His opinion was that your shutter was not opened to allow sufficient light for the conditions under which the pictures were taken. He was quite certain there was nothing basically wrong with your camera.

Under separate cover, I am sending you a roll of our high-speed film. May I suggest that you try this film next time you take shots on a cloudy day, opening your lens to at least F 4.5? I think this will help you get sharper and more satisfactory results.

Since your camera is already more than three years old, we feel we cannot replace it under our one-year guarantee. However, if you wish to have us examine it and make any necessary adjustments, we shall be pleased to do this for a nominal charge of $1.00 to cover the cost of handling.

Very sincerely yours,

Dear Miss Saunders,

Thank you for turning my difficult assignment into a most pleasant visit.

I assure you that my associates and myself deeply regret the loss of the statuette. The disappearance is one of those annoying mysteries that occur from time to time when one handles many precious items.

We think your proposal that we pay for the recasting of the statuette from an exact replica is a very fair one, and we are pleased to accept the responsibility for this charge.

I realize that this offer does not compensate for the inconvenience occasioned by this temporary loss, but I hope you will agree that under the circumstances it is the best possible solution.

Sincerely yours,

A "giving-in" letter.

I guess you're right, Joe Michaels.

Although I did feel sincerely that our charges for repair services were justified, your letter and a long talk with the crew who visited your shop convinces me that you are at last partially right. The flywheel must have had some defect to have given you so much trouble.

So I am instructing the bookeeping department to cancel all service charges last month.

I understand that everything is working smoothly now, but I want to assure you that we will continue to stand behind our product for the full two-year period.

Sincerely yours,
President

Helpful Sentences

Beginnings for adjustment letters

Please accept my sincere apology for the error in your May bill.
Thank you for bringing to our attention the defect in your . . .
We were sincerely sorry to learn that you were not completely satisfied with . . .
Thank you for writing (telling) us as frankly as you did about . . .
It was good of you to write and tell . . .
We appreciate your calling our attention to . . .
Thank you for your letter of . . .

The attached $2 Credit Allowance—made out in your name—has been approved by our accounting department. . . .
You were quite right! Your order did tell us to . . . and we are sincerely sorry that an oversight caused us to . . .
You did exactly the right thing when you . . .
A new shipment of _____ is on its way to you.
We can understand your annoyance . . .
I know just how you felt when you opened . . .
You were entirely right about . . .
We were very much distressed by . . .
We are most sorry . . .
I can't tell you how much I regret . . .
We greatly (very much) regret your dissatisfaction (unsatisfactory experience) with . . .
We always feel badly when a customer is not entirely (completely) satisfied . . .
I can't tell you how badly I feel about your letter . . .
Thank you for your letter giving us the opportunity to . . .
You (certainly) have every right to be angry (upset) by . . .
The inexcusable treatment by our salesman was . . .
Our greatest concern is to please you.
We appreciate your constructive criticism.

We are most anxious to adjust this satisfactorily and quietly.

Under these circumstances, will you reconsider your decision regarding XYZ products?

Closings for adjustment letters

Please let us know if you wish us to do anything further.

It is a pleasure to be able to give you this service.

We appreciate your calling this defect to our attention, for it is only by discovering these occasional imperfections that we can give our products the high-quality standards for which we strive.

We are looking forward to our next opportunity to be helpful. Meanwhile, we say thank you again.

Mr. Jones will drop in to see you soon and tell you personally how much we regret the oversight in your shipment.

Don't you agree this is a fair and equitable way to settle this matter?

The new set-up will speed up your deliveries by at least two days and thus enable you to guage your orders more carefully on a week-to-week basis.

CHAPTER 26

Routine Business Letters

A large portion of business correspondence consists of simple routine letters dealing with orders, changes of address, price increases, etc. Because these letters are routine, many companies give them scant attention and don't provide all the necessary facts, write with a lack of clarity, and tend toward inaccuracies. Overcoming these failings is usually only a matter of increased thought and attention.

To avoid some of these pitfalls, many firms have standard forms for orders, purchasing, making reservations, sending acknowledgments, etc. These provide blank spaces to be filled in with the various required elements so that the memorandum will be complete and correct.

Orders

The elements that orders should contain include:

1. A reference number so that the order may be identified and located easily at a future time.
2. The date.
3. A specific quantity of each item.
4. Specific descriptions of the goods including number, sizes, styles, color, and other specifications.
5. Price.
6. Directions for shipment.
7. Description of method of payment.

Gentlemen:

Please ship to us by express, prepaid, the following merchandise listed in your 1968 catalog:

3 dozen No. 4276 Formica tables at $14.98 each
          18 in yellow
          12 in red
           6 in mahogany
12 dozen chairs No. 4298 covered in plastic, at $2.87 each
          48 in yellow
          48 in red
          48 in blue

Charges should be made to our regular account and bills sent to ʊur Janesville office.

Delivery should be made as quickly as possible. If delivery cannot be made by August 10th, please cancel this order and wire us immediately.

Shipment should be made to our warehouse at 4762 Ohio Avenue, Greenville, Ohio.

Very truly yours,

Acknowledgments of orders

In some businesses, particularly those in which orders are not filled immediately, it is customary to acknowledge orders. Sometimes this is done by returning a carbon of the form on which the order is entered by the receiving firm. Sometimes a printed-form postcard is used. An acknowledgment by letter either repeats all the details of the order or merely acknowledges it and gives the date when merchandise will be delivered.

When an order cannot be filled or when some of the merchandise cannot be shipped immediately, the facts should be mentioned and the date when the merchandise will be available should be indicated.

Dear Sir:
  Thank you for your order No. 7427 dated June 7th.
  It is always a pleasure to hear from an old customer, particularly after so long a period.
  No. 4276 tables in yellow and red can be shipped immediately, and No. 4298 chairs will go out to you before August 1st.
  However, No. 4276 tables in mahogany will not go into production until August 15th. We would be pleased to ship these to you before August 22nd so that you could have them in stock by the end of the month. If this is satisfactory, will you please confirm this portion of your order?
  If you have a moment, will you take a look at the enclosed pre-

view of our fall line. We haven't released it yet to the trade, but we wanted you to get advance notice so that you can keep it in mind when you are making your plans for the future.

Very cordially,

Dear Sir:

Thank you for your order for three thermos bottles as advertised in the Sunday *Sentinel.*

Since we have no facilities for mailing merchandise on a C.O.D. basis, we must ask that you send a check or money order. The price of the three bottles is $12.75.

In the meantime, we are marking and placing your order aside with instructions to rush shipment to you as soon as your remittance arrives.

Very truly yours,

When the boss is away

A secretary is often required to reply to routine correspondence in the absence of her boss.

Dear Sir:

Your letter of June 4th addressed to Mr. Sidney Milton has come to my attention since he is out of town on an extended trip.

I know Mr. Milton will want to respond to your letter personally, but rather than wait for his return, I will answer those of your inquiries that appear to be the most urgent.

Our 24 gauge line is now in production and is being sold for delivery beginning June 1st. The prices will be similar to those of the 20 gauge line, with an approximate 2 per cent added for freight charges.

The No. 41 line in light woods has been discontinued, and only a few pieces remain in stock. I am enclosing a schedule of these items.

As soon as Mr. Milton returns to the office, I will bring your letter to his attention.

Yours truly,

Dear Mr. Saunders:

This will acknowledge your February 10th letter addressed to Mr. Tom Wilson.

Mr. Wilson is ill and is not expected to return to this office until about March 7th. As soon as he returns, I will bring your letter to his attention.

Very truly yours,

Making reservations

Reservation letters present problems in giving all the information and in getting the reservation confirmed. The latter is particularly necessary when accommodations are hard to get. It goes without saying that reservtaions should be made early, since they can always be canceled if not needed.

Gentlemen:
Please reserve a double room with twin beds and bath for Mr. and Mrs. Sidney A. Milton for April 7th, 8th, and 9th. An outside room is preferred.

Mr. Milton expects to arrive at 7 P.M. by train.

He will require the use of a car on April 7th and 8th and would appreciate your making arrangements for the rental at a local agency.

Please confirm by wire, collect, to Mr. Sidney Milton, Hotel Statler, Chicago.

Very truly yours,

Dear Sir:
Please reserve a Pullman seat on the Pacemaker to Albany, leaving Rome at 2:30 P.M. on Wednesday, April 3rd. The ticket and Pullman seat should be held in the name of Mr. Sidney Milton.

A messenger will pick up the tickets on April 2nd and will pay for them at that time.

Very truly yours,

Notice of a directors' meeting

Formal notices must be sent to directors prior to a meeting specified by law and the corporate by-laws. This notice must specify the time, place, and purpose of the meeting, and the group that is to meet. Often a waiver of notice or a proxy is enclosed in case directors cannot attend. If waivers are not requested, the sender usually files an affidavit that proper notice has been given.

There will be a meeting of the Board of Directors of the Saunders Products Corporation on Thursday, June 7th, at 10 A.M. at the office of the Corporation, 27 Cedar Street, Janesville, Ohio.

New contracts for executives will be discussed, and such other business as may come before the meeting will be acted upon.

If you cannot attend, please sign the enclosed waiver of notice.

Very truly yours,

TO OUR PRINTING
INDUSTRY FRIENDS

Greetings...

We apologize for the unfinished drawing shown above. We have some news and we want to get it to you as soon as possible so we told the artist to stop where he was.

First, some history -- in 1951 it was decided to expand our business and develop a line of offset presses. It was not an easy undertaking as the Miller reputation had to be upheld -- the presses had to be as modern and efficient as our Miller letter-presses, two of which were introduced in 1950 and three completely redesigned in 1951.

In order to speed this offset development, in 1952 we purchased the Printing Machinery Division of the Electric Boat Company and thereby acquired the 22x34 E.B.CO Offset Press. After redesigning to a degree we shipped the first Miller E.B.CO completely manufactured by Miller in 1953.

Since 1952, our engineers and production men have been designing and testing a Miller 22x34 Two-Color Perfector Press. This press will be introduced the latter part of March.

But, here's the big news. For the past two years our executives have been planning and working with M.A.N. in Augsburg, Germany, and after initial testing in Europe are now prepared to announce the Miller-M.A.N.* Offset Press in the United States. This new line will consist of:

30" x 42" (one to five color)
36" x 48" (one to five color)
40" x 56" (two to five color)

The Miller plant at Pittsburgh will continue to build small offset presses up to 22x34.

The letterpress department will also be expanded by the introduction of the Miller Poly, a cylinder press manufactured by M.A.N., taking a maximum sheet 14-1/2" x 20-1/2".

That's the news in brief form. If you are contemplating the purchase of an offset press within a month and you wish to discuss these new presses, write us a letter of your intention. We will be able to show you a machine on March 15th. We now have photographs and will be able to give you other pertinent data if you are interested.

Miller Printing Machinery Co.
Pittsburgh, Pennsylvania 15233

* The letters "M.A.N." should be individually pronounced -- do not pronounce them as the word "Man".

Price increase

Gentlemen:

This isn't a very easy letter to write, since we well realize that the price increases are not a welcome subject. For some time we've thought that sooner or later some changes would be inevitable, but up to now we haven't wanted to talk about such a possibility.

Unfortunately, we have no choice. Our production costs, inks, and labor costs have been going up almost daily, and as a result we've established an increased-price basis on printed cellophane sheets and rolls—effective immediately. All the orders we have on file were entered with a clause to the effect that prices prevailing as of date of shipment would apply. Accordingly, we are increasing prices on the orders you have on file with us. Corrected acknowledgments are attached. We assume this will be entirely satisfactory with you, but if by any chance it isn't, we'll appreciate your letting us know immediately.

Needless to say, we deeply regret the necessity for increased prices—it seems such a poor repayment for the many courtesies our customers have extended us. But we're sure you understand that the situation is beyond our control.

The business you're placing with us is indeed appreciated, and you may be sure we'll do everything in our power to take the best possible care of your requirements.

Sincerely yours,

Price reduction

YOU MADE IT POSSIBLE!
by your wonderful acceptance of our footlockers, enabling us to create greater production and thereby permitting us to manufacture at a lower cost. We are glad to pass this saivng on to you!

Change of address

Just to let you know
THAT OUR NEW TELEPHONE
NUMBER IS_____
Won't you jot it down in your
telephone-number booklet?
NAME_____
ADDRESS_____

One company used a really effective change of notice. With each memorandum they enclosed several stickers showing the correct new address and telephone number, to be pasted in the proper place in their directories.

WE ARE THANKING JOHN L. LEWIS
for telling us to move—

The United Mine Workers have bought the Chandler Building in which we have had our office for eleven years. John L. Lewis wants it for his pension-plan workers.

So we are moving into Colonel Ring's *new* Marsh Building, Office No. 119, 1832 M Street, N.W., Washington, D.C. Please change our address on your records (telephone number remains the same, REpublic 3433) and come to see us.

We began this business March 1, 1938, my partner and I, with a background of sound experience in publishing, association, travel, advertising-agency, and life-insurance advertising.

From the start, we determined on specialization in direct advertising and in promotion to help salesmen sell.

Our clients have prospered; so have we. In just one month in 1949 we did more work for our clients than in the entire first ten months of our business eleven years ago.

This year is to be a bigger year for most of us than any prewar year. Next year will be STILL BIGGER for those who have the foresight and action to make it so.

　　　　　　　　　　　　　　　　　　　Sincerely yours,

WE HAVE
MOVED
Dear Friend:

During the past fourteen years we were so crowded in our old location that sometimes customers who dropped in on us had to sit on typewriters.

　　　　　　　Nowadays—
you'll find it much easier to call on Taylor and Company. Easy parking facilities in our parking lot and pleasant offices will make it simple for you to get friendly folders and letters—in fact all types of direct mail—that will SELL MERCHANDISE.

　　　　　　　Production facilities are better, too!
We've just added larger presses and new hi-speed folders to give you better service in our mailing and printing departments.

If you'd like to visit our plant, just call Atwater 6366 and name the time.

We'll gladly pick you up!

Sincerely,

Refusing a price concession

I wish I could, but I just can't.

When Standard set up the 1969 price schedule last spring, we tried very hard to make the price on every number as low as possible. We set up a series of quantity discounts that reflected our costs and the savings we could make on big shipments. And we let all of our customers know exactly how little we could afford to charge. The whole schedule is based on a maximum value and an equitable price to everyone. So you see that if we charged less on one shipment, we would have to charge more on another. That would hardly be fair to other customers who, too, are "oldtimers" with us.

I know you will understand that our one-price schedule policy is the only way we can operate. It is a policy that assures you and all of those who trade with us that you are receiving maximum value for every dollar you spend.

Cordially,

CHAPTER 27

Showmanship, Tricks, and Gadgets

The personal letter that deals with a personal problem has a very good chance of receiving an answer. But business letters are in a very different category as we have mentioned previously.

Most of the letters received by the ordinary householder and an even greater proportion of the letters received by a businessman are form letters that have only a fair chance of being opened and a reltaively small chance of being read.

The competition for favorable attention has always taxed the ingenuity of letter writers and advertising men; indeed, it has given birth to a new industry for the production of ideas and material for unusual mailings.

In producing the letter, punctuation and spacing, type faces, rules and ornaments are often used to make the letter easier to read and to emphasize certain sections.

These typographic devices include:

1. headlines and subheads
2. underlinings
3. capital, bold-face, or italic type
4. variation of type faces
5. indentions
6. colored ink
7. display boxes containing a special message
8. listing special points and preceding them by numbers, symbols, or bullets
9. postscripts
10. marginal space for special notations
11. ellipses, asterisks, stars, etc., to break up the space

We offer you 8 MONTHS OF McCALL's

-- actual newsstand value $2.40 -

FOR ONLY $1!

That's right ...

YOU can get McCall's at HALF PRICE

if you act AT ONCE!

PRIVATE SALE BEGINNING TODAY FOR OUR
PREFERRED CHARGE ACCOUNT CUSTOMERS

as exciting as any in our history! Just look at the features!

FOR MEN: Reductions up to 20% on groups of Society Brand, Stein Bloch
and Roger Belmont suits, sports coats, slacks; and on all
Freeman Master Fitter and Bootmaker Guild sport shoes and
brown and black calf Oxfords. Groups of straw hats reduced
25%. Also $8.00 white broadcloth shirts at $5.95, or 5 for
$11.00; $1.50 broadcloth boxer shorts at $1.19, or 6 for
$7.00; $5.95 to $15.00 sport shirts at $5.15 to $11.65; and
similar reductions on pajamas, etc. etc.

FOR BOYS: Reductions up to 25% on groups of short-sleeve shirts; summer
pajamas from age 2; Junior and Cadet slacks and summer suits.

MR. MAGER

WHERE DO YOU FIND

"ORIGINAL" IDEAS

IN DIRECT MAIL?

Do you know any one who originated 2 selling ideas as good
as "send no money", and "examine free"?

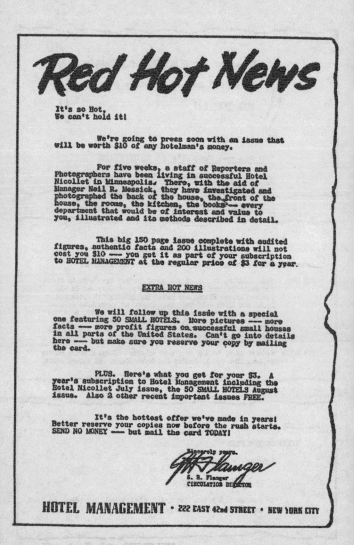

Red Hot News

It's so Hot,
We can't hold it!

We're going to press soon with an issue that
will be worth $10 of any hotelman's money.

For five weeks, a staff of Reporters and
Photographers have been living in successful Hotel
Nicollet in Minneapolis. There, with the aid of
Manager Neil R. Messick, they have investigated and
photographed the back of the house, the front of the
house, the rooms, the kitchen, the books—— every
department that would be of interest and value to
you, illustrated and its methods described in detail.

This big 150 page issue complete with audited
figures, authentic facts and 200 illustrations will not
cost you $10 —— you get it as part of your subscription
to HOTEL MANAGEMENT at the regular price of $3 for a year.

EXTRA HOT NEWS

We will follow up this issue with a special
one featuring 50 SMALL HOTELS. More pictures —— more
facts —— more profit figures on successful small houses
in all parts of the United States. Can't go into details
here —— but make sure you reserve your copy by mailing
the card.

PLUS. Here's what you get for your $3. A
year's subscription to Hotel Management including the
Hotel Nicollet July issue, the 50 SMALL HOTELS August
issue. Also 2 other recent important issues FREE.

It's the hottest offer we've made in years!
Better reserve your copies now before the rush starts.
SEND NO MONEY —— but mail the card TODAY!

Sincerely yours,

G. R. Flanger

G. R. Flanger
CIRCULATION DIRECTOR

HOTEL MANAGEMENT · 222 EAST 42nd STREET · NEW YORK CITY

Beyond these devices, the most obvious attention-getter, and one of the most widely used, is the addition of art work to the letter. Although art work attracts attention to a letter, it usually removes the personal element that is often important. Stock art work is available from many agencies, and several books containing material for reproduction are sold for a few dollars each.

Lacking a budget for art work, you may substitute, when appropriate, an ink blot or a thumbprint plus proper copy. The body of the letter may be processed upside down on the stationery or the type may be set in the shape of a bell, a flag, a question mark, a circle, or any other suitable shape.

One successful letter began with a signature and the following sentence:

You'll wonder why this letters starts with our signature. It's because the words "Sincerely yours" express just how we feel about you.

Handwriting the first few lines gives a letter a personal note that helps get further reading. The personalized written fill-in is particularly effective.

One recent letter on personal-size stationery came surrounded with a black border. It mourned the loss of an old customer. However, this technique must be used carefully, since it might strike many people as being in poor taste. Another company sent its message in "squared sense patterns"—blocks of type that conveyed the message simply and clearly. The Sheraton Hotel in Chicago promoted a new cocktail lounge with a letter in shorthand.

The paper you use can be another attention-getting device. Stock letterheads printed in four colors that show an interesting and appropriate scene may be purchased. The letter may be printed on graph paper, on paper with a background scene, or even on wallpaper. Paper with special finish or deckle edge, tissue paper, leatherette, wrapping paper, butcher paper, metallic paper, oil-cloth, or cotton all help take the letter out of the run-of-the-mill variety. One company used a laminated paper with a blue velvet finish to impress readers with the "S-M-O-O-T-H velvety performance your car needs . . ."

Printers' Ink

THE WEEKLY MAGAZINE OF ADVERTISING, MANAGEMENT AND SALES

205 East 42nd Street, New York, N.Y. 10017 Telephone: MUrray Hill 3-6500

Dear Mr. Mager:

The remark "I'd stand on my head to get it" may be just a flip phrase to some people . . .

But if acrobatics really will help me to win that coveted reply from you, here I am – upside down!

Or perhaps you have been holding out purposely to see the kind of letters we write. Now I say gently but firmly that we haven't much more leeway to continue unless your order is received.

The renewal was due weeks ago. However, I've mailed each issue since then in the hope you would not want to miss any copies of Printers' Ink. After all, renewal orders tell the story of the job our editors are doing – and every one counts.

This isn't entirely one-sided. Perhaps never before has there been so much stirring of importance to executives – and never before have we been so well equipped to cover these trends, to serve you. Printers' Ink holds first place in circulation because of its practical value; coming issues should pay high dividends on the modest investment.

But I can't hold out much longer, so please use the enclosed card today. Clowning aside, we do value your subscription and hope you will be with us for the coming issues. No need to send check now – invoice will follow later for payment at your convenience.

Cordially yours,

J. C. Chasin
Circulation Manager

The
SEASIDE
ATLANTIC CITY

The WORLD

seeks CHARM - yet overlooks
it. There's charm in the
earnest purpose of a
little boy building cas-
tles in the sand...There's
charm in the graceful curve
of a sea gull's wing........
There's charm in the joyous
laughter of the Boardwalk
throng on a clear, blue
summer   day.
FOR
YOU
and
YOUR FAMILY
THERE'S CHARM IN
A SUMMER VACATION AT
THE SEASIDE where you find
a blend of the old and new—
old fashioned hospitality with
modern vacation attractions....
'cycling on the Boardwalk, relaxation on the Sun Deck
....cool refreshment
in the Surf 'n Sand
Room, ...and
delightful dips
in the Ocean.
....
Why search
the world
for charm?
Come
down
to .. . . THE SEASIDE

A. G. Tower
General Manager

The
SEASIDE
ATLANTIC CITY

March 14, 19

A TOAST
to your
Spring Vacation!!

March in Atlantic City brings
more than a hint of Spring!!!
.....Here in our mild sea air
strolling along the Boardwalk
and basking on our Sun Decks,
MAY YOU enjoy to your heart's
content, a fore-taste of days
to come.........put away your
galoshes!...forget Winter!!
then for a few days enjoy
the benefits of a va-
cation-by-
the-
Sea!
Cordially,
THE SEASIDE.

Harrison Cook
Resident Manager

One method used occasionally is to write across a bill head:

You don't owe us a cent this month. Wish you did. How about more orders?

Occasionally it is important to get past a secretary whose tendency is to throw circular mail in the wastepaper basket. First-class postage, personally typed envelopes, and the word *Personal* typed on the envelope all help. A business man we know seals letters with wax, knowing that few secretaries will undertake breaking the seal.

An unusual or attractive envelope will also help to attract attention. Oversized envelopes, special stock, an interesting message printed on the envelope, a heavy enclosure such as a pencil or premium, have all been used successfully. A recent mailing that created quite a stir started an interesting story on the envelope with the note "continued inside."

Another mailer put his message on the outside of the envelope:

Don't open—THIS ENVELOPE IS EMPTY. Our product is on the outside of this envelope: YOUR NAME. We are mailing-list compilers. We help you to sell your product by supplying hard-hitting names of people with interest and buying-power. Our service is accurate and efficient; our list sources unlimited.

---

don't open don't open don't open - THIS ENVELOPE IS EMPTY

our product is on the outside of this envelope: YOUR NAME.

we are mailing list compilers. we help you to sell your
product by supplying hard hitting names of people with
interest and buying power.

our service is accurate and efficient; our list sources
unlimited.

The Zeller Company   15 east 26th street -- new york, n.y. 10010
murray hill 5-6278

PENNY LABEL COMPANY
9 MURRAY STREET
NEW YORK, N.Y. 10007

Don't gamble with DEADLINES!

You Touch These Almost
Every Day of Your Life

BUT RIGHT NOW
WITHOUT COUNTING
Can you tell how many buttons your shirt has?
4–5–6–7–8
Give Up?

If you didn't know, don't be alarmed. It's amazing how few of us
know the details of certain operations we perform every day of our
lives. We do so many things from habit that we overlook many important facts.

Isn't it time to take a look into your usual way of doing business?
In this day of the profit squeeze, why not investigate our Industrial
Division for lower costs, increased quality, added skills and facilities, new ideas and materials, an da way to expand. We build all
kinds of things for other manufacturers.

A few of the many AAA-1 rated companies that have taken advantage of our facilities are listed on the attached pages.

May we have a few minutes of your time to tell and show you
more of our story?

Call 994-4141.

Sincerely yours,
The Flexible Co.

P.S. The return of the attached card will bring you a brochure
along with a personal letter from one of our Account Executives. *Do It Now.*

Outdoor Life started a series of seven cartoon panels on
back of a No. 10 envelope. The first seven panels (on the
outside) showed a bear creeping up on a hunter, the gun
jams, the hunter is chased up a tree. . . . On the inside the
hunter gets out the jam with a .22-caliber rifle.

When requesting a response, it is best to make an answer
as easy as possible. If questions can be answered Yes or No,
a questionnaire may be enclosed. Otherwise space may be
provided for answering under each question. When a long
answer is required, the letter may be printed to the left side
of the page with a wide right margin for an answer. Enclosing
an order card or a return addressed stamped postcard or envelope will increase responses.

One device that has proved quite effective is the attached

reply card that slips into a transparent frame at the head of the letter. This forms the inside address and the return address on the coupon if it is mailed in. Variations on this are reply envelopes, reply invitations, reply labels, etc.

The XYZ Company has tossed seven of your letters in the basket. Perhaps they will respond to a simple letter, a questionnaire, a survey you are conducting about their needs, or a contest that induces definite action. The response to the questionnaire leads to an acknowledgment by you, perhaps their realization that you have just what their company needs and thus to a lifelong business friendship.

Simple but effective attention devices may be created with die cuts. The top of a letter head may be cut out in the shape of a telephone, a rocket ship, a gingerbread house. Or the stationery may have a die-cut top in the shape of a skyline, a motorcar, or a piece of furniture, with the illustration filling out the space. Pop-ups can be created with trick folds in two-page letters or with an extra flap on the side or on top.

Games integrated into the text of the letter create interest and keep your letter out of the wastebasket. Another series of gadgets is aimed at making the message harder to find and, therefore, more impressive when it is found. Enclosures may have copy printed in invisible ink that can only be read when dampened or when a lit cigarette is placed at a specified spot. One successful letter printed in black ink on black paper that was almost unreadable started "Are you working in the dark?"

Gadgets appropriate to the copy and attached to the letter are now widely used. These may be plastic, paper, wood, or metal miniatures, such as stamps, foreign money, or checks. A paper clip, a burnt match, or a swatch of fabric may be used.

An unusual or attractive envelope will also help to attract artificial snow. It tied in with a headline: "SNOW—and bitter cold, we know, make you think ahead to a HEAT WAVE! That's why we want to talk to you now about our specialized ability to get inquiries at a low cost." The mailing was sent out by Artwill Advertising Corporation during a period of snow flurries.

The Reader's Digest Association
PLEASANTVILLE, NEW YORK

LIFE IN THESE
UNITED STATES

"Mother, I wish I didn't look so flatchested," said my 15-year-old daughter as she stood before the mirror in her first formal dress.

I remedied the matter by inserting puffs of cotton in strategic places. Then I hung around Mary's neck a string of seed pearls—just as my grandmother had done for my mother and my mother for me.

At midnight her escort brought her home. The moment the door closed behind him Mary burst into tears. "I'm never going out with him again," she sobbed. "Mother, do you know what he said to me . . ."

(continued inside)

(continued from envelope) . . . He leaned across the table and said, "Gee, you look sharp tonight, Mary. Are those real?"

"I hope you told him they were," I said indignantly. "They've been in the family for three generations!"

My daughter stopped sobbing. "Oh, the pearls! Good heavens, I'd forgotten all about them."

(From "Life In These United States," a regular Reader's Digest feature.)

The Reader's Digest Association
PLEASANTVILLE, NEW YORK

LIFE IN THESE UNITED STATES

"Mother, I wish I didn't look so flatchested," said my 15-year-old daughter as she stood before the mirror in her first formal dress.

I remedied the matter by inserting puffs of cotton in strategic places. Then I hung around Mary's neck a string of seed pearls—just as two grandmothers had done for my mother and my mother for me.

At midnight her escort brought her home. The moment the door closed behind him Mary bent into tears. "I'm never going out with him again," she sobbed. "Mother, do you know what he said to me? . . ."   (continued inside)

have The Reader's
... HALF PRICE ...
(IF YOU ACT NOW!)

...usual offer?

...not a subscriber to The Reader's ...you to TRY it. Most folks who ...that they renew year after year. ...to make you this special

...vement for $1 later. All you need do is return the enclosed Card. For your convenience, here is a Postage Stamp that will speed the Card back to me by first-class mail ...

The CREAM of what's being written and thought today appears in the 35 or more articles condensed each month in The Reader's Digest. Its handy pocket size makes it easy to hold, convenient to carry, and enjoyable to read in those many odd moments that would otherwise be wasted.

This invitation cannot be extended again for at least two years. Therefore we urge you to act at once. Only by taking advantage of this opportunity now can you receive the next EIGHT issues of Reader's Digest for ONE DOLLAR.

Sincerely,

Carolyn Davis

CD/AB   For the Association

THE READER'S DIGEST ASSOCIATION ● PLEASANTVILLE, N.Y.

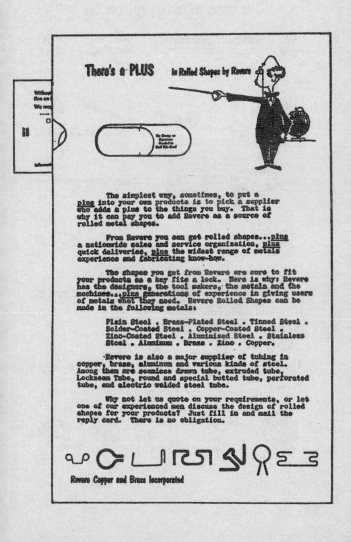

There's a PLUS in Rolled Shapes by Revere

The simplest way, sometimes, to put a plus into your own products is to pick a supplier who adds a plus to the things you buy. That is why it can pay you to add Revere as a source of rolled metal shapes.

From Revere you can get rolled shapes...plus a nationwide sales and service organization, plus quick deliveries, plus the widest range of metals experience and fabricating know-how.

The shapes you get from Revere are sure to fit your products as a key fits a lock. Here is why: Revere has the designers, the tool makers, the metals and the machines...plus generations of experience in giving users of metals what they need. Revere Rolled Shapes can be made in the following metals:

Plain Steel . Brass-Plated Steel . Tinned Steel . Solder-Coated Steel . Copper-Coated Steel . Zinc-Coated Steel . Aluminized Steel . Stainless Steel . Aluminum . Brass . Zinc . Copper.

Revere is also a major supplier of tubing in copper, brass, aluminum and various kinds of steel. Among them are seamless drawn tube, extruded tube, Lockseam Tube, round and special butted tube, perforated tube, and electric welded steel tube.

Why not let us quote on your requirements, or let one of our experienced men discuss the design of rolled shapes for your products? Just fill in and mail the reply card. There is no obligation.

Revere Copper and Brass Incorporated

GADGETS AVAILABLE FOR LETTERS

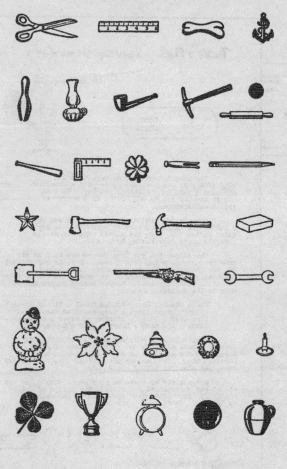

A novel use of coins was made in a change of address notice. The headline read:

LOOK
at our new phone number

Inside the two O's were nickels, the cost of a local call.

One mailing used an ordinary cotter pin (cost 20 for 1c) with copy starting: "You are now part owner of a car." A rubber band may tie in with "stretch your dollar." Here are some other effective tie-ins:

A strip of sandpaper: "Things are rough all over, but . . ."

An imitation blue bachelor button: Do you like a suit that has a smart metropolitan "flower-in-your-button-hole" air?

A campaign button: "This is a campaign letter, but it's different from any other campaign letter you'll receive this fall. We'll WAGER that."

A false mustache: "Handle-bar mustaches, like this one, went out of style years ago. And so did snug-fitting, tight-chested clothing for men."

A small silver spoon: "You don't have to be born with a silver spoon in your mouth to be able to afford . . ."

A rabbit's foot: "Luck has no part in good advertising or good results."

A miniature fireman's helmet: "Only 4% are interested in fire helmets, but . . ."

A compass: "Do you chart your course in advertising or just guess?"

A miniature wrench: "Tighten up on your advertising policy and eliminate waste."

The variety of attention-getting devices is as wide as the imagination, and creating a tie-in is not difficult. In preparing a gadget-mailing you may choose either of two approaches:

FITZJOHN
COACH COMPANY
BUILDERS OF FINE MOTOR COACHES

TELEPHONE 23-216

Muskegon, Michigan

With this cotter pin, you are now a part owner of a FITZJOHN DURALINER.

Under separate cover, we would _like_ to send you the rest of the bus for any test you care to make, being fully confident you would then _want_ to become sole owner of the entire bus——cotter key and all!

Our representatives travel in Fitzjohn Coaches, which they use to demonstrate these rolling moneymakers. Since we have a man in your area now it would be no trouble at all to roll a Duraliner your way—— BOUND to make you money.

There's nothing like seeing to become believing. Once you see the beautiful Duraliner and sense its passenger-appeal, sit in its comfortable and roomy seats, and look at this coach from the viewpoint of a passenger _you will realize its rider-appeal_. Once you drive and get the feel of the wheel you'll know why drivers like the Fitzjohn. And when you check the business end (figuratively speaking) you, as an operator will say: "That's my baby!" _For it's a low cost bus to begin with and most economical to maintain._

So why not write, wire or phone us long distance (reversing the charges) right now to send you the remainder of your Duraliner? Have us give you a demonstration or make some test runs.

Or, if you prefer, we'll send photos and literature of the Duraliner (or our other models——the Super Duraliner and Cityliner) and list of owners _though it costs nothing to look at the bus itself!_

Just remember——"IF IT'S MADE BY FITZJOHN, IT'S MADE TO MAKE YOU MONEY!" Ask any of the many users.

Very truly yours,

FITZJOHN COACH COMPANY

B. H. Measley

Sales Manager

"IF IT'S MADE BY FITZJOHN, IT'S MADE TO MAKE YOU MONEY"

(1) dream up an idea and then arrange to get someone to produce a suitable gadget; or (2) select an available gadget from a catalog of a manufacturer and adapt your copy to fit the device. Hundreds of items re available at prices ranging from ½c to 5c each: plastic locks, shovels, batons, stars, cigars, scissors, musical notes, tear drops, gun, numbers, felt flowers, shamrocks, horseshoes, animals, ladders, metal mirrors, clips, etc.

It is always desirable to have some drawing as a part of the device pasted on to the letter. A plastic boot used to kick a line-cut drawing of a comical character may carry the line: "We want you to get the point." A revolver appears to "hit the bull's eye." The plastic lariat in the hands of a cowboy helps you "round up new accounts."

A fund-raising letter may be printed on a legal mortgage form with a burnt match attached as an invitation to the burning of a mortgage. Confederate money, Chinese money, rubber money, foreign postage stamps, Band-aids, a safety pin, plastic toothpicks, buttons, a package of aspirin, an envelope full of sugar—have been used in successful mailings.

Tipped-in pictures can be effective as eye-catchers. One professional letter writer uses his own picture. A recent letter we saw used an enlarged photograph of an eye. Effective pictures are easily available from agencies carrying stock photographs of every subject.

One successful mailing used a live turtle to dramatize a point to customers who were "slow to recognize the market we have." The same idea was used with a collection letter that carried the message. "This feller has a reputation for being slow. Don't *you* build the same kind of reputation." Bees, frogs, certain types of worms, and live toads can also be sent through the mails.

Coupons in the form of stamps, checks, gold-imprinted certificates, or special discount cards not only act as attention-getters but help obtain responses. The copy often indicates that the coupon or stamp or check is something "special" that must be returned with the order to permit the advantage of the special, low, low price.

The ultimate in new ideas for attention value is the perfumed letter. This may be printed with perfumed ink or imbedded with a drop of essence added in the envelope. Fragrances are available to fit any conceivable type of product or copy—wood, leather, hay, flowers, chocolate, the odor of

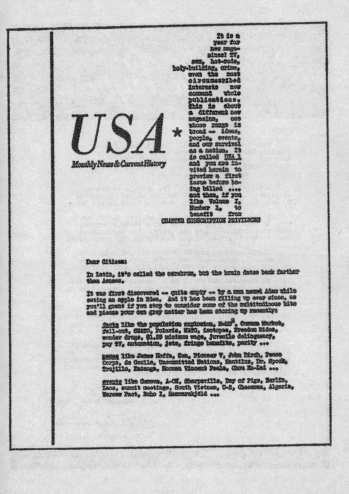

USA*

Monthly News & Current History

It is a
year for
new maga-
zines! TV,
sex, hot-rods,
body-building, crime,
even the most
circumscribed
interests now
command whole
publications.
This is about
a different new
magazine, one
whose range is
broad -- ideas,
people, events,
and our survival
as a nation. It
is called USA 1
and you are in-
vited herein to
preview a first
issue before be-
ing billed ....
and then, if you
like Volume I,
Number 1, to
benefit from

CHARTER SUBSCRIPTION PRIVILEGES

Dear Citizen:

In Latin, it's called the cerebrum, but the brain dates back farther
than Aeneas.

It was first discovered -- quite empty -- by a man named Adam while
eating an apple in Eden. And it has been filling up ever since, as
you'll grant if you stop to consider some of the multitudinous bits
and pieces your own gray matter has been storing up recently:

facts like the population explosion, E=MC², Common Market,
fall-out, SEATO, Polaris, NATO, isotopes, Freedom Rides,
wonder drugs, $1.25 minimum wage, juvenile delinquency,
pay TV, automation, jets, fringe benefits, parity ...

names like James Hoffa, Sen. Pioneer V, John Birch, Peace
Corps, de Gaulle, Uncommitted Nations, Nautilus, Dr. Spock,
Trujillo, Katanga, Norman Vincent Peale, Chou En-Lai ...

events like Geneva, A-OK, Sharpeville, Bay of Pigs, Berlin,
Laos, summit meetings, South Vietnam, U-2, Glennmen, Algeria,
Warsaw Pact, Echo I, Hammarskjöld ...

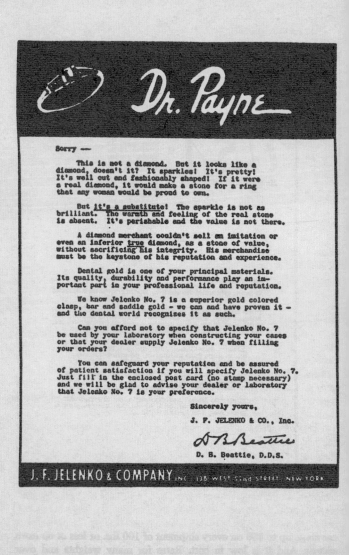

Dr. Payne

Sorry —

This is not a diamond. But it looks like a diamond, doesn't it? It sparkles! It's pretty! It's well cut and fashionably shaped! If it were a real diamond, it would make a stone for a ring that any woman would be proud to own.

But it's a substitute! The sparkle is not as brilliant. The warmth and feeling of the real stone is absent. It's perishable and the value is not there.

A diamond merchant couldn't sell an imitation or even an inferior true diamond, as a stone of value, without sacrificing his integrity. His merchandise must be the keystone of his reputation and experience.

Dental gold is one of your principal materials. Its quality, durability and performance play an important part in your professional life and reputation.

We know Jelenko No. 7 is a superior gold colored clasp, bar and saddle gold — we can and have proven it — and the dental world recognizes it as such.

Can you afford not to specify that Jelenko No. 7 be used by your laboratory when constructing your cases or that your dealer supply Jelenko No. 7 when filling your orders?

You can safeguard your reputation and be assured of patient satisfaction if you will specify Jelenko No. 7. Just fill in the enclosed post card (no stamp necessary) and we will be glad to advise your dealer or laboratory that Jelenko No. 7 is your preference.

Sincerely yours,

J. F. JELENKO & CO., Inc.

D B Beattie

D. B. Beattie, D.D.S.

J. F. JELENKO & COMPANY INC. 138 WEST 52nd STREET NEW YORK

smoke (for a fire sale), the aroma of freshly baked goods (for a bakery), the atmosphere of pine trees (for a resort), etc.

One recent mailing used the perfumed letter on pink stock, with a handwritten address and blue photo offset script in imitation of handwriting.

There is no limit to what can be used effectively for making a letter stand out in the morning mails and increasing its chance of being read. The task is to make it sufficiently different from the devices of many other imaginative letter writers to get and hold the reader's attention and convert this attention into the desired action.

One caution is suggested: Don't make your unusual mailing piece so clever that the recipient will remember your cleverness rather than your offer.

The main thing is to see your product with a fresh eye and to talk about it in a fresh style.

AIR EXPRESS
GET THERE FIRST

Here's An Old Trick of the Trade
That's Still As Good As New . . .

Being so close to the graphic arts, you undoubtedly know what a printer's hat looks like. And even if you've never made one, you'll find it's no trick at all to work one up by following the numbered instructions of the sheet enclosed.

Not only will it amuse your associates, but it will be handy for working around the house. And any time you want another, you can make one from a sheet of newspaper.

Which brings us to another trick of the trade . . . one that can give you added production time. It's Air Express . . . the fastest way to ship electros, engravings, mats, or anything else needed to meet an early deadline.

These two tricks have points in common. For example, a printer's hat has nothing on Air Express when it comes to *coverage, protection,* and *low cost*. All scheduled air lines carry Air Express, and your shipments go on the first scheduled flight direct by air to cover 1,800 airport cities and towns. And with the coordinated facilities of Railway Express—the world's largest ground shipping service, your shipments get fast handling to over 21,000 off-airline points as well. As for protection—Air Express gives you valuation coverage up to $50 on every shipment of 100 lbs. or less *at no extra charge*. And it is low in cost. Rates for many weights and over many distances are actually *under* those of other air-shipping services. So to get the most for *your* air-shipping dollar, call your local Railway Express Agency and ask for the Air Express Division.

Cordially,

With a package of seeds

> Thank you for the interest shown your association by recommending a new member.

In appreciation we would like to send you a bouquet of fresh flowers, but since we cannot send flowers to all, we shall resort to the next best.

Won't you plant these choice seeds and grow your own bouquet?

When they are in bloom, we would like you to consider them our special "thank you" for helping Liberty Federal grow.

Thank you again,

P.S. If you haven't received your anniversary souvenir, do stop for it at the reception desk the next time you are in.

Why
are
these
seeds
like
your
savings
account?

A package of seeds is
pasted in
this indicated space

They
are
dormant!

You planted a seed when you opened your savings account. At the time you probably had hopes that it would grow into a substantial amount. Your savings account at LIBERTY FEDERAL has not grown for over 2 years. Although we have added dividends (current rate 5½%), no effort was made on your part to help it grow by watering it with additional savings.

LET'S TRY THIS!

> Plant these zinnia seeds. As they grow, they will be a reminder to keep your account alive and growing.

To encourage growth, we have reserved a 54th Anniversary souvenir for you at our reception desk. Ask for it when come in.

Cordially yours,

With a usable trowel

Dear Sir:

The rugged little all-purpose trowel-cultivator on the folder cover looked to us like a real handy gadget to send you for spring, when most folks are polishing up their garden tools.

It's a mighty good time for all of us to polish up those *selling* tools, too—especially the ones that will help dig up some extra sales from the enclosed New Process Niblets Brand corn ad.

This new ad will appear in THIS WEEK Magazine in *your local newspaper*. That means a full-page of full-color advertising as local as your city hall.

THIS WEEK is circulated in leading *local newspapers* that give outstanding family coverage. (Details on back cover of gadget folder.)

All in all, it's a big chance to set up your ads and displays for a well-timed, well-coordinated mutual effort on Niblets Brand corn.

How about getting in your spadework right now? Look over the "tools" in the enclosed merchandising folder, check off the ones you want on the enclosed card, and return it today.

Sincerely yours,

Printers' Ink

The Weekly Magazine of Advertising, Management and Sales • 205 East 42nd Street, New York, N.Y. 10017

Dear Subscriber:

This forget-me-not...

... is by way of reminder that your renewal has not been received. We remembered to send copies, so you did not miss out, although the subscription has expired.

But now I need your say-so to continue if we are to avoid interruption. An O.K. on the attached card will enable me to do the needful. Please "do it now" as we are preparing our subscription list for future mailings.

Progress report: Printers' Ink keeps gathering momentum . . . many new subscribers added to the family. And the bouquets from old readers all over the country tell the same story - they like Printers' Ink a lot.

It will do even better in the future. I've seen what's cooking in the editorial department and the plans call for progressively higher standards for coming issues.

In these fast-moving times every issue is newsworthy, likely to be of special importance to you. Don't miss any copies of Printers' Ink - please return the enclosed card today.

Cordially yours,

J. C. Chasin
Circulation Manager

CE

Remington Rand
I N C.

SPRING 7-2000

315 FOURTH AVENUE, NEW YORK, N. Y. 10010

l👀king *for more business?*

- - - Read how this automotive wholesaler
underlined sales in seven months

Here's a timely case history report
that you as an automotive parts wholesaler won't want to miss. And you
needn't! The enclosed card will bring you a free copy - pronto!

☑ Bill Me   CREDIT APPROVED
CREDIT O.K.
☑ CHARGE IT
CREDIT
account OK - R.E.

...your *credit* is as good as gold

Dear Friend of LOOK:

Whatever your reason has been for delaying your LOOK renewal ..

... WE WANT YOU back -- and we want you back SOON!

How Much More
Will You Be Making
Two Years from Today?

That's a question of continuing interest to you, regardless
of your present income. And chances are you've thought about your

---

This entitles you
to one of the very first
copies of
"A New Concept in
Grinding Wheels"

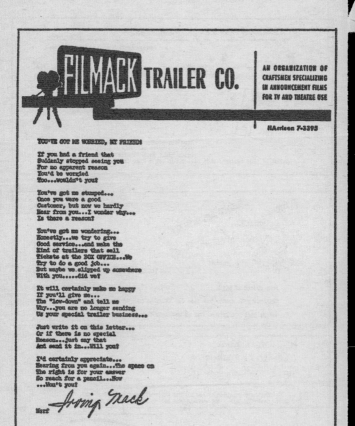

FILMACK TRAILER CO.

AN ORGANIZATION OF
CRAFTSMEN SPECIALIZING
IN ANNOUNCEMENT FILMS
FOR TV AND THEATRE USE

HArrison 7-3395

YOU'VE GOT ME WORRIED, MY FRIEND!

If you had a friend that
Suddenly stopped seeing you
For no apparent reason
You'd be worried
Too...wouldn't you?

You've got me stumped...
Once you were a good
Customer, but now we hardly
Hear from you...I wonder why...
Is there a reason?

You've got me wondering...
Honestly...we try to give
Good service...and make the
Kind of trailers that sell
Tickets at the BOX OFFICE...We
Try to do a good job...
But maybe we slipped up somewhere
With you.....did we?

It will certainly make me happy
If you'll give me...
The "low-down" and tell me
Why...you are no longer sending
Us your special trailer business...

Just write it on this letter...
Or if there is no special
Reason...just say that
And send it in...Will you?

I'd certainly appreciate...
Hearing from you again...The space on
The right is for your answer
So reach for a pencil...Now
...Won't you?

Irving Mack

Narf